Environmental Management in
Australia, 1788–1914

Environmental Management in Australia, 1788 – 1914

GUARDIANS, IMPROVERS AND PROFIT:
an Introductory Survey

J. M. POWELL

MELBOURNE • OXFORD UNIVERSITY PRESS

LONDON   WELLINGTON   NEW YORK

Oxford University Press

OXFORD   LONDON   GLASGOW   NEW YORK
TORONTO   MELBOURNE   WELLINGTON   CAPE TOWN
IBADAN   NAIROBI   DAR ES SALAAM   LUSAKA   ADDIS ABABA
KUALA LUMPUR   SINGAPORE   JAKARTA   HONG KONG   TOKYO
DELHI   BOMBAY   CALCUTTA   MADRAS   KARACHI

© *J. M. Powell 1976*

First published 1976

NATIONAL LIBRARY OF AUSTRALIA CATALOGUING IN PUBLICATION DATA

Powell, Joseph Michael
    Environmental   management   in   Australia,
    1788-1914.

    Index.
    ISBN 0 19 550478 x.
    ISBN 0 19 550479 8 *Paperback.*

    1. Environmental policy- Australia.
    2. Conservation of natural resources-
    Australia. I. Title.
    301.31'0994

PRINTED IN HONG KONG BY DAI NIPPON PRINTING CO. (H.K.) LTD.
PUBLISHED BY OXFORD UNIVERSITY PRESS, 7 BOWEN CRESCENT, MELBOURNE

For
Robert W. Steel
and
Richard Lawton

Contents

List of Illustrations

Preface

This work is intended as a brief introduction to some major themes in Australian environmental history and suggests some approaches to their interpretation. Although it is intended primarily for the use of students and teachers at various secondary and tertiary levels, its full purpose will not be achieved if it does not reach a more general readership. Accordingly, the book is presented as a descriptive-analytic narrative based upon a few convenient and simplistic divisions, and an attempt has been made to exclude most of the weightier type of factual data which a more complete and scholarly account would require. As an introductory survey much of the material is naturally a synthesis of existing literature and my profound debt to a wide range of writers will be immediately apparent from the inclusion of an extensive bibliography as a most essential part of the exercise. The bibliography is indeed my own best acknowledgement, therefore, of the influences of American, British and Australian authors upon this modest production.

The first section is an expanded and revised version of a discussion which originally appeared in *Australian Space Australian Time*, a volume of essays which I co-edited with Dr Michael Williams. I am grateful to Dr Williams and to the publishers, Oxford University Press, for allowing me to employ much of that material here. The writing was completed during the first part of my sabbatical year of 1974-75 and Professor Richard Lawton and his colleagues at the Department of Geography at Liverpool University provided generous hospitality during that time. I am also indebted to the staff and governing bodies of the Mitchell Library in Sydney; the National Library in Canberra; the State Library of Victoria, La Trobe Library and the libraries of Monash University and the State Rivers and Water Supply Commission, all in Melbourne; and the staffs of the British Library and Newspaper Library of the British Museum. The illustrations were prepared by my technical colleagues in the Department of Geography at Monash University under the direction of Jack Missen, Gary Swinton and Herve Alleaume, and I was also kindly assisted in this regard by the cartographers and photographers at Liverpool University.

In part, this investigation derives from lectures given to Bachelor's and Master's degree classes at Monash, and as usual I have gained considerably from the patience, interest and commitment of many students, too numerous to mention individually. I was particularly fortunate, however, in receiving sound assistance from my former students Heather Davies and Libby Henkel during an extraordinarily busy period of teaching and research, and there are important sections of the book which might never have been completed satisfactorily before my return to Australia had it not been for their timely support. My wife Suzie typed the manuscript and, as a third-generation Australian advising an adopted son of the country, she remains my most valued critic.

J. M. Powell
Liverpool, January 1975

Preface

An Historical-Cultural Approach to Environmental Management

WESTERN societies responded in various ways to the complex new setting which emerged during the nineteenth century, particularly to the conditions of urbanization, industrialism and the concomitant advances in science and technology. But for the peoples of the New World there were also the special features of unfamiliar, little-used territories and different, sometimes competing images of the new societies they hoped to create. For the British and European immigrants to Australia, the vast emptiness of the place and its predominantly subhumid, level and treeless environments provided a peculiarly difficult setting. Yet it was also a region of very recent settlement and its inhabitants were required to participate in a new era of Western progress long before there had been time to achieve more than a rudimentary grasp of the continent's most crucial ecological characteristics. There is surely great potential here for historical-cultural analyses.

Clearly, every society must exploit its physical environment in order to survive and, similarly, it should be expected that many human groups will act as dominating agents in the functioning of the ecosystems of their own habitats. It is now generally accepted by social scientists that

> Nature is always composed within a specific frame of motives and expectations: the habitats of human societies are not solely the function of ecosystem characteristics. Each human group develops its special collection of motives which designate the appropriate and inappropriate forms of conduct in regard to other men, other groups, and the nonhuman environment, and these selective perceptions determine whether the nonhuman environment will become a resource, a taboo, or remain unseen (Burch 1971: 51).

No less than for any other human group we must evaluate the consequences of the survival capacity of Australians *at any time* in terms of the nature of the existing social order, its symbolic directives, and the character and limitations of the local habitat. There is, therefore, no point in continuing to treat modern Australians and their forbears as morally reprehensible. In general terms (and borrowing again from Burch and other interpreters of the American experience) it could be said that the pre-European occupation of Australia was a situation of very gradual change in which habitat and social structure were reinforcing, whereas the replacement population of white Australians usually engaged in extreme exploitation in a setting of high instability, in which different kinds of traditional frames of reference no longer seemed to operate. Yet it is important to note that the following study should be seen as a preliminary sortie into an under-researched field, and that the term 'cultural' is therefore used in its widest sense throughout the book; the investigation includes, for example, some consideration of significant political and social contexts which might otherwise be judged better suited to more

3

specialist forms of inquiry.

Before the recent rapid diffusion of 'environmental history' courses on American campuses there were several geographers who were devoting a good deal of their own teaching efforts to the communication of the impact of American society on environmental change. But, following the lead of Hans Huth (1957), Samuel P. Hays (1957; 1972), Elmo R. Richardson (1962), Roderick Nash (1967) and others (Rakestraw 1972), the broader co-ordinating approach of a number of historians succeeded in mapping out a new teaching frontier with wide appeal, while too many of the geographers were preoccupied with their so-called 'quantitative revolution'. Discussing the development of his own very popular programme at the University of California at Santa Barbara, Nash (1972) disclosed a common emphasis in a number of these new history courses which distinguishes the special role of the conservation movement, *per se*. Drawing on his classic 'wilderness' treatise (1967), he argued that the motivation for conservation in the United States can be conveniently separated into three divisions; the *aesthetic* and *utilitarian* streams, which are both man-centred in so far as either 'man's stomach or man's spirit is the paramount concern', and the *ecological* stream, which 'puts man back into the biotic community, and its welfare, not that of *homo sapiens*, is given top priority' (Nash 1972: 368). The wider application of these divisions is reasonably acceptable to other social scientists, but some would anticipate the possibility of an unproductive and artificial separation, in teaching and research, of conservation itself from the general sphere of resource management. They could also point to the recent recognition of the *built environment* of rural and urban settlements, farming and industrial landscapes, as a most vital area for comprehensive environmental management—including vigorous development and re-development, as well as con-servation in its purest or 'preservationist' sense. The management of Austra-lia's built environment is treated as one of the major themes of this book.

Too often, as O'Riordan (1971) has indicated, historians have used the term 'conservation' to identify varous periods of political activity when the interests of certain resource-using groups were threatened, or when public policy was directed at the better management of resources. So there are said to be 'conservation eras' which 'coincided with public alarm over specific environmental crises, the emergence of a technical *élite*, and the dominance of a powerful and sympathetic President', yet the focus of official conservation policy has also moved from the preservation of public lands through regional multiple resource planning, national strategic safety and finally to 'environ-mental quality' and the 'dignity of life' (O'Riordan 1971: 8). The rather vague philosophy of conservation has clearly been subject to varying interpretations with changes in man's aspirations and his evaluation of the environment. Conservation must accordingly be viewed as a dynamic concept without precise definition, and none of the traditional disciplines can really expect to treat it adequately: a fusion of at least eight major approaches is required, ranging from economic, political, social and ecological perspectives to those of aesthetics, ethics, philosophy and science/technology (O'Riordan 1971).

My intention is to offer an exploratory survey of selected issues in the development of environmental appraisal and resource management in Australia before 1914, accepting the opinion that conservation, however narrowly defined, cannot be understood if it is divorced from this wider setting. As a simple introduction to the field for students from several disciplines, however, this study also attempts to illustrate that the growing body of American scholarship in this field will prove to be of inestimable value in the promotion of new and needed research in Australia; and indeed, the whole design of the book has obviously been deeply influenced by the same type of anthropocentric philosophy which has guided related research in that country, a philosophy which Nash has succinctly described.

> I would, rather, attempt a *history of attitude and action toward the land*. This would involve a description of environmental change, but my interest in it would be as evidence of man's values, ideals, ambitions, and fears. The environment, in other words, was an historical document. Rightly seen, it revealed a society's culture and traditions as surely as did a novel or a newspaper or a Fourth of July oration. The environment, after all, is synthetic—man made. Especially since the coming of technology man has shaped the face of the earth. In doing so he reveals himself. Even the unaltered or wild parts of the environment result from a conscious human choice. We deliberately let the land alone, displaying our ideas in the process (Nash 1972: 363; my italics).

'Environmental attitudes' will certainly be examined throughout this book. 'Attitude' is a familiar term in common discourse, but during the past century there has been an involved and controversial scientific pursuit of its function and meaning which has given it a much grander status. It is in a sense an interdisciplinary term: a bridge between sociology and psychology which is quite regularly used by the other social sciences. Complex problems of definition are involved and we cannot enter into a discussion of these here, but it is probably reasonably safe and sufficient to say that attitudes are related to, but must be distinguished from, both 'culture' and 'personality'; that an attitude essentially connotes a *disposition*; that it incorporates three connected components, *cognitive*, *affective* and *behavioural*, influencing the response towards objects and situations. The 'cognitive' element refers to aspects of awareness, knowledge, beliefs, ideas; 'affective' refers to feelings, likes, dislikes, fears; and these are influenced by, and in turn they also influence, 'behaviour'. But the use of the term 'disposition' is highly significant. By meticulous examination of contemporary opinions, taking great pains to offset the frustrating selectivity of the historical record, we may discover something significant about what people knew and felt about specific objects or situations, be they persons, trees, the city, the wilderness or whatever, but these findings will seldom explain all or even most of the behaviour patterns in which we are interested. We must also examine these very behaviour patterns in detail for their own sake—and then work back, as it were, to the causal mechanisms. Environmental behaviour (Nash's 'action toward') may appear to contradict specifically stated attitudinal postures because the behaviour was seen by the people involved in quite another light, perhaps in relation to another, stronger type of disposition which was unresearched. So the wilderness addict knows a great deal about that kind of environment and loves it dearly, but he may also have cherished objectives in his career, or for his family, which could severely restrict his use of wilderness, or he may not support the only political party campaigning (say) for more national parks because he disapproves of the rest of its platform, prefers to choose the competitor because of its strong educational programme, and so on. In short, we must also investigate relatively more stable or resistant *value orientations* which give a sort of 'ranking' to the whole suite of attitudes we may identify for an individual or group. Changes in these orientations, however motivated —by fear of some environmental catastrophe, a threat to the perceived 'quality of life', or through rising nationalism or simply group consciousness, for example—may introduce a wide range of other modifications in behavioural dispositions (for general guides to a fuller analysis see Creese 1966; Insko 1967; Gaffney and Hibbs 1968; Rokeach 1970; Proshansky *et al.* 1970; Tuan 1974). Naturally the identification of some of these basic processes of change forms a central objective of the present brief study, since it is concerned with an immigrant society relating to its strange environment over a period of more than a century.

*

Today's environmental issues are linked to the dynamics of political life because, by definition, the origins of 'resources' are to be found in society, not in the earth itself. Until very recently, the environmental values and attitudes of Australian society hardly differed from those of the nineteenth century, and although there are signs that we may be awakening to a new interpretation of our relationship with nature which can yield a more secure basis for community survival, all too often we are content to blame the politician and to demand solutions of the scientists and bureaucrats. Essentially this book is an examination of the potentials of one type of historical-cultural approach which may usefully document our progress towards this dangerous position. During the formative period 1788 to 1914 the Australian environment was irrevocably altered for future generations. Complex ecosystems were totally destroyed or rendered unproductive from any viewpoint, and others were so dangerously modified as to pose serious problems even for the sophisticated techniques of modern management. Similarly, specific and general orientations of the Australian public towards native fauna, flora and landscapes, and to a lesser extent towards the built environment, became deeply entrenched.

We may not welcome the inheritance now, but to understand its origins and to read, as we must, the warnings it surely contains, we are obliged to see it all through the eyes of its creators, the people of the day. For the same reasons, it is also vitally necessary to examine the counteracting process by which certain groups and individuals gradually won some success in contributing towards the 'modernization' of what was then a type of 'underdeveloped' country by promoting important principles of conservation and resource management and by injecting what they called 'efficiency', 'expertise' and 'system' into the working of public policy. The most tangible result of the latter process was the emergence of distinct bureaucratic agencies for various aspects of resource management, a peculiarly neglected field of research for this heavily bureaucratized nation.

II Man and Nature in Australia, 1788–1860

FOR Australia's Aboriginal cultures religion provided the central co-ordinating theme which gave meaning to their lives, and the pivot of that religion was man's intimate, reciprocal connection with the land. Extensive anthropological research indicates that in all parts of the continent various interpretations of this fundamental relationship guided the complex development of social organization and structure; styles of living were considered to have been set in train for all time by the great spirit beings of the past, and this belief was incorporated into the general recognition and employment of a remarkably intricate 'totemic' landscape in the determination of a wide range of territorial and social divisions (Berndt and Berndt 1965; Strehlow 1970). The apparent rigidity of this control is frequently overstated. As a matter of survival, Aborigines certainly required the very detailed knowledge of their own area which was fostered by the operation of the totemic system, but successful harmonic adjustment between population and resources also required more flexible social and territorial arrangements to permit the geographic mobility of some individuals and families, in order to diffuse at least a broad understanding within each group of the wider region beyond their original hearth and to facilitate redistributions of populations from time to time. Yet it is indeed fair to claim that the successful resource management techniques developed by the first Australians owed a great deal to their philosophy of land and life. Game animals and food plants were protected against reckless exploitation by totemic prohibitions, and even in severe and prolonged drought conditions in the interior the same process maintained excellent water-holes as inviolable sanctuaries, so that a reservoir of wild creatures was supported until the rains returned and the inland again displayed its celebration of new life.

Of the remarkable inhabitants of the desert heart, it has been asserted that 'Totemic religion gave them a feeling of oneness with Nature that has rarely been equalled, and never surpassed in other parts of the world' (Strehlow 1965: 144). On the other hand, the popular modern image goes much further in assuming an ideal 'natural' pre-European environment over the entire continent, and this grossly underestimates the massive ecological impact of some 30,000 years of Aboriginal technology. The broad vegetational zones within which the first European settlers were obliged to work, and in which they undoubtedly wrought so much havoc, had already been profoundly modified by the hunting, food-gathering and widespread fire-using activities of the Aboriginal inhabitants (Mulvaney 1971). Fire in particular, 'man's first extra-corporeal muscle' (Jones 1969: 228), was an integral part of the Aboriginal economy which attracted the attention of Cook and other explorers, and its high ecological significance in Australia's open plains and thin savanna woodlands was quickly recognized and communicated by the most perceptive of the nineteenth-century commentators.

> There is no subject connected with New South Wales, or Australia, less under-
> stood in England than the character and condition of the aboriginal natives.
> They have been described as the lowest in the scale of humanity, yet I found
> those who accompanied me superior in penetration and judgement to the white
> men composing my party. Their means of subsistence and their habits are both
> extremely simple; but they are adjusted with admirable fitness to the few re-
> sources afforded by such a country in its wild state. What these resources are,
> and how they are economised by the natives, can only be learnt by an acquaint-
> ance with the interior . . .
>   Fire, grass, kangaroos, and human inhabitants, seem all dependent on each
> other for existence in Australia; for any one of these being wanting, the others
> would no longer continue. Fire is necessary to burn the grass, and form those
> open forests, in which we find the large forest-kangaroo; the native applies
> that fire to the grass at certain seasons, in order that a young green crop may
> subsequently spring up, and so attract and enable him to kill or take the kangaroo
> with nets. In summer, the burning of the long grass also discloses vermin, birds'
> nests, etc., on which the females and children, who chiefly burn the grass, feed.
> But for this simple process, the Australian woods had probably contained as
> thick a jungle as those of New Zealand or America . . . (Mitchell 1848: 412).

Heathcote (1972) has identified three principal, mutually interacting components which influenced what the invading Europeans understood of ecological relationships in this strange environment as their own less intimate form
of stewardship, so often accompanied by blind inhumanity, supplanted that of
their Aboriginal predecessors. These components were (i) the *basic geographical characteristics of the continent itself*, (ii) the types of *observers* and (iii) the
media by which information was communicated to those observers.

   (i)   The remote location of Australia influenced the late arrival of European settlement and greatly handicapped the rapid transfer of all types of
news and opinions in either direction; the compactness of the huge continent
offered very few opportunities for rapid penetration by sea and overland
travel was particularly difficult and expensive before the introduction of the
railway. Approximately half of the area was arid, effectively discouraging and
delaying inland exploration, which was scarcely completed until the early
years of the twentieth century. Also, climatic conditions were generally
variable and extremely difficult to interpret, especially in terms of the current
confused thinking and relatively low level of technological expertise in the
subject in general throughout the world, and the heavy reliance which had to
be placed upon the fragmented and impressionistic accounts of private and
official exploration parties. Similarly, the complete novelty of the native flora
and fauna postponed their most effective employment as indices for environmental appraisal, including the assessment of seasonal variability and settlement potential (Blainey 1966; Spate 1971; Heathcote 1965, 1972). This last
point can be overemphasized, however.

   (ii)   The observers were influenced by their own training, experiences,
objectives and motivations, and strictly for convenience it could be said that
most individual observers belonged to one or more of the following type-
categories. Early British officials were rather more inclined towards the
search for promising sources of supply of naval stores, the strategic geo-

graphies of land and water, or likely sites for the establishment of free or convict settlers. Promoters and some politicians looked for the chances of speculative gains and commercial success, and frequently overstated their cases. The learned societies and individual specialists in applied science engaged in detailed and honest field investigations in the pursuit of useful knowledge. The official explorers were often restricted by the specifications of their commissions or by their own interpretations of the immediate or ultimate purpose of the trek, either for their own careers or for the progress and prosperity of the country. For the most part, the pioneer settlers were naturally engrossed in establishing a foothold and this acted as a primary filter which influenced the type and amount of information they sought, received and transmitted to fellow colonists and contacts in the home country.

(iii)   Resource information, including commentary on the processes of exploration and the modes of settlement which were transforming the environment 'captured' from the Aborigines, was extensively documented in a wide range of literary and graphic sources at official and private levels—the 'media' of the day. For Europeans without the controlling measure of actual experience in the country, the literary sources proved dangerous guides because of the bewildering and infuriating contemporary practice of reasoning from analogy and the equally confusing semantic problem. The first is best illustrated in the abuse of grossly simplified latitudinal zoning theories to predict suitable climatic regions for white settlement, and the second in the long-continued use of familiar and totally inappropriate terminology for the description of Australian topography (Heathcote 1965: 18-20; for a Western Australian example, see Cameron 1974).

It is obviously impossible to reconstruct the entire perceptual environment with the full and varied range of contradictory views which must have been present; yet some approximation—however crude—must be attempted, for there is no other way of discovering environmental attitudes and behaviour with any degree of accuracy and promise of further utility. There is some consolation and assistance in the relative homogeneity of the population before 1850, with important local exceptions: the original inhabitants were few, scattered, weakly organized, rapidly pushed aside or largely ignored, and in comparison with several other regions of recent settlement Australia's white population was drawn almost exclusively from a single source before the gold rushes in mid-century. That source was Britain, and the tight nexus between the two countries was never really broken until the period following the Second World War. In addition, the penal and military nature of the earliest forms of British settlement resulted in a deliberate effort being made to impose strong, centralized and unifying control over the appraisal and utilization of the Australian continent. Difficult as it is to unravel the complexities of the changing perceptual environment, the enduring attraction of the coastal and intermediate districts, especially in the better-favoured southeastern crescent which accommodated the vast majority of settlers, does help to focus the enquiry.

1 The British and the Bush, 1788–1830

THE principle of comprehensive government responsibility for the primary decisions of resource management arrived with the First Fleet in 1788 and quickly became a contentious feature of colonial life. British military personnel, including the Governors and their appointed 'experts', built the foundations of Australia's bureaucratic system during their early experience of geographical and botanical exploration and the control of settlement initiation and expansion, town planning and the provision of water supplies, all of which they administered with varying degrees of success and public support.

Utility and Perversity

British colonial policy was not invariably empirical or *ad hoc* in character as is so often assumed. It was always influenced to some degree by theoretical considerations and the origins of British attitudes towards the colonies must be sought in contemporary economic and social requirements in the home country, together with the official response to the need to harmonize changing British demands with the altered role of particular colonies within the Empire as a whole (Blainey 1966; Burroughs 1967; Dallas 1969). The establishment of a convict settlement in Australia clearly provided a reasonably simple solution to some basic problems then facing the British penal system, but the south-eastern coast of the continent was also thought to be strategically and economically valuable to European expansion in the entire Pacific region. Whaling, sealing and the supply of naval timber proved to be immensely important enterprises, though as yet surprisingly little is known about the timber trade and the first two industries have been virtually ignored by most researchers.

All too often, Cook's voyages have been described exclusively in terms of their relationship with pure scientific research. They borrowed, of course, from a whole suite of recent scientific advances and repaid in full by means of innumerable direct and authoritative observations of nature in newly discovered regions. But there may also have been a good deal of *applied* science in the original motivation for the voyages, definitely in their more practical results; and above all, commercial and strategic possibilities were obviously greatly extended by Cook's brilliant demonstration of new precision in ocean navigation. Despite the painstaking research of K. M. Dallas over twenty years ago, this was until recently a strangely neglected feature in interpretations of Australia's early settlement; the long history of commercial warfare between Britain and France was certainly beginning to focus on the India and China trade, and the subsequent entry of aggressive Yankees into the region posed a further threat to British interests (Dallas 1969; Wace and Lovett 1973). Britain was engaged in wars with the United States and France at various times before and during the first generation of settlement in Australia (from the War of American Independence, 1775-83, until the Battle of Waterloo in 1815) and it is inconceivable that strategic considerations should be so underestimated in the critical assessment of the initial choice and subsequent employment of Australia as a principal locational resource in the maintenance and extension of British interests.

This emphasis on utilitarian motivations is merely to balance or clarify, not to contest, the observations of several scholars who have pointed out that the chief importance of early Australia in intellectual and cultural terms was as a new field for science: the discovery of the new continent greatly excited botanists, geographers, zoologists and geologists everywhere, and the main preoccupation of the best-educated settlers was also with matters of scientific interest. It is an undisputed finding which should indeed be given more prominence in the assessment of the supposedly very limited artistic and practical accomplishments of the first colonists (Serle 1973)—not only because some of the best energies of the most accomplished men of the day were focussed on what we would now call the field sciences, but also because it is simply futile to attempt to separate the aesthetic and scientific appraisals of *any* new environment during this period. From the present perspective these activities, both small and great, merit our special attention because they contributed immensely to the formation of public and private images of the Australian environment.

A common belief concerning the new country in the late eighteenth and early nineteenth centuries was that its primary characteristics were the extremely 'odd', even grotesque, 'antipodean perversities'; born of scientific ignorance and the prejudice of the exile, this pervasive notion was subsequently entitled 'the concept of the reversal of Nature' (Green 1961). The elementary loss of seasonal indicators would have been sufficient to confuse the brutalized majority of the population in the penal settlement, but environmental anomalies were quickly seized upon and publicized by every commentator—the egg-laying mammals, the marsupials and the incomprehensible methods of reproduction were frequent topics of debate, not to mention the flightless emu, so large that 'a side-bone of it will dine three real carnivorous Englishmen' (Smith 1854, quoted in Smith 1960: 17). Peron's *Voyage of Discovery* (1809) also helped to popularize the idea that nature in Australia was freakish, even whimsical in its operation. Sydney was backed by a mountain chain: why then, he asked, should it be parched by hot westerly winds in the summer—did this mean that Australia had its own natural laws, peculiar to itself? He also noted with consternation the irregular flooding of the Hawkesbury River near Sydney and complained that this was quite inexplicable, according to known principles: 'It must be allowed that, in this, as in many other phenomena New Holland defies our conclusions from comparisons, mocks our studies, and shakes to their foundations the most firmly established and most universally admitted of our scientific opinions'. It was all very bewildering.

> . . . rare conservatory plants were commonplace; the appearance of light-green meadows lured squatters into swamps where their sheep contracted rot, trees retained their leaves and shed their bark instead, the more frequent the trees, the more sterile the soil, the birds did not sing, the swans were black, the eagles white, the bees were stingless, some mammals had pockets, others laid eggs,

it was warmest on the hills and coolest in the valleys, even the blackberries [wild raspberries] were red, and to crown it all the greatest rogue may be converted into the most useful citizen: such is *Terra Australis* (Martin 1838: 123).

As Smith (1960, 1962) and Heathcote (1972) have indicated, these 'curiosities' were simply matters of information for the enthusiastic recorders of natural history and their meticulous draughtsmen, but for the *interpreters*, prejudice often obscured their judgement and the data so carefully gleaned was repeatedly exploited in a series of emotional outbursts. Australia was by no means easily loved, and this is the crux of the matter. The first colonists were committed to the country before they came to understand it; modern Australians find the place more attractive because their forbears learned first how to live with it, then to accept it and finally to appreciate it. They have been assisted in this learning process, this problem of adjustment, by the priceless insights of a few poets, writers and painters (Wright 1965; Powell 1972; Serle 1973). In the early years, however, as Smith's (1960) classic statement on this theme illustrates, the artistic evaluation of the strange new landscapes was bound to reflect the general environmental ignorance and the transplantation of inherited standards of aesthetic judgement. A few examples will perhaps suffice to make this point. Australian readers should find them very familiar, since this part of the story has been well taught and researched.

The first book of verse printed in Australia was written in 1819 by Barron Field (1786-1846), a Judge of the Supreme Court in Sydney. In this book and in his *Geographical Memoirs of New South Wales*, Field actually complained that there had been too much scientific description and that the monotony of the eucalypt forests encouraged too little poetry ('botanists are many, and good cheap'!). To be narrow-leaved, virtually shadeless and evergreen was perverse in any tree: 'There is a dry harshness about the perennial leaf, that does not savour of humanity in my eyes. There is no flesh and blood in it: it is not of us, and is nothing to us ... without January, in my mind, there can be no May'. So the whining song of the exile continued: seasons were 'picturesque' to the painters, 'emblems' for the poets, and lacking these, the Australian landscape was bereft of inspiration: 'I can therefore hold no fellowship with Australian foliage, but will cleave to the British oak through all the bareness of winter' (Field 1825: 425, 441). At least Field recognized that he faced a problem in perception, or *conditioned* literary perception. The contrary view of some native-born poets who bewailed 'the rude invasions of the falling axe' (Tompson 1826) was much less acceptable to a literary *élite* which was steeped in the pastoral literature of another place, in another century. With the crossing of the Blue Mountains in 1813 and the discovery of the vast interior plains, the aesthetic prospect was no brighter. The dull uniformity of the eastern forests merely gave way to such a massive monotony that the coastal districts gradually became better regarded simply because they were far exceeded in this burdensome Australian defect: 'A variety of wretchedness is at all times preferable to one unvarying cause of pain and distress' (Oxley 1820: 113).

As Brian Elliott has demonstrated on more than one occasion, it is inevitable that the early phases of poetic literature in any new country will

THE PICTURESQUE AND THE PRACTICAL.

Mr. Cobalt having made a pleasing sketch of a picturesque gum-tree, returns two days afterwards to complete the picture, but finds the aspect of his subject has materially changed in the interval.

1 'The Picturesque and the Practical', *Melbourne Punch,* 1858

be concerned with establishing the essential machinery of 'effective sugges-tion': a type of selective picture-making based upon recognizably *native* emblems was required. Charles Harpur (1813-68), the Australian son of British convicts, was perhaps the first to produce these useful 'creative clichés' or acceptable emblems of the bush; but although they clearly owed a great deal to his early experience in the forest and open country, his poems really belong to a later period. It was admittedly very ordinary fare and in a sense too self-consciously patriotic, yet commanded no audience in Harpur's own day. Amid the continuing groans and irrelevancies of the sojourners and transplanted Britons, however, his work was distinguished by its acceptance of the harsh realities of the Australian scene as integral parts of the beauty of life itself (Normington-Rawling 1962; Wright 1963; Elliott 1967).

Aesthetic appreciation is for many the foundation of a more specialized appraisal of the environment and this was clearly a major barrier in Australia during the first generation of settlement; the country had to be accepted first of all for what it was (Moon 1969, 1970). Yet at the level of practical settlement there were many other colonists who chose with Harpur to respond more positively to the challenge of the new environment and there were some, no doubt, who embraced the bush as ardently as he. For them, the embrace may be said to have been a matter of plain survival, rather than celebration. But who would define survival?

The Role of Botanical Exploration

In 1753 the *Species plantarum* of the Swedish botanist Linnaeus (Carolus von Linné 1707-78) established a binomial nomenclature for flowering plants based upon the identification of the genus and a simple qualifying word, usually a simple enough adjective denoting the locational characteristics, even the identity of the first classifier, and so on. It was a rigid, 'artificial' system, scientifically inferior to a 'natural' basis proposed by earlier workers which was ultimately very well developed in the classic works of the de Candolles, George Bentham and Sir Joseph Dalton Hooker (Green 1909). But the supreme quality of the Linnaean taxonomy was that it was very easily understood and peculiarly well timed to service the rapid botanical investigation of newly-discovered territories, especially Australia.

Gilbert (1966, 1970, 1971) has carefully demonstrated that the natural environment around the initial penal settlement was intensively explored to fulfil three interrelated functions: to supply a variety of pressing needs for the young society, to satisfy general curiosity and to further scientific enquiry. From the outset all classes, bond and free, were involved in a busy exploration which was inevitably concentrated upon the primary botanical characteristics. The most important aspect of these early expeditions was the search for a reliable staple, particularly timber and flax for naval supplies, but the basic and immediate requirements of the colonists were also extremely important in promoting an urgent reconnaissance of the local environment. By the crudest form of empirical testing and deduction from apparent British analogies, settlers discovered an amazing variety of uses for bush materials. Saturday was established as the regular 'vegetable' collecting day within the first year of settlement, according to Gilbert (1970: 17) and the bush was quickly made to yield building materials, food and fuel, medicines, cordage and even hats. The cabbage-tree palm (*Livistona australis*), plentiful around the original settlement at Port Jackson, provided good straight trunks for walls and its leaves were excellent for fodder, roofing and hat-making. The *Casuarina* species were easily split into shingles, various stringy-barks and iron-barks provided excellent material for slabs and beams, and convicts were regularly dispatched to collect wild fruit, grass-tree (*Xanthorrhea*) leaves, bulrushes and the like. The native currant or acid berry (*Leptomeria acida*) was highly prized as an anti-scorbutic in the overworked hospital and the climbing native sarsaparilla (*Smilax glyciphylla*) provided a popular beverage which was also judged to be extremely valuable as a pectoral and anti-scorbutic.

The entire Pacific region presented a fascinating challenge for studies of the relationship between man and nature, and apart from Charles Darwin, the commanding scientific personality in these endeavours was Sir Joseph Banks, president of the Royal Society for over forty years and a generous patron of Australian research (Francis 1972). In close association with the Earl of Bathurst, Secretary of State for the Colonies, Banks strongly influenced official appointments and exploration activity: he sponsored Matthew Flinders' Australian voyages, for example, and secured the appointment of the brilliant young botanist Robert Brown to accompany Flinders. This enabled Brown to establish his own claim as a leader in the field with the publication in 1810 of the first great botanical work on Australia, *Prodomus Florae Novae Hollandiae*. Specimens collected by a host of amateurs and professionals in Australia were usually channelled to England through the resident 'King's Botanist' or 'Colonial Botanist' and through interested

Governors. Most of the material was deposited for research in the Banksian Herbarium at Kew Gardens and some essential system was thereby injected into the colonial data by experienced and highly respected international authorities. These links were further strengthened after the development of a Botanic Garden at Sydney and by the supply of a succession of well-trained young botanists and horticulturalists from Kew to high administrative and research appointments in Australia. In 1841 Sir William J. Hooker brought his own botanical collection to Kew on becoming Director, and the demand for herbarium specimens and living plants grew thereafter exponentially (Turill 1959; Chadwick 1966; Bligh 1973).

'Botany Bay' was indeed well-named! When Darwin's theory of evolution became better-known after the publication of his *Origin of Species* in 1859, the native fauna and the Aboriginal population could be more intensively studied (Mozley 1967); until that time, the Australian flora inevitably held most scientific attraction. One most interesting feature is that botanical knowledge was directly and indirectly increased by the very fact that the tree cover and other primary botanical fixtures were quickly and naively accepted as incredibly versatile indices of carrying capacity, soil quality, the presence of underground water and the availability of certain minerals (Powell 1968a, 1969; Gilbert 1971). Similarly, the success of the great expeditions of inland exploration came to depend very heavily upon their efficient employment of the techniques of botanical observation. From the beginning, trained botanists were occasionally included in the official parties, but the point was also established independently time and again by a few gifted expedition leaders. Although their first objective was usually to fill in the huge blanks on the Australian map, the value of an acceptable frame of reference in completely unknown country was supremely important in the daily welfare of the expedition parties as well as in the successful pursuit of their major tasks and the leaders' subsequent communication of the findings.

Australia's native grasses were not generally understood, however, until commercial livestock farming was initiated. In the early years of settlement, the most valued fodder was provided by the 'oat grass'—almost certainly Kangaroo grass (*Themeda Australis*)—which was originally widely available in large tufts or stands, often a few feet tall, interspersed with more or less bare or relatively useless patches. This mode of occurrence prompted several early attempts to introduce English grasses in order to improve stocking intensities; most of these efforts failed and although the experiments continued, there were a few far-sighted individuals who argued for an alternative solution which bore fruit two generations later. Robert Dawson, for example, as Chief Agent of the Australian Agricultural Company, suggested the selection and widespread cultivation of combinations of drought-resisting native species which had already proven their worth in their regions of origin (Dawson 1831: 404). But the pressure for introduced grasses continued, relenting only in the worst depths of drought conditions and rising again with every good season.

Conservation and Pollution Control

The official promotion of botanical investigation was obviously assisted by the recent acceleration in scientific interest and expertise in the subject, but above all it was prompted by utilitarian considerations. This is also true of the earliest measures for conservation and pollution control which concerned the Colony's water and timber supplies. On 15 May 1788 Governor Phillip chose Sydney Cove as the landing place for the First Fleet because it was the only satisfactory site thus far encountered which appeared to have a reliable stream of fresh water. Baron Augustus Theodore Henry Alt, a well-seasoned military engineer, designed and supervized the essential buildings and public works and was largely responsible for the deepening of the river and the excavation of tanks in its sandstone bed, thereby ensuring the capacity of the 'Tank Stream' to provide Sydney's only public water supply for about forty years. From another perspective these activities could be taken to mark the beginning of a remarkably fruitful and enduring union between the Australian engineering profession and the public authorities: an intimate, virtually exclusive partnership, with fundamental social and political implications. A succession of Governors and public servants attempted thereafter to direct the residential, agricultural and industrial land-use decisions of all classes in order to preserve the Tank Stream from serious pollution and erosion. Within the first five years of settlement regulations were passed forbidding the felling of trees within fifty feet of the stream, and fences and intercepting ditches were placed on both banks for further protection (Corbett 1957, 1969, 1973; for additional contemporary comment see Tench 1961; *Historical Records New South Wales* 1893: 326 and 1895: 10-11, 206, 518, 531). But Australia's first legislation for the protection of a vital catchment area met with little success. The inhabitants who depended upon the Tank Stream were for some reason quite content to employ it as a drain for various types of industrial and domestic effluent, as some of the comments in the Governors' despatches angrily record. So Governor King, for example, informed his superiors in 1802 that vigorous action was to be taken against polluters:

> If any person whatever is detected throwing any filth into the Stream of fresh Water, cleaning Fish, Washing, erecting pig-styes near it, or taking water up but at the Tanks, on conviction before a Magistrate, their Houses will be taken down and forfeit £5 for each Offence to the Orphan Fund . . . (*Historical Records of Australia,* hereafter cited as *H.R.A.,* Series 1, vol. 4: 321-2).

In terms of its locational utility the Botany Bay settlement fulfilled several overlapping functions. Principally it was a simple penal outpost of the Empire, a service and supply base for ships and crews, and the forerunner of a series of 'limpet ports' which helped to establish Britain's claim and to initiate useful reconnaissance into the unknown territory. Timber was an essential requisite in the foundation and maintenance of the settlement itself, but it was also intended for export and for the repair of visiting ships and, accordingly, there were frequent reports on the character and availability of local timber supplies from the reconnaissance expeditions along the coast. The colonial authorities possibly knew far more about Australian timber than about any other element in the local physical environment—or at least they showed rather more interest, especially where British naval supplies seemed to be involved. As early as 1795 an enclosure to a despatch from Governor Hunter to the Duke of Portland deplored the indiscriminate felling of useful timber along the Hawkesbury and its tributaries and declared:

> ... it is hereby strictly ordered that no timber whatever be cut down on ground which is not marked out or allotted to individuals on either of the banks or creeks of the aforementioned river. And in order to preserve as much as possible [of] such timber as may be of use either for building or for naval purposes, the King's mark will be forthwith put on all such timber, after which any person or persons offending against this Order will be prosecuted (*H.R.A.*, I, vol. 1: 683).

The Order continued to explain that the regulations were concerned only with Crown land; where land had already been granted to individuals a clause had been inserted, apparently with little effect, which reserved to the Crown 'such timber as may be growing or to grow thereafter, upon the said land which may be deemed fit for naval purposes'. It was also recommended that some of the convict ships should return with cedar, stringy-bark and box from New South Wales to help to relieve the shortage of ships' timber in Britain (*H.R.A.*, I, vol. 3: 571). Colonial cedar was particularly highly regarded and the authorities found it hard to contain the illegal trade in cedar-cutting in the country districts.

> It having been represented to the Governor that some of the Settlers at the Hawkesbury are making a traffic of the Cedar growing on or about that River, he strictly forbids any Cedar being cut down but by his particular permission to the Officer commanding at that place; And if any Cedar Logs or Planks are brought from any part of that River to any other Settlement without the Governor's permission, such Logs or Planks will be seized for the purposes of Government, and the Boats or Carts containing them confiscated to the public use (*H.R.A.*, I, vol. 3: 619).

Specialist research should disclose the reasons for the limited success achieved by these measures and the serious implications for landscape and society. The dominating utilitarian motives notwithstanding, dramatic and concentrated environmental degradation could not fail to alert some of the early Governors to the ecological dangers inherent in a management system which permitted the uncontrolled clearing of trees. King was particularly disturbed by the short-sighted, exploitative attitude taken by those colonists who were ignorantly increasing the natural flood hazard along the Hawkesbury and in 1803 he attempted to enforce protective measures.

> From the improvident method taken by the first Settlers on the side of the Hawkesbury and creeks in cutting down timber and cultivating the banks, many acres of ground have been removed, lands inundated, houses, stacks of wheat, and stock washed away by former floods, which might have been prevented in some measure if the trees and other native plants had been suffered to remain, and instead of cutting any down to have planted others to bind the soil of the banks closer, and render them less liable to be carried away by every inconsiderable flood.

> ... it is hereby directed that no settler or other person to whom ground is granted or leased on the sides of any river or creek where timber is now growing, do on any account cut down or destroy, by barking or otherwise, any tree or shrub growing within two rods of the edge of the bank, except for an opening one rod wide to have access to the water (*H.R.A.*, I, vol. 4: 67).

A considerable fine of fifty shillings per felled tree was to be imposed, with the penalty to be awarded in a similarly un-Australian way to the informant; here again, however, it is not yet possible to do more than to suggest that the directive probably had little or no durable effect.

2 Environmental Appraisal and Resource Management, 1830–50

IN close association with the accelerating changes in resource assessment and utilization during the Industrial Revolution, there was an increasing appreciation of the individual and collective promise of the great New World territories. This resulted in what might fairly be called a 'New World Revolution' with a story of its own, in which special environmental problems and potentials were identified and exploited by innovative management techniques, but significant cultural, financial, political and other links with the European hearth were always retained. For Australia, it is convenient for our present purposes to distinguish a second phase of settlement evolution in which an essential ingredient in the New World Revolution, the tension between Home and Colonial interests, was forcefully expressed in every major facet of environmental management.

For the people of Britain, an important back-drop to these developments was the promotion of an attractive new vision of Australia by Samuel Sidney, Charles Dickens and other popular writers. Coral Lansbury (1970) has shown how the image of Botany Bay was slowly changed from that of a small and distant cesspool of depravity to a veritable Arcady in which a Golden Age of rural prosperity and individual dignity might be recaptured. It is not difficult to accept her argument that there was indeed an assertion in English popular fiction that Arcady *was already established* in Australia and that Sidney's contribution towards the promulgation of the myth was paramount. The very boldness and apparent conviction expressed in his repeated claims must have contributed to the success of Sidney's campaign to market the idea of Australia in Britain.

> Australia—New South Wales—Botany Bay—these are the names under which, within the memory of men of middle age, a great island-continent at the antipodes has been explored, settled and advanced from the condition of a mere gaol, or sink, on which our surplus felonry was poured—a sheepwalk tended by nomadic burglars to be the wealthiest offset of the British crown—a land of promise for the adventurous—a home of peace and independence for the industrious—an El Dorado and an Arcadia combined, where the hardest and the easiest, best paid employments are to be found, where every striving man who rears a race of industrious children, may sit under the shadow of his own vine and his own fig tree—not without work, but with little care—living on his own land, looking down to the valleys to his herds—towards the hills to his flocks, amid the humming of bees, which know no winters (Sidney 1852: 17).

The discovery of gold in the 1850s brought scores of British travel writers to Australia, but the literary delineation of the continent was by that time so well established that no amount of personal experience could greatly modify it. Lansbury cites the case of Henry Kingsley's novel *The Recollections of Geoffry Hamlyn*—which, though set in Australia, could well have been written in London, despite the author's colonial experiences. Kingsley was writing commercially, for an established market, and his book was crammed from cover to cover with the accepted clichés and the familiar underplaying of natural hazards, particularly drought. He knew better, but the stereotyped formula proved to be a financial success.

> Australia was the Arcadian settlement of verdant plains and wooded heights, seamed with gold, where small farmers dwelt in rustic content supplying food to the diggers. The young pastoralists galloped freely through the bush, no whit different in appearance from the humblest shedhand or shearer. It was an expression of English social aspiration that men had no desire to see fulfilled in England itself, and an elegy to the way of life that had passed away before an age of industry and machines (Lansbury 1970: 121-2).

Australia was therefore subjected to the concentrated attention of some of Britain's most influential writers at a most crucial period in its history. It would have required a writer with the contemporary prestige of Dickens himself to change the image of Australia in English literature, but Dickens had no equal in his field. He refused an offer to tour Australia in 1862—the visit would surely have changed his whole concept of the country—and he maintained his rustic vision until the end. In the last quarter of the century, English farmers were struggling against the competition of imported produce from the New World. Workers could no longer 'look back to the land' which offered such insecurity, but forward to co-operative strength in trade unionism, in which they might force society to change according to their needs. Socialist doctrines proclaimed the liberation of the worker, and the elementary palliative of emigration was rejected. But Lansbury maintains that as the Arcadian myth became unacceptable to the rapidly industrialized urban societies of Britain, it was transferred to Australia, where it maintained a vigorous literary existence. Evidence will be offered later to qualify Lansbury's thesis and to suggest that the myth was in fact a virile hybrid of British and Australian stock. Its British characteristics are best seen in the root structure, certainly, but we should therefore be wary of over-exposure. The largest and most attractive part of the plant became thoroughly Australian. It was adapted to, and for, the political and social environment of the new nation, and there is no doubt that a major factor in its healthy growth was the continued learning process of identifying, interpreting and communicating the qualities of the Australian landscape.

At present, we must be more concerned with some of the developments supported in part by this literary promotion. This second phase of settlement was characterized initially by the introduction of certain mechanisms of 'Systematic Colonization' which were to be regulated by the sale of colonial land in regions of concentrated development; it ended with the discovery of gold and the separation of the Colony of Victoria from New South Wales. It will become clear that the precise dates bounding this complex phase should be accepted as no more than very rough guides.

Regional Planning, in Theory and Practice

The detailed management of Australia's greatest natural resource, the public lands, was bound to be influenced by the general ignorance of environmental conditions and the confused mixture of goals and attitudes. Above all it reflected a complicated interplay centred upon the senior local officials, who strove to make sense of their vague directives from London while at the same time resisting the claims of the most powerful local interest group, the big pastoralists or 'squatters'.

This situation is nicely illustrated in the theory and practice of settlement control by prior survey and land valuation. From the third decade of the nineteenth century Australia's isolation, natural environment and small population fitted it admirably for the extensive production of wool for the Yorkshire mills, then on the verge of a great expansion. Yet some of the most creative independent action of the early Governors had been directed towards the establishment of nursery-colonies of small farmers in selected localities (Jeans 1966a). Subsequently, the London authorities appear to have spent rather more of their own energies in fostering intensive cultivation and mixed farming, at the same time insisting upon the evils inherent in settlement dispersion and the 'civilizing' effects to be obtained from confining settlement within pre-determined geographical limits. The publicized official programme was also far more elaborate than its modest, flexible, spontaneous and often merely 'expedient' predecessors. The rationale of what transpired to be a rather ambigious policy was particularly rigorously stated in the 'thirties and 'forties, after the successful promotion of Edward Gibbon Wakefield's schemes for Systematic Colonization had emphasized a very full range of reciprocal benefits to be derived for Home and Colony from the introduction of a complicated method of controlled emigration and settlement, funded by carefully regulated land sales (Mills 1968; Philipp 1971).

Although Britain's armchair theorists succeeded in defining the familiar coastal, intermediate and interior or outback divisions of the country, their crude regionalization was obviously based upon a careless or naive acceptance of quite primitive locational controls and it was frequently queried and modified by the Governors (Jeans 1966a). The importance of pastoralism as a viable and long-term commercial land-use was completely underestimated, it seems, yet the industry had developed far too quickly to be ignored and the squatters were therefore charged a nominal rent without security of tenure, while the colonial authorities were directed to concentrate almost entirely upon the preparation of land within the pale for purchase and intensive settlement.

One of the first great projects to facilitate the expansion of farming settlement in the coastal districts involved the introduction of a rectangular land survey system after the American style, which for a time was highly esteemed in London for its apparent speed, cheapness and simplicity. The early Australian Governors occasionally did their best to honour their official instructions regarding the implementation of the programme, but by accident and design the field surveyors introduced their own variations. In addition, some Governors chose to ignore or manipulate their instructions, or boldly charged that the project was totally inapplicable to Australian conditions (Jeans 1966b). In North America the rectilinear grid survived to become widely extended as 'a striking example of geometry triumphant over physical geography' (Pattison 1964: 1), but the organization of land sub-division in the Australian Colonies followed a mixture of styles. There were strictly

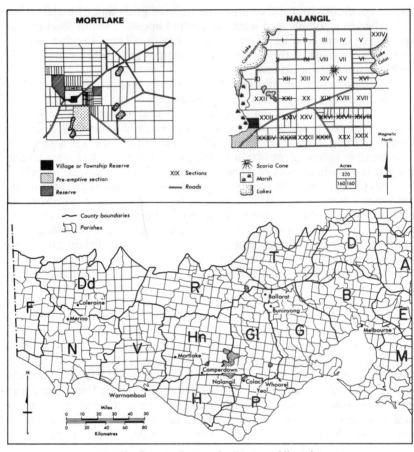

2   The Survey System in Western Victoria

Top
Mortlake, a type of 'parkland' town, and the planned suburban and country
sub-divisions in the surrounding parish; Nalangil parish, illustrating a Victorian modification of the American-style 'rectangular' survey pattern.

Lower
The uppermost divisions of the survey hierarchy, showing counties and parish
divisions. F—Follett county; Dd—Dundas; N—Normanby; V—Villiers;
R—Ripon; Hn—Hampden; H—Heytesbury; P—Polwarth; Gl—Grenville;
T—Talbot; G—Grant; B—Bourke; D—Dalhousie; A—Anglesey; E—Evelyn;
M—Mornington. The locations of Melbourne and of Mortlake and Nalangil
parishes are shown, together with a selection of other representative areas
discussed in detail in Powell 1970a: 32-55; 1970b.

local examples of almost pure rectangulation in which the survey lines could
not be extended to meet those of adjacent regions supposedly administered
under the same principle. In later years elsewhere, particularly in Wakefieldian South Australia, but also in Victoria, survey units were laid out
in an elementary hierarchy of sizes (Williams 1966a, 1966b; Meinig 1970;

Powell 1970b). The latter schemes were usually intended to complement the traditional regional planning framework for south-eastern Australia as a whole by providing for the gradual penetration of intensive settlement into the interior, at the same time varying the sizes of farm-blocks according to location and land quality (Figure 2).

Gipps and the 'Patrimony of the People'

The official-popular interplay which marked the earliest years of settlement became more intricate during this period of expansion. One major focus for the new research required to clarify the evolution of associated resource management practices is, indeed, the analysis of the direct and indirect roles taken by the Governors and their senior advisors. There is space for only a brief elaboration here.

The isolated but very powerful figure of Governor Sir George Gipps dominated the land policy of New South Wales between 1838 and 1849. Pleasing neither party, he chose to stand between the theorists of the Colonial Office and their most inflential opponents, the Port Phillip (Victorian) squatters. Gipps rejected the Wakefield-style plan to regulate the sale of highly priced land so as to ensure a gradual movement of labourers towards the ownership of small cultivated farms in regions of concentrated settlement. Ridiculing the 'contrivances' of the theory, he substituted an interesting common sense refinement of the relationship between lot size, location and price, which resulted in a novel Thünian sub-division around the town of Melbourne. The management decisions of Governor Gipps were also significant in the planning of Brisbane, but the nineteenth-century design in the case of the future capital of Queensland proved an unwelcome inheritance in several respects. It has directly contributed, for example, to the increasing problem of flooding in modern times, since one of Gipps' main decisions was to restrict the amount of urban open space, which might have reduced the hazard potential in the city (Laverty 1971, 1972).

Above all, Gipps repeatedly emphasized that some variant of the current mode of pastoral occupation would long be the mainstay of the Australian economy.

> The Theory of forcing persons to cultivate, or even to occupy lands in the order of their natural advantages, seems altogether to fail in Australia, where not the hundredth part of the land sold by the Government is purchased with any intention of cultivating it, and where scarcely one acre in a thousand is cultivated, of the land that is occupied without being purchased . . .

> But if the theory, by which it is sought to make persons cultivate lands in Australia in the natural order of their advantages, be altogether incapable of good, that which would seek to prevent the dispersion of the people is only capable of mischief, because it is utterly impossible to reduce it to practice. As well might it be attempted to confine the Arabs of the desert within a circle, traced upon their sands, as to confine the Graziers or Woolgrowers of New South Wales within any bounds that can possibly be assigned to them; and as certainly as the Arabs would be starved, so also would the flocks and herds of New South Wales, if they were confined, and the prosperity of the Country be at an end (*H.R.A.*, I, vol. 21: 127).

And so, to add to their problems of deciphering the new environment, the Imperial authorities were actually faced with two contrasting colonial views concerning the preferred management of the public domain: those of the Governor, and those of the squatters, who held almost revolutionary attitudes, born of a frontier pride in hard-won achievements.

> It was true, no doubt, in point of law, that these spacious domains, which formed the squatting stations of the country, did rest in the Crown by virtue of its prerogatives; but the Crown was but the trustee for the public. It was evident that all the value of this country, whether of the city or of its remotest acres, has been imported to it by its population; and consequently the country itself is our rightful and first inheritance . . . these wilds belong to us, and not to the British Government (*Sydney Morning Herald,* 10 April 1844).

But Gipps held dearly to the opinion that the same 'wilds' were 'the rightful patrimony of all the people of the United Kingdom', and he successfully argued that the granting of long leases to the pastoralists would ultimately create a dangerous and uneconomic monopoly (*H.R.A.,* 1, vol. 24: 782). Governor Gipps, acting in the role he had identified for himself as the most central of 'resource managers', received this eloquent support from the Bishop of Australia:

> Considering the numbers, station, and influence of those who compose the squatting interest, and that they have already a predominant interest in the Legislative Council, do you not clearly perceive that the effect of such measures, as we have been considering, must be to throw the whole power of the country into the hands of those few persons, in whom the bulk of real property will be vested? And what will this be but to create a democratic oligarchy, which will not long be denied the control and disposal of what are now the revenues of the Crown, in trust for the whole people of the United Kingdom? What can the Crown oppose to such a power? And what can the people do when they require land, and find that the whole is monopolised by a few, so that the many cannot obtain a single acre without coming to them, and agreeing to take it upon their own terms? (*H.R.A.,* I, vol. 24: 786).

The situation could indeed be interpreted as bristling with threatening implications: despite Gipps' passionate appeal on behalf of future generations there was far more than a straightforward 'conservation' issue here. Yet it is obvious that the conduct of all forms of resource management, *in any period*, can never be adequately portrayed as a marriage of coldblooded economics and the facts or theories of environmental science. It is demonstrably clear from the small amount that is presently known of Gipps' period of office that such matters as the assessment of personality and political and social interaction should be included in any serious analysis. The squatters were not entirely blocked in their efforts to lock up the lands, but in lieu of a reliable management scheme for the enlightened disposal of the public domain, Gipps had chosen to move independently to win a valuable breathing space. One is compelled to speculate that over large areas, the changing landscape must have borne the marks of the management decisions of this leading actor in the settlement process.

Profit and Loss: the Squatter and the Environment

Over vast areas of Australia beyond the coastal fringe, the pastoralists'

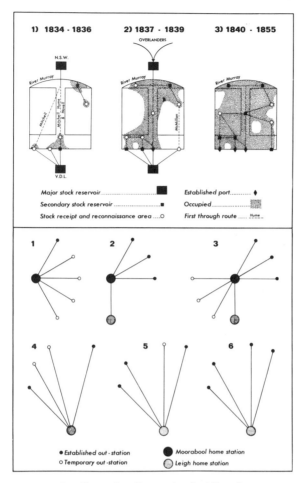

3   Squatting Expansion in Victoria

Top
A schematic representation of the patterns and processes involved in the expansion of the squatting frontier, emphasizing the locational significance of major points of entry and initial routes of penetration by exploration parties (Hume and Hovell, Mitchell), the basic physical differences between the Eastern and Western divisions of the Colony and the contributions made by the two older Colonies, Van Diemen's Land (Tasmania) and New South Wales.

Lower
Empirical testing on a major pioneer sheep-station, the Clyde Company's holding in Western Victoria, based on the initial choice of a base in the Moorabool Valley and its gradual replacement by the Leigh home-station, after a complicated process of 'testing' in both valleys, using a number of out-stations. The processes described briefly here are discussed in more detail in Powell 1968a, 1969, 1970a: 3-31.

independent, individualistic, mobile and opportunistic mode of settlement resulted in the first regional appraisals of land capability, which made a broad but valuable contribution towards environmental awareness by adding considerably to the piecemeal resource inventory compiled by the local officials. Small farmers and squatters alike became thoroughly experienced in the unavoidable empiricism of the current mode of environmental appraisal:

> Every settler is under the necessity of becoming a geologist; he must also be a geographer, that he may find water and not lose himself in the bush; and it must, indeed, be admitted that the intelligence of the native youth, in all such matters, is little inferior to that of the aborigines (Mitchell 1839, 2: 325).

The pastoralist was, however, the supreme exponent of this somewhat exaggerated art, and his contribution was best displayed in Victoria, originally the Port Phillip District of New South Wales—an area as large as England, and explored and occupied by a host of pioneer squatters in little more than fifteen years (Powell 1969). Before the close of an amazing period of expansion from 1834 to 1850, commercial sheep-farmers had brought the major regions of modern Victoria into focus by the simple process of empirical testing on each holding, coupled with individual and group reconnaissance of the surrounding country (Figure 3).

There is no form of exclusive concentration upon a single enterprise which could ever have served to elucidate the detailed environmental diversity of such immense new farming areas over the southern half of the continent. Yet much of this vast area was patently suited to extensive livestock management, principally for wool, since it was relatively subhumid country dominated by open grassland plains and thin savanna woodland. The squatters were not encouraged by their insecure tenure to undertake more than a small amount of experimentation in techniques of clearing, draining, fencing, cultivation and water supply, yet eventually this activity also accumulated useful information and support for their contemporaries and successors. This is particularly well displayed in the detailed regional distinctions which were emphasized by the determination of livestock-carrying capacities per holding, under the terms of the Orders-in-Councils of 1847-48 (Powell 1970a: 26-30).

By the late 'forties and early 'fifties the pastoralists formed an exceedingly powerful class, especially since scores of them had purchased freehold rights over their extensive holdings and had moved to positions of the highest social, economic and political rank. Individually and as a group they had progressed far more rapidly than most of the other colonists towards an understanding of the Australian environment and (when they were impartial) their considered appraisals deserved a great deal of respect. They were all justifiably proud of their frontiering and a few were already settling into new lives in new landscapes of their own making, soon to become splendid antipodean squires in opulent mansions set in landscaped parks—with high tea, tenant farmers, boarding schools and Oxford and Cambridge, a convivial hunt club and their own estate villages, no less, replete with churches and subservient clerics to suit their own persuasion (Kiddle 1961).

The 'reflective attitude' towards nature, which was encouraged in Europe by Alexander von Humboldt (1769-1859) and other great scholars, was already beginning to assist painters, writers and poets, whether residents or visitors, towards a new appreciation of the Australian landscape. Stressing the importance of these developments, conservationists who espouse the 'new nationalism' of the 1970s commonly attack the unpardonably resilient 'British' preferences of Australia's nineteenth-century *élitists*, presumably because they alone had possessed the power and the opportunity to ensure the preservation of much of the 'native' scenery. The futility of such arguments has already been indicated, but as a simple matter of record it is relevant to point to one important contribution of the squatters as a major *élitist* group towards landscape transformation. Beginning early in the century among the Tasmanians, who enjoyed the most temperate of local environments, there was a growing interest in landscaped parks and gardens which, for good or ill, added some valued comfort and familiar decoration to the Australian scene. It was nevertheless tragic that the economic and aesthetic arguments of Thomas Shepherd, one of the most perceptive and creative of Australia's early landscape gardeners, were largely wasted on the pastoralists.

> We have a few orchards it is true, and some romantically situated country residences, most embellished within the last few years, where attention appears to have been paid to the principles of this delightful art [landscape gardening] by gentlemen of taste and capital. But there is certainly much [that] remains to be effected ... In place of cutting down our splendid forests right forward without distinction, we have only to thin out, and tastefully arrange and dispose them, to produce the most pleasing effects. The country could by this means, at a very small cost, and with less labour than is required by the indiscriminate destruction of our native trees, present an exterior to the eye of the stranger and the resident in the Colony, such as no other country in the world I believe could furnish. Besides the pastoral nature of this country would favour such embellishments, as not an acre of ground would be lost—sheep might feed on our lawns and parks, adding the pleasure of seeing living objects enjoy the benefits of improved scenery (Shepherd 1836, quoted in Spooner 1974: 4).

There was in addition a definite *negative* contribution in the exploitative, trial and error procedures of the years of pastoral pioneering and this was extremely damaging: certainly for the Victorian environment, and possibly for that of other areas which are less well documented. Following the first big impact of the gold rushes of the 'fifties, Lieutenant Governor Charles Joseph La Trobe compiled an invaluable collection of reminiscences from old pioneers of the pastoral era and although there is surprisingly little of specific interest for the student of environmental history in this familiar but underused material, in several places La Trobe's correspondents clearly reveal some of the immediate and long-term consequences of the squatters' rough invasion (Bride 1969). Whereas C. B. Hall, for example, preferred to remember the 'pleasure of exploring'—of observing rather than transforming the face of nature, 'which heterodox as the opinion in these days may seem was, to my eye, more beautiful than in its present aspect of national pretensions and magnificence'—he also wistfully recalled the abundance of emu, geese, swans, kangaroos, quail, bush turkeys and other 'game' (Bride 1969: 268). Similarly, the blunt and egocentric Captain Foster Fyans, a former Commissioner of Crown Lands in the Pastoral District of Portland Bay, chose to emphasize a basic distinction between the 'gentlemen' squatters and those who were merely 'a kind of shop-boys', and the award of either description to any individual squatter was only partially dependent upon the degree of hospitality the good Commissioner had received during his period of office. His favoured gentlemen 'of undoubted character and well connected at home' did indeed combine in regular enjoyment of some of the pleasures of the more privileged of British country folk.

> Mount Emu is a beautiful country. A noble pack of hounds was kept up by gentlemen squatters who met every season, hunting twice and thrice a week, and meeting at each others' houses, where good cheer and good and happy society were ever to be met . . . at daybreak the master of the hounds, a squatter, sounded his bugle; shortly after, his second, for breakfast; and in half an hour his third bugle, when a fine pack of dogs let loose from the kennel appeared, full of life and glee, led away by the well-known master of the hounds, Compton Ferrers, followed by thirty well-mounted gentlemen squatters (Bride 1969: 185-6).

Fyans was far from impressed with the flood of immigrants in the early 'fifties ('You are aware of the goldfields—the ruin of the colony') and his ridiculous class prejudices never permitted him to consider laying any of the blame for the decimation of wildlife at the doors of those gentlemen 'sportsmen' who shared his own love of shooting.

> Emus and kangaroos on our arrival were plentiful in all parts of the district; also bustards in large flocks of from ten to thirty or forty, or perhaps more. The bustards now are scarce, and only met with in distance places. The kangaroo and emu are nearly extinct in the [Western] district; the country is almost void of game. Quails in years gone by were plentiful, but I think are fast disappearing; snipe we have in the season, but not in the same abundance as in other countries; we also have the painted snipe, the same bird that is met with in all parts of India; black ducks, large, and a delicacy; also various small ducks, and wood ducks, etc; the bronzewing pigeon, a fine game bird, fully equal to an English partridge; black swans,—useless and ugly; snakes of many descriptions, and some exceedingly bold—the more so than I have known them in India . . . For an idler or a sportman, this country affords nothing, and for a military officer it is the most damnable quarter in the world. There is nothing in the shape of sport except in the season a few snipe and quail; then it ends until the next September (Bride 1969: 191-2).

Even today, deliberate persecution, and certainly *controlled* hunting, would be largely discounted as serious problems in fauna conservation except in such special circumstances as those of proved or suspected rarity, the high scientific or community-endorsed value of some type of distribution and so on. But it is a fact that except for some early moves to restrict the shooting seasons the notion of any true form of legal protection for native animals arrived very late indeed in Australia, and the sentiments underlying Fyans' remarks were representative of public attitudes towards wildlife until the most recent years. It seems that three major species were recognized in the middle of the nineteenth century: 'vermin', 'edible' and 'game'. The kangaroo and the wallaby had the singular bad fortune to belong to each of these classifications, yet they easily survived in this period in most localities and may even have increased where more reliable water supplies were provided for stock and domestic use. The European rabbit, more so than in any other country, is now firmly placed in the first of the three categories. It was probably originally introduced into the Australian region by whalers and sealers, the first of our ecological marauders, to improve the food supply of relatively isolated and hitherto undisturbed off-shore islands. But it is known that a few pairs were deliberately imported from Britain in 1859 to provide comfortable and familiar sport on the pastoral stations of Victoria's Western District and their subsequent diffusion across the continent, successfully competing with many native and introduced domestic species, provides one of the world's most remarkable and disturbing examples of ill-considered acclimatization.

Without more detailed research into the fate of our indigenous fauna during the squatting mode of occupation, there is no point in introducing modern predilections to take the case further. It would be a particularly unreasonable complaint to suggest, for instance, that the pastoralists should have been able to draw upon a peculiarly wide experience of these and other types of environmental change in Australia, as well as the power to press for some control. They were then deeply engrossed in a complex variety of political and economic issues, and obviously, neither they nor any of their fellow colonists can be blamed for activities which had the full sanction of their own times. Again, it is perfectly fair to say that fauna conservation depends primarily upon two factors: the preservation of habitat, which was principally threatened in the intensively settled coastal region, and a detailed knowledge, which was not widely available for many years, of the effects of habitat modifications on animal populations.

Where soil, water and vegetation were concerned, however, the profound deterioration of a number of properties over a brief period of grazing occupation was far more tangible and challenging to the early pastoralists: it was registered annually, in their account books and even daily, on their consciences. Mistakes were bound to be made, especially in difficult territory which was eventually judged to be 'marginal' in the prevailing technical and economic climate. So the bewildered John G. Robertson, shortly before his return to Scotland, wrote to La Trobe of the marked decline of his 50,000 acres in the south-west of Victoria.

Many of our herbaceous plants began to disappear from the pasture land; the silk-grass began to show itself in the edge of the bush track, and in patches here and there on the hill. The patches have grown larger every year; herbaceous plants and grasses give way for the silk-grass and the little annuals, beneath which are annual peas, and die in our deep clay soil with a few hot days in spring, and nothing returns to supply their place until later in the winter following. The consequence is that the long deep-rooted grasses that held our strong clay hill together have died out; the ground is now exposed to the sun, and it has cracked in all directions, and the clay hills are slipping in all directions; also the sides of precipitous creeks—long slips taking trees and all with them. When I first came here, I knew of but two land-slips, both of which I went to see; now there are hundreds found within the last three years. A rather strange thing is going on now. One day all the creeks and little watercourses were covered with a large tussocky grass, with other grasses and plants, to the middle of every watercourse but the Glenelg and Wannon, and in many places of these rivers; now that the only soil is getting trodden hard with stock, springs of salt water are bursting out in every hollow or watercourse, and as it trickles down the watercourses in summer, the strong tussocky grasses die before it with all others. The clay is left perfectly bare in summer. The strong clay cracks; the winter rain washes out the clay; now mostly every little gully has a deep rut; when rain falls it runs off the hard ground, rushes down these ruts, runs into the larger creeks, and is carrying earth, trees and all before it. Over Wannon country is now as difficult a ride as if it were fenced. Ruts, seven, eight, and ten feet deep and as wide, are found for miles, where two years ago it was covered with tussocky grass like a land marsh (Bride 1969: 168-9).

We urgently require a thorough evaluation of the profits and losses to the Australian environment which were registered in the major years of pastoral expansion and in the succeeding confusion of mining activity during the 'fifties. Superficially, this might appear to involve a process of accounting which demands a higher level of interdisciplinary co-operation than we have come to expect in Australia, yet several of the necessary skills are already represented within Geography itself! Hasten the day when biogeographers, geomorphologists and historical geographers combine to interpret and communicate the ecological impact of both the 'Squatting Age' and the 'Golden Age'.

3 Vandals and Scientists: the 'Fifties

THE population of Australia grew from 438,000 in 1851 to 1,168,000 in 1861 and in Victoria, which experienced the maximum impact of the gold-mining developments of this time, the total population soared from 77,000 in 1851 to 460,000 in 1857 and 540,000 at the end of the decade—principally because of a massive immigration which all but swamped the existing society and made, in a sense, 'a new, large, self-governing county, automatically recreating British institutions and re-forming familiar clubs and societies' (Serle 1963: 381). The braking effect of this rapid influx upon the previous development of Australian patriotism can be overstated, but the external signs were plain enough for most contemporary observers.

> ... [in] spite of foreign vegetation, the English stamp and English character are on all their settlements. They are English houses, English enclosures that you see; English farms, English gardens, English cattle and horses, English fowls about the yards, English flowers and plants carefully cultivated. You see great bushes of furze, even by the rudest settlers' cottages. There are hedges of sweet-briar around their gardens, bushes of holly ... There are hawthorns and young oaks in the shrubberies. There are cowslips and oxslips now in flower in the gardens, but no primroses that I have yet seen ... England reproduces herself in new lands; and how feeble seem the native races against the sinewy, plucky, pushing, predominating Englishman (Howitt 1972: 57).

In fact, it could also have been said that some of Victoria's regional land-scapes, like those of the Midlands and Northern England, quickly suffered the disastrous consequences of uncontrolled urbanization and rapacious mining operations. But there was still a very *Australian* flavour to the successes and failures of environmental appraisal and management throughout the 'fifties.

Melbourne, Polluted and Profitable

By 1861 about 46 per cent of Australia's population lived in Victoria and for some time the Colony had been producing about one-sixth of Britain's imports of wool and one-third of the world's gold. From a small port of 20,000 inhabitants at the end of the 'forties, an insignificant outpost of the Empire without decent roads, pavements, sanitation, water or gas supplies, frequently reeking of the appalling stench of busy tallow works, Melbourne became a bustling commercial centre with 125,000 residents, the hub of a growing import and export trade, the headquarters of Australian banking, the country's major reception centre for immigrants, and the capital of the most celebrated of Britain's colonies. Before the end of the decade the urban area had all the trappings of a comparatively well-administered industrial and commercial centre, including a useful transport system, reticulated water and gas, the beginnings of a promising local government network, an Art Gallery, Public Library and University. There was still a great deal to do, but the town had made remarkable progress, partly in response to an experience of extremely low and deteriorating living conditions in the early years of the boom.

Initially, Melbourne grew haphazardly and some parts of the city were horribly polluted. This was mainly due to the absence of rigorous planning controls, and above all the need for an adequate zoning scheme to ensure the separation of industrial and residential land-uses and the isolation of 'noxious trades'. The Yarra, long since renowned as an 'upside-down river', fully deserved its reputation at this time. In 1852 Howitt described the worst of several activities leading to a vile corruption of the natural watercourse:

> The most revolting sights which I have seen here are the slaughter-houses, which are placed exactly on the riverside, so that anyone coming up by the steamer is treated to a view of them. They are wooden buildings with a fenced-in yard on one side, in which stand the poor wretched victims, amid mountains of the heads of their predecessors, from which a host of pigs are rending the flesh. On the other side, and half in the river, are equal heaps of entrails and garbage, which other swine are rending. Altogether, the filth, the blood, the piles of heads of cattle, either stripped of their flesh or in the process of it, and the crowds of poor animals standing in the midst, patiently awaiting their fate, is one of the most shocking and disgusting scenes that can be conceived. In the hot weather the stench and danger of contagion must be of no ordinary kind . . . At present it is in the very front and prominence of the approach to this El-Dorado capital (Howitt 1972: 38-9; cf. Potts and Potts 1970: 17).

Howitt blamed it all on the rush to be rich: 'the one great principle of the colony is the Dutchman's maxim:—"Get honestly, if you can; but at all events get!"'. People avow the principle. They come here, in fact, as they go to India, to make fortunes, and then, "go home"' (Howitt 1972: 37). He probably did encounter many of these 'servants of mammon' living in a sort of temporary exile, but it was unfair to generalize so easily: it is known, for example, that of some 300,000 entering Victoria from Britain in the 'fifties little more than 15 per cent returned. But it was true, none the less, that it was a heavily materialistic society—with so much gold and such a large proportion of eager new immigrants it could hardly have been otherwise. Success in Victoria had always depended to a high degree on elements of chance, as well as upon skill and application. All types of speculation had been virtually endemic since the first frantic land sales in 1837, continuing through the 'land rushes' of the early days of squatting and the subsequent repeated gambling with markets and seasons. The 'fifties provided unique opportunities, however, for large-scale speculation in the building industry and in urban real estate, and the results are still deeply ingrained in the fabric of Melbourne's townscape.

Adelaide was far better served by Colonel William Light's ideas for the divided focus of the central district, the geometrical arrangement of streets, blocks and squares, the reservation of the riverine strips and his enlightened provision of a 'parkland' belt separating the city and its suburbs. It was a carefully planned city for an intricately planned Colony and its design mirrored the ideals of the Colony's founders. Unfortunately this excellent plan was later less successfully used as a model for hundreds of smaller townships in the country districts (Williams 1966b) and the leading citizens of the capital itself became increasingly complacent about their sacrosanct park-land, resisting every effort to extend the philosophy behind the original idea to the expanding suburban districts. In comparison, Sydney was permitted to grow more or less haphazardly in the early years, although (like Hobart) it had the marked advantage of a singularly beautiful natural setting. Melbourne's site was less well-endowed by nature, and although the early reservation of some central parks relieved the monotony of its flat and gently rolling topography, the lax supervision of expansion ensured that the Adelaide model was not repeated in Victoria.

The depressing suburban sprawl which now overpowers the Australian city had its major origins in the speculative process which consumed Melbourne. There was a rapid acceleration in the migration of the wealthier classes from the expanding central business district 'to live in the manner of our London and Liverpool merchants, so far as their wealth and taste enable them' (Horne 1859: 148), in ornate villas in St Kilda, Richmond, Prahran, Hawthorn and Heidelberg, all within reasonable carriage-distance of town. Commuting was quickly established as a major feature of the Melbourne scene, as development expanded into the southern and south-eastern sectors.

> If, morning or evening, you go out into the great roads in the vicinity, especially that leading to Prahran, St. Kilda and Brighton, you find a continuous chain of drays, omnibuses, carriages, and people, reaching for miles; on all sides hundreds and thousands of clerks and men of business are marching in in the morning, or out in the evening in groups, and knots of acquaintances and neighbours, bound for the numberless rural dwellings which stud the vicinity for miles round. All seem to cling to their English habits of getting out of the city as soon as the counting-house stool is abandoned, and breathing the air, and enjoying the quiet of the country. Therefore Melbourne has its great living tide, night and morning, flowing towards it, and again ebbing from it, as regularly as London has (Howitt 1972: 310).

In fact, Liverpool, Chicago and other new commercial creations of the nineteenth century offer closer spatial comparisons than London, which had captured or engulfed several pre-existing settlements during its long and continuing period of expansion (Spate 1951; Briggs 1971; Ward 1971). Lacking a cheap public transport system and with the Victorian Government refusing to offer more urban land for sale to counter spiralling prices, the working-class residents were forced to choose tiny allotments in locations close to the centre. The major immigrant quarters in Collingwood, South and North Melbourne, Fitzroy and Carlton were at first amazing spectacles of rampant jerry-building: 'Money was so plentiful and accommodation so urgent, that Building became a natural mania: almost anything constituted a "House", and in those days, canvas and paper wrought miracles' (*Australasian Builder and Land Advertiser*, 7 August 1856: 182). It was well said of the Melbournians that 'They go ahead in everything excepting order, cleanliness, effective police, good taste, and security of property' (Howitt 1972: 39), for there was nothing very progressive or civilizing about an urban management system which permitted the rapid construction of expensive new slums in the inner districts.

Here is a new settlement in all its newness. The houses are some of them complete, others are just erecting. A balder and more unattractive scene cannot
meet the eye of man. Every single tree has been levelled to the ground; it is one
hard bare expanse, bare of all nature's attractions, a wilderness of wooden huts
of Lilliputian dimensions; and everywhere around and amongst them, timber
and rubbish, delightfully interspersed with pigs, geese, hens, goats, and dogs
innumerable. The streets, so called, which all run in the true gridiron or rather
hurdle style, are not roads but quagmires, through which bullock drays drag
fresh materials, with enormous labour ploughing the muddy soil up to their
very axles. There is not the trace even of the idea of a garden amongst the whole
of them. These diminutive tenements are set down on the open field, as if they
were the abodes of a race of squatters, *but they are all built on purchased allotments* (Howitt 1972: 15; my italics).

Howitt's final qualification is important: the little they had was at least
their own. Similarly, the young economist William Stanley Jevons, in his
interesting manuscript notes for the unfinished and overly class-conscious
'Social Map of Sydney', found himself wavering between aesthetic revulsion
and grudging appreciation for the colonial production.

But nowhere except in Australia could be seen collections of such hastily erected
frail and small habitation[s], devoid of even a pretence to ornament and in
many or most cases belonging to and built by those who inhabit them. Almost
every labourer and mechanic here has his own residence on freehold or lease-
hold land and unpretending as it is to any conveniences or beauties, it yet satisfies
him better than the brick built, closely packed and rented houses of English
towns. An Australian second or third class suburb would not be taken for a
permanent part of a town at all; it more resembles the wooden huts of a military
encampment (Jevons 1858: 28).

Chicago's famous school of urban studies in the 1920s was preoccupied
with researching the impersonal forces which shaped the urban environment.
There has recently been a major reaction to this emphasis even within the
more traditional quarters of urban geography, leading to the promotion of
alternative explanatory schemes highlighting the organizing processes involved in community values and action. The variable development of Australia's
cities offers good support for this viewpoint. The 'built environment' of the
city influences the distributions of people and institutions in so far as it sets
limits (which may not be perceived) to the kind of cultural values that can
be developed or maintained, and within these limits it 'provides scope for
the expression of these values in certain ways but not in others' (Martin
1970: 302). Under prolonged conditions of rampant speculation in the
less desirable living areas of Melbourne, the original sub-divisions
became progressively smaller even before there was a substantial resident
population. Only in the smaller and much older Rocks district were conditions worse than this: Jevons remarked that although he was 'acquainted
with the worst parts of London ... and with the most unhealthy parts of
Liverpool, Paris' and other European centres, he had never before encountered 'such a retreat for filth and vice as "the Rocks" of Sydney ... the
highest disgrace both to the municipal authorities and the landlords of the
neighbourhood' (Jevons 1858: 22).

These problems were of course exacerbated by the absence of firm civic planning and, while many speculators grew wealthy on the immediate profits, the enormous long-term losses accrued to the Victorian and Australian communities in general, and most of all to the unfortunate local residents, who were able to achieve only a limited amount of success in their struggles against the cynical forces of nineteenth-century 'realism' (Barrett 1971).

The situation improved after the introduction of the *Municipal Corporations Act* of December 1854, which established the English 'urban district' as the model for local government in Victoria. In the following two years, twelve new councils were proclaimed and elected, struck their first rates, received supplementary aid from the first self-governing Victorian Parliament and began the construction of vital public works. By 1860 there were fifty-six municipal districts providing, in theory, dramatically improved opportunities for democratic political activity to contribute towards the making of the cultural landscape in Melbourne and throughout the Colony. As yet, there has been no full-scale investigation of the planning activities of these bodies.

The Environmental Impact of Gold-Mining

Where the winning of a quick profit was patently the sole motivation, on the diggings themselves, visual pollution and environmental degradation reached appalling levels. Howitt complained that Ballarat, like Melbourne, was becoming a veritable bottle-dump, and although he was frequently drawn to express his excited admiration for the wonderful rapidity of the transformation of the mining landscape, he ruefully noted the passing of the wilderness: 'Every tree is felled; every feature of Nature is annihilated' (Howitt 1972: 252; the habit had been established earlier, however—cf. Meredith 1844: 56). It may be that the worst feature of this period—and it is no better for being inevitable—was that the mining interests, great and small, were permitted so much control over the Colony's forest and water resources at a time when there was general ignorance at every level of the full extent of those resources and their future significance.

Most of the gold-fields were situated in wooded hills, ranges and valleys which hitherto had been lightly used or virtually ignored, and these quite finely balanced ecosystems were maintained by a mutual adjustment of slopes, drainage and vegetation cover which could not survive the amazing destruction wrought by the miners.

The diggers seem to have two especial propensities, those of firing guns and felling trees. It is amazing what a number of trees they fell. No sooner have they done their day's work, than they commence felling trees, which you hear falling continually with a crash, on one side of you or another. In fact, the stringy-bark is the most useful tree conceivable, for the diggers as well as for squatters. Its bark easily peels off, and forms large sheets, which become hard as boards, from half an inch to an inch thick. These make sides and roofs of huts. They make also floors for them, and for tents. They make seats and tables, one of which we have laid on two trestles in our tent. It forms boats, and spouts and shoots for water. You see large shoots of it to convey the water from the diggers' holes, or to their washing places. A few sheets of canvas, or a few blankets, eked out by sheets of stringy-bark, form numbers of temporary abodes at the diggings. You see numbers of stringy-bark trees standing with their bark stripped off for six or eight feet high, and others felled, and completely stripped. The wood is not less useful. It has the property of easily cleaving, and splits up readily into posts and rails, into slabs for the walls of huts, or into anything that you want. Therefore, there is great destruction of this tree, and fortunately there is no lack of it. It burns very well quite green, so that it supplies fuel at hand (Howitt 1972: 176-7).

In their living state the trees were less highly regarded, for they disguised important microgeological features which served the miners very well in lieu of adequate topographical maps and scientific data, and in any case they obviously restricted the working operations then in vogue (cf. Report 1856-7). The practice of clear-felling undoubtedly initiated the process of accelerated erosion, especially the savage gullying which scars wide areas of the old diggings today. Further injury was inflicted directly and indirectly by each of the ruling techniques of mining. Before the discovery of quartz reefs and 'deep leads' (underground, in ancient valleys), *surfacing* and *shallow sinking* predominated. The first of these concerned the washing of the thin covering of gold-bearing earth from the higher slopes and hill-tops; the second was the practice of sinking shallow pits in the deeper deposits at lower relative elevations closer to the streams and even in the very river-beds. During the subsequent processes, a great deal of·water was required to sort the gold from the 'washdirt'. In the early years, individuals and small groups could perform these tasks satisfactorily with the aid of a spade and small wooden 'puddling-tubs' and 'cradles'. Later, the horse-driven puddling-machine was introduced wherever the local prospects and water supply could support it, and this quickly led to more thorough operations on the new deposits and a frantic re-working of some of the older fields.

There was profit and good employment in all of this, of course. In the peak year of puddling in 1858 over 5,000 of the machines were used in Victoria and, at Bendigo alone, some 10,000 men and 5,000 horses worked 2,000 machines. Beautiful valley-sides were literally stripped to the bone, their flesh digested in the puddlers and the unwanted residue flushed downstream. In later years, even the great rivers of New Zealand's Westland region were hard-pressed to withstand the additional load imposed by gold-mining operations (McCaskill 1966). Few Australian streams could ever have survived without permanent injury to their function in the natural drainage system and their original ability to maintain a variety of life forms. At Bendigo vast quantities of sludge moved down the valley, frequently blocking all the natural watercourses, inundating agricultural and residental land and greatly increasing the damage wrought in the town by the occasional flash floods, which would have been reasonably well controlled under normal drainage conditions (Smyth 1869: 93).

'*Hydraulic mining*', including a variety of *sluicing* operations, was introduced into Victoria's north-eastern fields by Californian miners. The method depended upon reliable water supplies of good volume and was not widely employed elsewhere. Its most devastating procedure involved the undercutting of hillsides and steep stream banks down to bed-rock, using powerful jets fed by water races which stretched for between three and twenty miles across the rough countryside. Depending on the nature of the material

4 The Port Phillip and Colonial Gold Mining Company, Clunes (from Smyth, 1869)

involved, hydraulic sluicing enabled a single worker to shift between fifty and over one hundred cubic yards, twice the amount obtained by other sluicing methods, in a normal winter's day. *Deep sinking, tunnelling* and *quartz mining*, which became more common in the late 'fifties and early 'sixties, are usually noted for their contribution towards increasingly capitalistic modes of organization and the resultant social and political transformations. Their disruptive ecological role has not yet been examined and was not perceived at the time: greater demands were made on the forests for pit props, fuel and general equipment; similarly the deep shafts and various types of tunnelling must have disturbed local water tables and the side effects of these processes may still be accumulating. There was also a larger scale to the mining operations which emphasized these effects and, in addition, showed great efficiency in building up spoil into innumerable 'mullock heaps' to disfigure the landscape and totally confound the local working of the natural system.

A better example of secure and productive water-use was available in the Chinese market gardens in the vicinities of each of the main settlements, and the attitudes and actions of the thrifty gardeners certainly attracted far more favourable attention than the painstaking thoroughness of the Chinese miners—which was probably no kinder towards the environment than the activities of the Europeans. The irrigated market gardens hinted at great potentials for increased productivity and intensive settlement, but this was overshadowed by the mining boom. For the Victorian and Australian community in general, however, mining did eventually highlight the vital significance of water as a resource and distinguished some of the major legal, political and administrative implications inherent in its management in a dry continent. In several districts during the 'fifties, race-holders spurned the toils of mining itself and made a good living from the 'sale' of water rights, contrary to the spirit and purpose of the original vague legislation which had been developed too casually to link the specified rights of using the water to directly productive activities.

> Looking at the authority under which races were originally occupied, it is obvious that the claimholder had granted to him only an easement—a privilege. It is true that he has from time to time endeavoured to strengthen his title. The water diverted in the first instance in order to work a particular claim then in his occupation was subsequently used to work some other piece of ground. Afterwards he ceased to be a miner, or continued to be so only in name; but believing that he had an exclusive right to the enjoyment of the water over which he had had control for a long period, he did not hesitate to sell it; and in this manner, by slow growth as it were, *the claimholder was transformed into an owner of water*. Regarding his own interests, entirely indifferent to the wants and requirements of the miners, and not hesitating when necessary to encroach on their privileges, the race-owner was looked upon with jealousy and distrust. He, believing that he had an equitable if not a legal right to the water, was exacting; and the miner, knowing the nature of the title, was not slow to avail himself of its weakness, and to thwart and annoy him by damaging his race and diverting the water (Smyth 1869: 398; my italics).

The Victorian Government had neither the financial strength, technical expertise, nor even the political opportunity or inclination, to move quickly to regularize this chaotic situation. New legislation was eventually passed in the 'sixties, however, to permit the issue of more clearly defined licences for races and reservoirs in order to preserve the rights of the mining community as a whole over those of the individual, and subsidies were granted to encourage the construction of water storages and reticulation systems under the control of the local district bodies. In reality, the convenient 'democratization' of water-use was seldom achieved by this form of decentralized administration, which remained open to considerable manipulation by local worthies and especially by the mining companies. But the principle of *public ownership* of a crucial resource had been given a good hearing and the new regulations established a useful precedent for future management decisions.

The diggers loom massively in Australia's social and political history, but their contribution was also crucial, yet far more ambiguous, in the history of environmental management. The most difficult aspect of this is possibly that there were so many of them who surely achieved their own type of competence in 'bushmanship'—including a deep respect as well as intimate knowledge—during their lonely treks and makeshift efforts for food and shelter in the wilds of the new country. We know too little as yet of the type of environmental attitudes later imparted by those miners who entered the business of pioneer farming; there is still, however, that disconcerting record in the ruins of the gold-fields.

> Little more than a year ago, the whole of this valley on the Bendigo Creek, seven miles long by one and a half wide, was an unbroken wood! It is now perfectly bare of trees, and the whole of it riddled with holes of from ten to eighty feet deep—all one huge chaos of clay, gravel, stones, and pipe-clay, thrown up out of the bowels of the earth! So much has been done on this one

forest in one year; and not only so much but a dozen other valleys as large . . .
It is thus that a few months sees the most wonderful metamorphosis of the
country where gold is. It is thus that one of those tremendous rushes which
takes place whenever there is the least rumour of success anywhere, brings tens
and tens of thousands speedily together, like a flight of locusts, who tear up
and leave the earth desert in a few weeks (Howitt 1972: 47-8).

Urbanization, the New Bureaucracy and the Learned Societies

We have neither art nor the reminiscences of the past. Even nature itself is tame
and destitute of poetry. The only food for imagination is the *future*—and the
idea that *that* future may be moulded and influenced, and directed, so as to
produce what is great and glorious, by our individual exertions . . . Were I in
England I should only regard myself an unit in twenty six millions of my fellow
beings, impotent for any design to benefit the race to which I belonged. *Here*
on the contrary I am enabled to exercise the small modicum of ability that God
has granted me, in a way that may to some extent be useful to those who may
live ages hence. No man need wrap up his talent in a napkin and hide it—but
may employ it with usury. *Here* we have to lay the foundations of a social
edifice—that may endure for good or evil as long as the race to which we belong
may inhabit this planet. This aspect of our peculiar and special condition ac-
quires additional force with me every day—and reconciles me to what would
otherwise be a prosaic and often intolerable life (Charles Nicholson, quoted in
Dyster 1965: 304).

There was an equally significant and more accurately perceived transformation of Australia's *social* environment during these years. During the
'forties, the increasing dominance of the urban centres, particularly the
capitals, had been apparent to many leading contemporaries. In Sydney,
especially, there was a strong belief in the future of the city as a hearth of
enterprise and innovation, and several influential figures were questioning
the traditional view of urban dependence upon the country, proclaiming or
demanding the full and immediate commitment of their respective urban-
based professions to the pursuit of 'progress', 'development' and the application of 'expertise' (Dyster 1965). Australia's mining boom attracted men of
confirmed standing in several diverse fields. It also helped to launch the
careers of others who came to participate, perhaps to lead, in the construction of the new urban community, and it supplied the *opportunity* for many
more, whether or not they were directly or indirectly concerned in mining,
to find and develop their best talents. The 'American'-style declaration
quoted above was made by one of Sydney's civic leaders on the eve of the
boom, but it was, after all, simply the articulation of an *immigrant's* perception of a personal challenge, and must have applied with equal force in
the other emergent cities. It is a useful reminder that location theory can never
fully explain the processes of urbanization: the very *response* to the
new locational condition must also be accounted an integral part of the
causal mechanisms involved—according to the nature of that response, it
may even have exerted a significant braking, accelerating or reorientating
effect upon the fundamental geographical and social facts of increasing
population concentration. In employing this type of humanistic interpretation, we can only be concerned here with the consequences for influential

contemporary views on the appraisal and management of both the natural and the built environments. The reaction to the new situation was probably better illustrated in Victoria than in New South Wales, yet the large mining settlements of Victoria are really special cases of urbanization in the Australian context and considering present limitations, the selection of Melbourne alone for some detailed commentary does appear to offer a more 'representative' example.

At first the Australian response to urbanization naturally fed on the same sources of inspiration which fuelled the great debate on the British city during the nineteenth century (Briggs 1971: 59-87), but a recognizably Australian flavour was always maintained. In Britain the critics of the city were largely those who favoured and promoted the countryside or various types of model communities as alternatives, and those who sought instead the radical 'improvement' of the existing fabric (Coleman 1973). One reason for the most trenchant criticism concerned the loss of power to the established religion, which had previously depended on personal contact and on stable, stratified community life; another related concern was the threat posed by the city to the traditional politics of personal or family influence. The case *for* the city was of course based precisely on these same grounds, and proudly asserted the new values of economic competition and social individualism. But it is important to note that although the controversy in Britain had more or less reached 'an age of equipoise', mildly fluctuating between phases of optimism and pessimism, but without the extremes of earlier or later years (Coleman 1973: 2), the immigrants to Victoria brought these same arguments with them—with the full range of sub-themes, ranging from Chartism through to Social Environmentalism, including Public Hygiene and a fresh spirit of social enquiry which had been generated by the great debate itself and by the continuing observation of a community experiencing rapid urbanization. The study of 'Political Economy', for example, had been introduced in Britain to satisfy the curiosity about the new industrialism and this initiated a wide-reaching statistical and impressionistic investigation of urban society. The old arguments were enlivened in Victoria at the end of the 'fifties (as they were frequently enlivened in Britain during the century) when general social and economic prospects looked comparatively gloomy. But before that happened, the educated and articulate classes were already busying themselves in 'improving' city life and in monitoring the changing situation of the Colony.

Among the most interesting products of the 'Age of Improvement' were the Mechanics' Institutes, founded in Britain in the late eighteenth century and subsequently turning up in every nook and cranny throughout the English-speaking world (Briggs 1969). Australia's Mechanics' Institutes performed a valuable service in the 'diffusion of knowledge', especially among the working classes, but there was considerably greater civic and cultural importance attached to the more pretentious bodies which served the local cultural *élite*. Within the first few years of Separation, intellectual activity rapidly expanded under the vital patronage of Lieutenant-Governor La Trobe and, while the Mother Colony of New South Wales languished far behind, organized science in Victoria rivalled, then outstripped, the commendable achievements of the Tasmanians. By the end of the decade Austra-

5 'Yan Yean Impurities' (from the *Melbourne Punch*)

Engineers, physicians and other technical experts, disagreeing over the quality of Melbourne's public water supply, bring a major issue in resource management under public scrutiny. A letter on the subject from a real or imaginary citizen had appeared a few weeks earlier in the same journal—

Sir—I have observed in the daily papers lately a great deal of correspondence and discussion about the purity or impurity of the Yan Yean water, and I perceive that a scientific gentleman recommends the admixture of two and a half grains of ter-sulphate of alumina to the gallon, by way of guarding against all ill-effects.

Not being scientific myself, I have not tried that experiment, nor do I know exactly what ter-sulphate of alumina is, but as a practical man I have found the following recipe makes the Yan Yean water very palatable:—to two thirds of a tumbler of Yan Yean water, hot, add one-third of pale French brandy and two lumps of white sugar (*Melbourne Punch*, 19 August 1858).

lian science in general was far less parochial than it had ever been; it was in fact rapidly maturing and 'the period of the collector, the dilettante scientist and the individual worker, for so long characteristic features of colonial science, was soon to be superseded' (Hoare 1967: 8; see also Hoare 1968). Victoria's scientific progress in the 'fifties constituted an indispensable transitional stage in this process, and it provides a very suitable topic to close this section.

La Trobe's appointment of a number of scientists to administer Victoria's new bureaucratic departments is a vital distinguishing feature. Exposed to public opinion and official scrutiny, these men were compelled to question their own goals and determine the means of communicating their findings to an untrained and occasionally hostile colonial audience. In addition, the close social and professional links which were built between the new 'experts' inevitably assisted in the establishment and maintenance of formal scientific societies. After the demise of an ambitious but short-lived Geological Society in 1853, a Museum of Economic Geology was established in Melbourne. In July 1854 the Victorian Institute for the Advancement of Science was founded to follow the pattern of the British Association for the Advancement of Science, and the Philosophical Society of Victoria was formed to provide a colonial copy of the Royal Society of London; the two societies combined in July 1855. Doctors, engineers and leading public servants were prominent contributors to the local scientific and philosophical journals, and the subjects favoured ranged from agriculture, botany, engineering, exploration and lunar physics, to optics, palaeontology, phonetics, statistics, linguistics and the development of public utilities. All in all, the emphasis appears to have been upon steering a middle course between 'useful' and 'abstract' science, as befitted the times: 'In all probability the advancement of science in a new country is better obtained by constructing good roads and excellent railways than by setting up telescopes and gazing at the stars' (*Illustrated Journal of Australasia* 1857; quoted in Hoare 1967: 8). Utilitarian objectives could never be forgotten.

The great scientific controversy of the day concerned the proposal to build the large Yan Yean reservoir, to supply the expanding city of Melbourne and to use the excess water for irrigation and hydraulic power. At first the scheme was presented solely as a viable engineering solution to a problem of acute and growing shortage, but it was challenged on medical grounds and the Philosophical Society appointed a Special Committee to evaluate the project. The close involvement of the Government is evident in all of these transactions—for instance Surveyor-General Andrew Clarke was, significantly, Vice-President of the Institute and at the same time President of the Philosophical Society. The Committee consisted of three engineers and the Society's Secretary. It produced a detailed investigation of the discharge, evaporation and physiographical characteristics of the basins which were to supply the reservoir and reported their cautious support, while querying the quality of the water to be obtained from two extensive swamps. One of the engineers (Clement Hodgkinson, an excellent Deputy Surveyor-General in the later 'fifties) resigned in protest, deploring the Committee's naive reliance on British data 'corrected' as far as possible to meet supposed conditions in the Colony. Hodgkinson pointed out that Australian climatic conditions demanded thorough independent research and authoritative, directly relevant meteorological statistics, that scientists and technicians trained elsewhere were indeed dangerously ignorant of the Australian environment. In support of this view Robert Brough Smyth, who was currently engaged in introducing European recording techniques to investigate Victorian weather conditions, provided a lengthy statement on the relationship between local physiography and climate, which was published by the Society. Smyth's grasp of the works of Charles Lyell (1797-1875) and Alexander von Humboldt's magnificent *Cosmos* (1848-58) was clearly indicated in his preference for microclimatological influences rather than elementary latitudinal position on precipitation and evaporation. He also stressed the significance of Australia's short periodic rains as the major supply source and made a strong appeal for complete daily hygrometric readings and intensive research into run-off and discharge (Smyth 1855). Smyth later became Secretary of Mines and Secretary to the Board of Science, which was appointed in 1858 to advise the Victorian Government on the scientific advancement of the Colony. His earlier efforts in climatic research were surpassed only by those of the brilliant young economist William Stanley Jevons, who eventually produced an excellent regionalization of the continent in 1859 (La Nauze 1949: 26-44; Perry 1966; for a general discussion see Jevons 1886).

This fruitful debate was continued for some time by the Medical Society of Victoria and it frequently supplied material for the *Australian Medical Journal*, but at the level of Government consideration the original Yan Yean proposal was generally vindicated by a Select Committee, although it was insisted that stringent measures should be taken to preserve water quality. The furore nevertheless succeeded in focussing scientific and popular interest on local water resources and home-grown expertise (Figure 5). Methods of catchment analysis and water quality control were quickly improved and engineers were persuaded to look more closely into geology and hydrology. Weather forecasting and climatological interpretation also received attention, scientists and technicians combined more readily to provide an essential community service and, eventually, the links with the elected Government were also strengthened.

In the later 'fifties 'acclimatization' was vicariously pursued as one of the 'useful' goals of the learned societies. The journalist Edward Wilson used the Institute's *Transactions* to promote the introduction of British song birds and the transfer of Murray Cod to the Yarra system, and after the Royal Park Zoological Society began to falter Wilson reconstituted it in 1861 as the Acclimatization Society of Victoria and more serious work commenced. Wilson's philosophy was that man had every right to intervene to 'improve' the balance of nature if it made human life more comfortable and that it was not only fit and proper but also essential and possible to do this in Victoria: 'a virgin country, an Italian climate, and British institutions to lend force and intelligence' to the immigrants' efforts (Hoare 1967: 21). His more interesting demand for prompt action by the Government to create a State Department of Agriculture and a number of experimental farms received some support, but the early official moves in this direction were disappointing (Powell 1970a: 68, 117).

Victoria was singularly fortunate in that a number of excellent professionals took command of the public service in these foundation years. Through their dedication to their official duties and their active support of the learned societies, they succeeded in making a unique contribution as a group towards an assessment of the developing personality of the Colony.

The work of the Registrars-General, particularly of William Henry Archer, is notable here for the institution and supervision of an extraordinary body of detailed data which rivalled the best efforts of British and European statisticians. Agricultural statistics, for example, were for a time collected for parish units some eight years before similar returns were introduced on a regular basis in England, and the local enumerators were also required to submit detailed reports on the progress of agriculture and rural settlement in each district. This valuable background data added to the store of information which was then being compiled as part of a new discovery of Victoria by private individuals and public servants: a discovery founded on industrious field research, leading to a vastly improved understanding of the regional variety of the physical environment.

Gold-mining naturally gave a boost to practical surveying and applied geological research. In 1852 Alfred R. C. Selwyn was appointed as Geological Surveyor. With seven years experience in the English Geological Survey, Selwyn proposed to introduce the same system into Victoria and although he was always critically short of funds and qualified assistants he did very well indeed in his first few years, producing a simple sketch-map of the Colony and a few detailed maps of selected areas. In January 1857 Professor Georg Balthasar von Neumayer, a distinguished German astronomer, meteorologist and physicist, arrived armed with testimonials from the British Association and from an array of European luminaries, including Humboldt, Justus von Liebig and Johann von Lamont, and displaying up to date instruments supplied by the King of Bavaria. He soon established an observatory in Melbourne for magnetic and meteorological recordings and in addition employed it to offer valuable service for coastal navigation. Before Neumayer returned to Germany after six productive years in Victoria, a successful local campaign for a thoroughly modern observatory was directed by R. L. J. Ellery, who subsequently introduced the Geodetic Survey to regularize and simplify the management of land sub-division during the succeeding decades of settlement expansion.

One of the most interesting of La Trobe's early appointments was that of Dr Ferdinand Mueller. Although he received his doctorate in botany at the University of Kiel in 1846, Mueller was also well trained in chemistry and pharmacy and for a time contemplated a medical career. His astonishing research energy and complete dedication to detailed observation were fully exhibited soon after his arrival in Adelaide in 1847. For the next few years he conducted extensive botanical explorations along the South Australian coast, in the hill country near Adelaide and in the Flinders Rangers, culminating in the first of his many scientific papers on Australian flora. In 1852, on the recommendation of the eminent British botanist Sir William Hooker, La Trobe decided to appoint Mueller to the position of Victoria's first Government Botanist. It is no exaggeration to say that this was the beginning of a new era in the scientific appraisal of the Australian environment; for botany in particular it meant that the direction of research at both scientific and utilitarian levels came to be determined in Australia rather than in England.

Melbourne's Botanic Gardens were then being developed on their present site near the Yarra River, on a former Aboriginal reserve, and Mueller's duties were to be wholly scientific, complementing the work of the Curator, John Dallachy. Mueller lost no time in taking full advantage of the opportunities provided. Usually alone, but sometimes accompanied by Dallachy and other field assistants, he successfully completed the first botanical investigation of the Eastern Highlands, much of the little-known Gippsland region, Wilson's Promontory, the Grampians, the Mallee fringe and the Murray Valley. Before the end of the 'fifties he had established the broad vegetational divisions of the Colony and demonstrated their principal connections with the South Australian and Tasmanian distributions. He had also built the foundations of an enduring and mutually rewarding correspondence with Sir William Hooker and the Kew Herbarium, which was regularly supplied until Mueller's death with samples of his newly discovered specimens (Daley 1924; Willis 1949).

Scientific knowledge, as the great Humboldt had declared, was to be seen as an invaluable 'natural' resource, a central part of any nation's wealth, which must be properly developed and exploited if stagnation and decay were to be avoided. It is difficult to imagine Ferdinand Mueller ever agreeing with his countryman's rejection of contemporary religious attitudes, but there is no question that he also believed passionately in this view of the role of science in modern society. A strong inclination towards a search for practical applications in his devoted and inspired work enlivened Mueller's official reports during this period and continued to do so during his long and productive life. There can be few doubts about the multiple origins of this inclination: firstly, it continued his early interests and training; secondly, as as a devout Lutheran he welcomed the opportunity to render dutiful service to the community; in addition, Mueller might thereby justify a senior scientific appointment in the eyes of his lay contemporaries, including his paymasters in parliament. Further research into Mueller's correspondence with his most significant peer group, at Kew Gardens, may show that this last factor was far more important than was ever realized by either his Australian contemporaries or his modern interpreters. Yet the quest for utilitarian goals should also be seen as a simple reflection of the talents, aspirations and predilections. of this extraordinary individual—certainly, another facet of his own image of this pioneering role was that of an active research worker earnestly making his way in the national and international scientific fraternity, while at the same time staking a claim as a most *professional* career scientist engaged in an essential public service. Drawing upon his varied scientific background in Europe and South Australia, Mueller diligently recorded the medical and industrial properties of the plants he encountered during the 'fifties. The economic value of the native timber, for example, and the availability of tannin from the acacias, were frequently mentioned in his reports and in his papers presented to the local societies, in which he played a leading part.

At the height of his distinguished career, Mueller's Australian and overseas mail reached an astonishing annual average of 3,000 items, yet each was quickly dealt with by the man himself, efficiently dispensing advice, identifying and despatching seeds and specimens. Thus he strove, with some success, to reduce those pains of isolation which must have severely handicapped most of his Australian colleagues. A perfect complement to his proven research skills, it was perhaps this amazing capacity for maintaining and encouraging regular communication which also ensured the survival of the Mueller legend in Australia. His influence pervaded various types of official policy throughout the continent until the early twentieth century, but it extended far beyond his adopted country. He was deeply involved, for example, in the successful promotion of the 'sanitary influences' of the Australian eucalypt, especially the blue gum, which came to be accepted as 'the great fever-tree' to counteract the malarial 'miasmas' of Central Italy and California (Thompson 1970). This notion first emerged in 1854 from his association with Joseph Bosisto in the invention of a process for distilling medicinal oils from eucalyptus leaves, which led to the development of a sizeable local industry. In the following year he served as phytographic naturalist on Augustus Gregory's expedition to the Northern Territory, covered 5,000 miles of difficult country in sixteen months and discovered 800 species new to Australia. He was a leading patron or member of virtually every important scientific society in Australia, became one of Victoria's first Fellows of the Royal Society, and was made both a British Knight and a German Baron. At the time of his death in 1896 Baron Sir Ferdinand Jakob Heinrich von Mueller was credited with at least 800 botanical and other scientific publications; through his long association with the public service he had also made an inestimable practical contribution towards the continuing assessment of the Australian environment. We will meet 'the Baron' again in the next section.

*

Progress in the appraisal and management of the Australian environment during the period 1788 to 1860 reflected the precarious and variable development of aesthetic, ecological and utilitarian streams of thought towards an increasingly more intimate and therefore more independently 'Australian' approach by a rapidly evolving immigrant society. A dominating utilitarian motivation strongly influenced artistic and scientific evocations or interpretations of the Australian environment, but the interlinkages of these three streams were maintained throughout: they are best shown in the key periods and centres of activity and in the contributions of certain groups and individuals, particularly those based in the cities. As an integral part of settlement expansion and the process of discovering man's role in vital ecological linkages, which is often ambiguously entitled 'adaptation', the focus of most colonial efforts was concentrated predominantly upon the south-eastern crescent of the continent. But Tasmania and Western Australia were by no means forgotten, pastoralists were already following the explorers towards the north and centre, and the separation of Queensland from New South Wales in 1859 meant that the problem of white settlement in the tropics was soon to provide a very controversial theme for further speculation on man-environment relationships.

Until the end of this period natural science was long on facts and short on theory, and the prevailing encyclopaedic or 'gazetteer' approach permitted, even invited, wide participation. Botanical exploration was therefore peculiarly well suited to assist in the interpretation of Australia, since it could offer an established elementary 'system' to guide all practitioners. For a time, the spatial isolation and the comparative independence of the separate political units encouraged a surprising amount of good local work in botany and several other fields when there was strong leadership for inspiration and co-ordination. Above all, the development of the learned societies in the capital cities, especially in Tasmania and Victoria, vastly improved the status of organized science and helped to prepare Australians for important post-Darwinian adventures into deeper theoretical investigations of the natural world. Environmental management at both the official and popular levels was carried out by empirical testing, occasionally *ad hoc* decisions and frequently great irresponsibility. In the search for profit, the natural scene was irrevocably disfigured over wide areas; uniquely Australian ecosystems, fragile and robust, were either totally destroyed or placed in jeopardy, and the design of introduced artificial systems had yet to mature. On the other hand a great deal had been learned, often through the very observation of these transforming processes, and in Victoria, the hub of most of Australia's commercial, industrial and political life, science and technology were making a recognized contribution towards the building of a new bureaucracy.

III Forests and Farms, 1860–80

THE attitudes of Australians towards their environment can be identified as products of the interplay between a European heritage, individual and group aspirations, an evolving sense of national identity and the matrix of problems and prospects actually or apparently inherent in the southern continent at any point in time. From the more specific but closely related viewpoint of conservation and resource management—a 'behavioural' outcome, it could be said, of changing environmental attitudes—the foundation of that matrix was undoubtedly the progress of science and technology, and particularly the work of leading specialists in the public service.

Yet Australia's writers, poets and painters also played a major role in what might be described either as a 'learning process', or simply the experience of 'relationship' with Australian nature. They effectively evoked a variety of images of the natural and built environments which at the highest level of interpretation advanced from hostility through confusion towards a general acceptance of some 'unique' characteristics. Whether deliberately or unconsciously, these contributions towards an aesthetic appraisal of Australia also assisted the adaptation and orientation of the emerging nation, for they were closely linked with other images, notably political and social, which accommodated, precipitated and succeeded social change. In the United States, pioneering conditions may indeed have promoted nationalism, as originally hypothesized by historians of the Turner school, but for Australia at least this view is too simplistic; the sentiment of nationalism was clearly a very complex and potent force which fed upon *and also encouraged* the romanticization of the Australian frontier. In fact the 'bush ethos' was born in the earliest days of empirical testing in the convict settlement, was nurtured later by pioneer settlers and by an itinerant rural proletariat, and was then annexed by a type of nationalist movement in the last quarter of the century during conditions of rapid urbanization. Cultural historians and literary critics have been engaged for some time in investigations of various aspects of the bush ethos and their major findings are now well known (see, for example, Ward 1958; Turner 1964; Elliott 1967; Serle 1973; for the geographer's interpretation see Heathcote 1972; Powell 1972).

Although the next section of this book will show that there were undoubtedly important social and political implications for environmental management in the evolution of the familiar bush ethos, at this point we must be mainly concerned with the impact of some new developments in science and technology on the Australian scene, for this is still a comparatively neglected field. And in this respect the better-documented experiences of that other immigrant society in North America again provide useful guidelines for the modern researcher, as indeed they did for some leading Australian contemporaries, who were greatly influenced by the activities of their American cousins.

53

4 The Gospel of Efficiency in North America

It is not entirely extravagant to claim that, with the exception of Charles Darwin's *Origin of Species* and the Bible itself, no book has had more direct and indirect influence upon Western man's perception and use of his environment than George Perkins Marsh's *Man and Nature*, published in New York in 1864. The fifth and final volume of Humboldt's *Cosmos* was completed shortly before the publication of *Origin of Species* in 1859, yet the title of Marsh's book was originally to be *Man the Disturber of Nature's Harmonies*: as David Lowenthal indicated in his introduction to the centenary edition, Marsh shared the view of other highly educated men of his time—he believed in a more or less static natural harmony. But he surpassed both Humboldt and Darwin in communicating the almost revolutionary concept that man's dominant role in nature displayed an immense, unrecognized and largely destructive power. According to the accepted Christian ethic man was God's own terrestrial steward, given special powers to subdue and cultivate the earth, and there was something very modern in the way Marsh challenged this fundamental assumption:

> Man has too long forgotten that the earth was given to him for usufruct alone, not for consumption, still less for profligate waste. Nature has provided against the absolute destruction of any of her elementary matter, the raw material of her works; the thunderbolt and the tornado, the most convulsive throes of even the volcano and the earthquake, being only phenomena of decomposition and re-composition. But she has left it within the power of man irreparably to change the combinations of inorganic matter and of organic life, which through the night of aeons she had been proportioning and balancing to prepare the earth for his habitation, when, in the fulness of time, his Creator should call him forth to enter into its possession (Marsh 1964: 36).

Marsh was born in 1801 in the frontier township of Woodstock, Vermont. He witnessed and participated in the transformation of that heavily wooded region through his legal practice, political involvement and varied business interests, and his influential social contacts and amazing versatility as a scholar and linguist persuaded Lincoln to appoint him as ambassador to Italy, a post which he retained from 1861 until his death in 1882. This position gave him the opportunity for extensive travel and wide reading which confirmed the lessons learned from his experience of environmental degradation in North America, and he had sufficient lesiure to organize his thoughts into the argument which formed the basis of *Man and Nature* (Lowenthal 1958). Although he must have been severely handicapped by his lack of formal training in natural science, Marsh was extraordinarily conversant with the leading French, Italian, German and other authorities on such matters as the ecological effects of overgrazing and deforestation. He was less knowledgeable about the physics and chemistry of pollution and soil exhaustion *per se*, partly because of the small amount of scientific literature on these subjects and its highly technical nature.

Man and Nature is now judged to be Marsh's finest work and a major landmark in the evolution of modern geographical thought, especially for its insistence upon the pivotal role of man as an agent of geographical change. Like Alexander von Humboldt, 'the father of physical geography', he saw nature as a whole and man as a part of that whole, but he was rather more concerned with researching the interface between what we might now distinguish as the 'human' and 'physical' branches of the subject. He never regarded himself as a geographer and his contemporaries were certainly more inclined to see him as a linguist, historian or *litterateur* who could hold a distinguished place in any Old World company; but he had a profound love of nature and a practical, realistic 'commitment', born of his New World origins, towards what he saw to be an urgently necessary change in environmental attitudes. His great book is universally acknowledged as the very fountain-head of the conservation movement in North America and was a major influence in the rest of the Western World, principally because of its full and competent discussion of the damage resulting from the destruction of natural forest cover and the range of lasting benefits to be gained from the vigorous promotion of scientific forestry operations. Yet Marsh also discussed other problems in *Man and Nature*—the 'Transfer, Modification, and Extirpation of Vegetable and Animal Species'; the various potentials, limitations and landscape consequences of existing and projected schemes for water conservation, irrigation, drainage and flood protection; the high significance of reclamation and protection measures to combat coastal erosion and sand drifts; speculative notions concerning the possible environmental side-effects of the construction of the Suez and Panama Canals, and some of the other visionary enterprises of the day.

But the centre-piece of the book was indeed the chapter on 'The Woods', which provided over one-third of the total text. Marsh succeeded admirably in communicating his passionate conviction that man's dominating role in dangerously changing the face of the earth depended primarily upon his attitude towards the rapid and widespread removal of the tree cover. Excessive erosion, violent fluctuations in run-off and seasonal floods, and the loss of valuable springs, fauna and flora, were all attributed to the clearing of the forest. The felling of trees usually presented the most obvious local cue for popular and scientific explanations of broader environmental change, and Marsh offered an impressive summary of contemporary ideas from all sectors of the globe. While he was sure that a good tree cover conserved moisture and provided a safeguard against temperature extremes, Marsh was far more reluctant to support the current growing conviction that the total amount of precipitation was in some way closely associated with the local extent of forest or woodland vegetation: it was this type of balanced assessment which immensely broadened the appeal of *Man and Nature*. In Europe long-standing traditions of environmental management were then being challenged by urbanization and industrialization, yet a sound foundation had already been laid for modern forestry and Marsh's ideas were quite readily adopted in enlightened circles. The confident peoples of the New World found it more difficult to accept the basic proposition that the earth's fundamental resources were being quickly exhausted or misused. An immediate impact was certainly felt, however, in American forestry—especially since the book served to reinforce recent predictions of a timber famine—and according to Lowenthal, it directly inspired an 1873 memorial which led to the establishment of government forest reserves and a national forestry commission (Lowenthal 1964: xxii).

Despite its minor literary and scientific defects, Man and Nature was essentially a timely and comprehensible call to action, and this is the real measure of its achievement. It included innumerable bold 'revelations' which Marsh widely publicized in attractive style, but he clearly had great faith in the power of man to redeem himself by restoring his natural support-systems and fulfilling his moral obligation to bequeath them intact to his descendants. This marked commitment to the future was not only an American characteristic; it has probably been fairly common in most immigrant societies, including that of Australia.

Conservation did not emerge as a social movement in the United States until the early years of the twentieth century, but the germinal concepts of a truly conservationist philosophy can be seen to be of much older vintage, particularly if we accept the introductory argument of the present book that conservation is best understood within the general context of resource management. For our purposes it will suffice to point to the broad characteristics of certain periods. In the colonial era, the abundance of resources 'engendered a spendthrift attitude' and the wilderness was regarded as a profane space which had to be made over to 'civilized' usage. During the growth of the young republic, from 1781 to 1870, the National Government acquired control of a vast public domain of over 1,807,681,000 acres, which it proceeded to sell to individuals, groups and companies in order to raise revenue and, according to the most seductive rhetoric of the day, to build a new society of independent freeholders. There was then a lengthy 'period of awakening', beginning in the 'seventies, when the settlement explosion of the previous period was increasingly questioned and monitored, and some attempts were made to control it. This was followed, in the 1930s and post-war years, by a time of 'implementation', characterized by a rising technology and the proliferation of powerful official resource management agencies to introduce several of the principles which had been thrashed out during the earlier years (Highsmith et al. 1962: 1-25). The latest chapter began in the 1960s. It has been marked by the rediscovery of old problems and the realization that while these have reached appalling new dimensions, they are also tied more closely than ever before to various interpretations of the fundamental question of survival—pollution, the diminution of non-renewable resources, the upgrading of aesthetic and other non-economic considerations with the growth of 'participatory democracy' in the planning process, and so on.

After 1850 major advances were made in the application of science and technology to manufacturing and transportation, and the associated processes of industrialization and urbanization brought chain reactions in resource demands for fuels and raw materials in the United States. In short, the progress of the national economy was such that the American's ability to convert resources to use moved far beyond his ability or concern to maintain or improve the productivity of those resources. The chaotic westward expansion of rural settlement, especially after the passage of the *Homestead Act* of 1862, also meant that the potentials of the national resource base tended to decline. There was no store of experimentation to guide the myriad decisions which had to be made at every level and each settler was left to discover his own management techniques by trial and error, at the expense of his local environment. Above all, however, there was still a dominating penchant for speculation and, together with the continued lure of virgin territory, this bred in the American pioneer an overwhelming passion for locational mobility. Marsh was only one of several commentators to emphasize this trait, but his special concern was with the implications of this mode of behaviour for the formation or reinforcement of exploitative, or non-conservationist, environmental attitudes. Calling for 'some abatement in the restless love of change which characterizes us, and makes us almost a nomade [*sic*] rather than a sedentary people', Marsh insisted that 'This life of incessant flitting is unfavourable for the execution of permanent improvements of every sort, and especially of those which, like the forest, are slow in repaying any part of the capital expended in them' (Marsh 1964: 280).

There were also other gifted men and women who deplored the dominant public approach to the American environment. Some, like John Muir, promoted an aesthetic and ethical philosophy to build a new value system which would not support the dangerous prevailing attitudes (Huth 1957; Leighly 1958; Nash 1967); others strove for a more immediate impact by influencing public policy at the highest possible level. Samuel P. Hays (1972), in what is acknowledged as one of the most authoritative accounts of the activities of this latter group, emphasizes that the historical role of conservation in the United States arises from the implications of science and technology in modern society: in the last one-third of the nineteenth century, conservation was essentially a scientific movement and its leaders came from such fields as anthropology, agrostology, forestry, geology and hydrology. With some important exceptions, it could be said that loyalty to their professional ideals rather than a close association with the 'grass-roots' public set the tone of their contribution towards government policy, and the principal goal they shared was the injection of the idea of 'efficiency' and 'rational development' into the management of all natural resources. These conservationists envisaged a political system guided by the ideal of efficiency and dominated by the technicians and scientists who could best determine how to achieve it (Hays 1972: 3). They did not realize all of their aims, but the new types of expertise, bureaucratization and centralization which ultimately emerged from their efforts were certainly representative of the kind of 'modernization' they wished to impart to American society.

Notwithstanding the widespread social and political consequences of the revival of the Arcadian ideal in urban America after the turn of the century (Schmitt 1969), one of the most notable features of the period as a whole is certainly the remarkable spatial impact made by the activities of certain key individuals and small groups. This was particularly well illustrated in the reservation of the first National Parks (Huth 1957: 148-64; Ise 1961); similarly, the innovative work of John Wesley Powell, first Director of the Geological Survey, provided a comprehensive appraisal of the agricultural potential of the arid and semi-arid West (Powell 1879) and this led to the *Reclamation Act* of 1902 which was designed to promote the conservation and efficient use of the water resources of that region.

The administration of forest resources was strongly influenced by all of these developments, and some early schemes for preservation and rigidly controlled exploitation were fostered by the work of the American Association for the Advancement of Science; the appointment of European-trained foresters to high government positions; and occasionally by the enlightened approach of some mining and sawmilling firms which held a major controlling interest in the nation's timber resources. In 1891 about thirteen million acres were set aside in forest reserves, but although this area was subsequently considerably extended, no systematic plan for forest management was laid down; until 1905 the national forests were administered by the General Land Office of the Department of the Interior, while the Division (later the Bureau) of Forestry remained as a small body of technical advisors working within the Department of Agriculture. Nevertheless, under the inspired leadership of Gifford Pinchot, a dedicated individual with wide practical experience in Europe and America, modern management was successfully introduced into a new Forest Service. When Pinchot retired in 1910 there were nearly one hundred and fifty million acres in national forests, several forestry schools had been established and the now familiar concepts of 'multiple use' and strictly controlled exploitation were widely accepted and employed (Pinchot 1947).

The culmination of these primarily scientific and utilitarian achievements was President Theodore Roosevelt's famous White House Conference of 1908, a giant landmark in the history of conservation and resource management. In attendance were the President and Vice-President with members of Cabinet and Congress, a number of scientists, the Governors or their representatives of forty-one States, leading public servants and interested citizens. A direct outcome was the appointment of a National Conservation Commission under the chairmanship of Pinchot and the formation of a further ninety-two Conservation Commissions to represent the States and various national organizations, and the three-volume national resources inventory quickly produced by Pinchot's team in 1909 was an immensely valuable document.

Students of environmental history in Australia cannot draw upon a rich tradition of local scholarship in their chosen field and it seems reasonable to suggest that an examination of the American experience should provide an indispensable general perspective. Indeed, many leading figures in conservation and resource management in Australia were (and are) keen observers of the American scene. But there is a distinct temptation, in this as in several other matters, to allow simply for the familiar 'cultural lag' and to press on with a 'comparative' approach for Australia. The dangers are obvious enough—the special environmental problems facing Australians, and their sustained relationship with Britain, for instance, must never be discounted. The remainder of this exploratory section is therefore deliberately concentrated upon the management of forests and the disposal of the public lands, in order to allow a reasonably full treatment of the play of both local and international influences.

5 An Australian Awakening

It is disputed whether either the mean or the extremes of temperature, the periods of the seasons, or the amount or distribution of precipitation and of evaporation, in any country whose annals are known, have undergone any change during the historical period. It is, indeed, impossible to doubt that many of the operations of the pioneer settler tend to produce great modifications in atmospheric humidity, temperature and electricity; but we are at present unable to determine how far one set of effects is neutralized by another, or compensated by unknown agencies. This question scientific research is inadequate to solve, for want of the necessary data; but well conducted observation, in regions now first brought under the occupation of man, combined with such historical evidence as still exists, may be expected at no distant period to throw much light on this subject.

Australia is, perhaps, the country from which we have a right to expect the fullest elucidation of these difficult and disputable problems. Its colonization did not commence until the physical sciences had become matter of almost universal attention, and, is, indeed, so recent that the memory of living men embraces the principal epochs of its history; the peculiarities of its fauna, its flora, and its geology are such as to have excited for it the liveliest interest of the notaries of natural science; its mines have given its people the necessary wealth for procuring the means of instrumental observation, and the leisure required for the pursuit of scientific research; and large tracts of virgin forest and natural meadow are rapidly passing under the control of civilized man. Here, then, exist greater facilities and stronger motives for the careful study of the topics in question than have ever been found combined in any other theatre of European colonization (Marsh 1964: 48-9).

While some of the leading scientists of the day seemed to be asserting that the earth had made man, Marsh provided an elaborate but practical and challenging synthesis which was in comparison far less threatening to established modes of thought. Slowly and painfully, the ecological vision of Humboldt's *Cosmos* and Darwin's *Origin of Species* was transforming man's concept of the organic world, but even today there is some resistance. Scientists and churchmen have had to make the change in their own ways, in the face of powerful metaphysical and traditionalist attitudes, and ideological beliefs; initially, some of them chose to resist the challenge by every means at their disposal. Evolutionary theory in particular was not widely accepted in Australia until the beginning of the twentieth century, despite the vast amount of corroborative work in the preceding decades and the gradual accommodation made in Britain by scientists and clergymen of all descriptions. One of the reasons for this, according to Mozley (1967), was the vigorous opposition of some of Australia's most influential scientists, who shared with their local churches the traditional theological concept of a universe of design and purpose based on William Paley's standard university texts, *The Principles of Moral and Political Philosophy* (1785), *A View of the Evidences of Christianity* (1794) and *Natural Theology* (1802). The *Origin of Species* did not form the subject of public debate in any of the Colonies during the nine-

59

teenth century, and comment in the scientific societies was extremely reserved. Indeed, Sir Henry Barkly, Victoria's Governor and President of its Royal Society, chose instead to urge the scientific fraternity to refute by every scholarly means a theory 'so pernicious to the very existence of Christianity', and Ferdinand Mueller himself felt constrained to decline to assist Darwin in his botanical experiments, clinging tenaciously to his Lutheran convictions and his belief in the fixity of species. In the young Australian universities, the foundation professors of science were also staunch and articulate anti-evolutionists. Frederick McCoy, for example, who occupied Australia's first Chair of Natural History at the University of Melbourne, was a devout Anglican and an absolute creationist who gave authoritative force to the anti-Darwinism movement rooted in the Victorian capital. There were some important independent thinkers, particularly in Adelaide and Sydney, but in general the reception was either muted or hostile for forty years or more (for a fuller discussion, from which the above comments are drawn, see Goodwin 1964 and Mozley 1967).

Man and Nature provided less dangerous fare and was enthusiastically received, not least because it examined some very familiar issues which had been attracting local attention during the previous decade and communicated the 'latest knowledge' in a fluent, almost casual style, free of obscurantism and inscrutable scientific jargon, and admirably suited to a wider diffusion in the astonishing proliferation of journals and newspapers, the mass media of the day. And the isolated Australian public was in fact very well served in several respects by the flowering of professional journalism in the latter half of the nineteenth century. With little competition from other sources, journalists then had a unique opportunity to influence public opinion and to depict and interpret contemporary social, intellectual and cultural preoccupations, rather than concentrate solely on matters of topical significance. British and American literature was frequently and competently reviewed, sometimes even serialized, and the 'principal events' in the wider world were carefully chronicled and given perspective by a variety of gifted local commentators. There was a ready audience for *Man and Nature* in Australia. It soon provided the substance of leading articles and editorials, was regularly quoted and plagiarized in parliamentary debates and reports, and inspired a wide range of public speakers over the next forty years.

Crusading: the Case for Conservation in the Fertile Crescent

Environmental degradation and especially the need for forest conservation were frequent topics of discussion in Victoria and South Australia in the 'sixties, when the old arguments concerning the climatic influence of the tree cover, the relationship between forests and water supply and the demand for an assured supply of mining timber, gained strength from the locally-recorded international success of *Man and Nature*. There were echoes of Marsh throughout this discussion, though it seldom incorporated his careful qualifications. The Melbourne *Age* was particularly intemperate in its judgement, though its views were undoubtedly widely shared.

Sprung from a country where the natural humidity of the climate and the abundance of coal combine to render the exhaustion or the destruction of the native woods matters of comparative unimportance, we are apt to undervalue the lamentable consequences which must inevitably ensue if our present heedlessness is persisted in. Indeed, it requires no great discrimination to perceive that if rigorous measures are not speedily taken to check the present prodigality and abuse, the existing generation will hardly have passed away ere climatic changes and the increasing price of one of the necessaries of life must painfully remind the colonist of the inconsiderable and injudicious profusion [*sic*] of the earlier settlers. If preservation of the woods be necessary in temperate regions, it is imperatively called for in a semi-tropical climate like our own, where the supply of water, and consequently of animal and cereal produce, is in a great degree dependent on the existence of forests, especially in the elevated parts of the colony. And, moreover, the fact that nature has but sparingly endowed this hemisphere with rivers and watercourses, and the unpleasant recurrence of droughts, ought to impart an additional spur to our exertions in the conservation of an indispensable adjunct to our social existence. The destruction which is proceeding in the ranges [that is in and around the goldfields] must not only tend to diminish appreciably the amount of rainfall throughout the colony, but must also be the means of baring the sources of the springs from which the few permanent rivers and streamlets with which the colony is provided take their origin. We have it from incontrovertible authority that such a denudation of the sources of springs is frequently attended by a total cessation of the flow of the derivative streams or rivers, and invariably by a large diminution in their volume. Recent examples, both from the old and new world, are not wanting to remind us of the terrible consequences which have resulted from a wholesale extirpation of the natural screen of the earth (*Age*, 3 October 1865).

And so the editorial continued, recounting the examples given in Marsh's famous third chapter, and calling for an official forestry programme to introduce selected exotic trees for commercial timber. Under the guidance of the enthusiastic naturalist Edward Wilson, the rival metropolitan daily, the *Argus*, took a substantially similar line, but it displayed a much better grasp of Marsh's central thesis, relating it very well indeed to the Victorian situation.

Over and over again we have urged that steps should be taken to protect our forest lands, not only because extravagance will lead to scarcity, but also because the local climate will be affected in all those places where the forests are removed. In protecting the forests we do more than increase the growth of timber—we prevent waste of soil, we conserve the natural streams, it is not improbable that we prevent decrease in the rainfall, and it is certain that we largely affect the distribution of storm waters. A covering of shrubs and grass protects the loose soil from being carried away by floods. Anyone who has looked at the wheel-ruts in the friable soil covering our palaeozoic rocks must have observed how rapidly the rain, having once found its way under the roots of the grass, cuts large unsightly channels in places where for ages there has been but a slight depression. The physiognomy of many districts of the colony has been greatly changed in this manner. But far more effective in altering the physiognomy of a country is the removal of forest timber. The Italian hydrographers have made mention very often of the disastrous results attendant on destruction of forests—Frisi relates that when the natural woods were removed from the declivities of the Upper Val d'Arno, in Tuscany, the soil of the hills was washed down into the Arno in vast quantities, to the great injury of the riparian proprietors. Some districts of Catalonia have suffered even more by the incautious operations of man; and, on the other hand, we know by what has been done in Italy, in France, in Germany and in Algeria, how much the local climate may be ameliorated, and the fruitfulness of gardens and fields increased by judicious planting. *In a new country such as this, one can see to what extent man is a levelling agent, and how easily he can disturb the harmonies of nature.* Mining, ploughing, roadmaking, the cutting of drains, the formation of tracks, all aid in diminishing the conservative powers of the natural herbage, and it is not surprising that our best streams, such as the Loddon, Campaspe, and Avoca, are fast becoming mere channels for the efflux of sludge and sand. Even in those parts not touched by the gold-miner, the rivers are rapidly changing their character. The mere occupation of the country for pastoral purposes has produced great changes, and it is well to consider whether anything can be done to compensate for, if we cannot check, this kind of devastation. The reservation of large tracts of forest land is our first duty. By keeping the hills clothed we may make fruitful the valleys, and provide stores of moisture for the parched plains. As in America, we find in this colony the finest forest lands in those parts where the rainfall is largest ... As necessary as fertile soil or moisture is shelter; and that could easily be obtained. Becquerel states that 'a simple hedge, two metres in height, is a sufficient protection for a distance of 22 metres' [directly taken from Marsh 1964: 132], and these plains might easily be clothed with forest trees if the young plantations were protected by hedges of prickly acacia or poplar. In this country no regard is paid to the laws which regulate the growth of forest trees. Sawmills are at work from Wood's Point to Warrenheip, and trees are cut down and maimed and barked, as if nature could produce as fast as man can destroy. The distillers collect the leaves and barks of aromatic shrubs and trees with no more judgment than guides the opossum, and unless steps be taken by the Legislature to protect the property of the state in its forests and to regulate and control the labours of licensed woodcutters, we shall soon reduce vast areas now covered with magnificent trees to mere unhealthy and unprofitable shrubberies, such as we find in the vicinity of the gold workings at Castlemaine and Maryborough. Carefully managed, we have much wealth in our forests. The miner, the agriculturalist, and the housebuilder, notwithstanding that their demands are large, can be fully supplied if extravagance be checked and waste be prevented. As the old trees are removed others should be planted. We may with advantage take a lesson from Mehemet Ali and Ibrahim Pacha, who planted more than 20 millions of trees in Egypt [cf. Marsh 1964: 164]. But even in this there is need of discrimination. We should not plant unwisely. While protecting the forests on the mountains, we might clear the valleys and river basins between the coast and the main [Dividing] range, so as to allow the cool sea breezes—moisture laden—to flow freely to the hills. On the more fertile well-watered lands the chestnut, the hickory, the umbrella pine, the pitch pine, the white cedar of Virginia, the valuable cypress of the Himalayas, would grow and flourish, and serve at once to enrich the country and adorn the landscape. Nor should the farmer neglect his fields. Shelter is necessary to the well doing of his crops, and if he plant judiciously the ground will not be used unprofitably. In Europe and in America the pasture beech and the pasture oak give better wood when grown in the open field than in the forest; and it would be easy to name a list of trees which would be suitable to the requirements of the vine-grower, and profitable to the gardener and the agriculturalist. The conservation of the forest lands, and the extension and improvement of them, concern alike the landholder and the miner, and should occupy the attention of everyone who has leisure and means to become a co-worker with nature (*Argus*, 16 October 1865; my italics).

At various times during the same year, other perceptive editorials in the

Argus applied the thesis further to additional examples of destruction and negligence in Victoria: the paper chose to highlight the lack of adequate water storage facilities, for example, and reckoned the continued waste of town sewage even more scandalous (*Argus*, 8 and 11 November 1865). These were very pertinent observations during a decade which was marked by the urgent promotion of intensive rural settlement via a succession of 'Land Selection Acts' (Powell 1970a: 59-190). At the official level the local success of the forty-second section of the 1865 *Amending Land Act*, which established hundreds of miners and others on wooded allotments near the gold-fields, caused great concern in some circles and prompted the convening of a special committee to investigate the whole issue of forest conservation in Victoria. Significantly, the members of this committee were Clement Hodgkinson, the Assistant Commissioner of Lands and Survey, with Robert Brough Smyth, then the Secretary for Mines —both of whom had been very active contributors to conservation debates in the 'fifties—and Charles Whybrow Ligar, the Surveyor-General. In the first week of November their report was laid on the table of the House. It was a remarkably detailed document, in spite of its rapid production, but it was as distinguished by its heavy reliance upon the international review in *Man and Nature* as by its direct commentary on Victorian affairs. The dominating utilitarian concern was with the 'needless destruction of timber' and the committee recommended that Victoria should follow the lead of those several countries mentioned by Marsh which had 'obtained the assistance of scientific men in repairing the injuries done thoughtlessly in past times'. The continuing wasteful ways of the 'improvident diggers' (then about 85,000 strong) were now matched and sometimes surpassed by those of pioneer settlers and a host of bush workers.

> We believe that much of the prosperity now so evident on the goldfields of Victoria is due to the circumstances that claimholders and lessees of Crown Lands have the opportunity of procuring timber from indigenous forests at small cost. They require wood, both for underground operations and for engines; and it has been ascertained that any considerable increase in the price of timber would cause works to be abandoned as unprofitable, which now yield to the miner considerable sums over and above the cost of working. A great number of persons employ themselves in cutting timber for the mines. They fell the best, and destroy more than they use, consequently there is unnecessary waste. Persons resident on the gold fields destroy also an immense number of fine trees, by taking sheets of bark from them for roofing their huts. Instead of at once felling a tree, and removing from it several sheets of bark of the required size, they generally take one sheet of bark only from each tree, which is left standing with a portion of its trunk entirely denuded of bark; and it soon perishes, and ultimately becomes a prey to bush fires (Report on Forests 1865).

The committee recommended the proclamation of an extension to the existing forest reserve near Ballarat in order to protect the timber resources on and north of the Dividing Range; further large reserves were suggested for each of the busiest mining centres and an interesting proposal was made for the afforestation of the open basaltic plains south-west of Rokewood with native and exotic species. The *Argus* warmly applauded the report, but kept up the pressure for more comprehensive environmental planning schemes, proudly but justifiably identifying the important role to be played by the colonial press in reforming public attitudes.

State forests would be a future provision for the wants of the miner because they would admit of periodical thinning under proper superintendence. But such reserves will need to be provided for in other localities as well for the danger of a check to our gold-field enterprise, serious as it is, is after all quite insignificant in comparison with the danger of a deterioration of climate—that calamity of aridity and consequent sterility which has befallen every semi-tropical land when deprived of its woods.

The Australian climate is already too dry, and it is the danger of increasing this tendency to drought which we are called upon to guard against. And now that we are on the eve of measures to preserve a suitable amount of forest, the question suggests itself, is it quite safe to have the drainage of our marshes and numerous water-covered flats undertaken at the present moment? The Government are about to issue leases for a great number of these wastes, with the view of having them reclaimed by the lessees; but it certainly would be prudent to consider the project more carefully, and, perhaps, postpone it until the proposed forest arrangements have been some time in operation, and until it is seen that they are practically effective in checking denudation within the prescribed localities. When in each division of the country the inhabitants can be quite sure of retaining a sufficiency of woodland for the creation of moisture, the drainage of the marshes will unquestionably be a great public boon; but until then there is little doubt that they perform a useful part in influencing the climate. The morasses of Victoria are not miasmatic, like those of most parts of the world; and, as the author of 'Nature and Man', a scientific work last year published in London, observes, 'The drainage of lakes and marshes and other superficial accumulations of moisture reduces the water surface of a country, and of course the evaporation from it. [...] Hence, if carried out on too extensive a scale, it must affect the temperature of the atmosphere and the rainfall' [Slightly misquoted, see Marsh 1964: 304]. We cannot help concluding, therefore, that the present is not the most propitious moment for proceeding with the undertaking we refer to, useful as it might prove at a more favourable opportunity.

The success of any forest regulations will greatly depend on the hearty cooperation of the public, and it is only by the press that a just conception of the urgency for such regulations can be popularised ... Nature will not have her harmonies violated with impunity, and after dearly-bought experience, it is at last recognized that forests are absolutely requisite to mitigate the extremes of climate: that, more than anything else, they are the great moisture gatherers; that, they feed the clouds, and protect and enlarge the springs and streams. Deplorable, indeed, have been the consequences in nearly every country where nature's economy has been deranged by their indiscriminate destruction ... (*Argus*, 13 November 1865).

Similar protests were being made with less clamour in New South Wales, where the emphasis was being laid squarely on the threat to future timber supplies from the indigenous forests and Charles Moore (1820-1905), Director of Sydney's Botanic Gardens, pointed the bone at the pioneer farmer: 'The axe of the settler has no discrimination; — every tree disappears under its rude sway when the land is required for a homestead'. But this was no time, of course, for the type of bitter confrontation between conservationist and developmental interests to which we have become accustomed in the 1970s, for that degree of polarization required the perception and articulation of

6   G. W. Goyder (1826-98)

many more threat situations to rally support for each side. Today, the developmental interests are forced increasingly to compromise and to modify,
if not to abandon, their schemes. One hundred years earlier, long before the
battle lines were so severely drawn, very few of the champions of conservation would have seriously or consistently questioned the need for development. Their concept of 'progress' was simply different, proceeded from an
alternative base, and their unifying aim was to correct the course of develop-

ment, to turn it to what they deemed to be better purposes and more lasting results.

The South Australians were less hard-pressed than their Victorian neighbours by the varied demands of a major mining industry, but their agricultural economy was rapidly expanding and the Colony was particularly poorly endowed with natural woodland. Several leading politicians and public servants campaigned throughout the 'sixties for the promotion of new plantations and the reservation of large areas of natural forest. Foremost among these were the Surveyor-General, George Woodruffe Goyder (Figure 6), R. Schomburgk, Director of Adelaide's Botanic Gardens, and F.E.H.W. Krichauff, a long-serving Member of the House of Assembly (Jacobs 1957). In 1870 these three associates recommended the reservation of some 300,000 acres of forest in the southern, central and northern districts, and Schomburgk suggested a reduction in local rates for landholders who planted trees on their properties. With loyal support from Krichauff the scheme for major reservations was incorporated, with modifications, into the *Forest Trees Act* of 1873 and the *Forest Board Act* of 1875 (Report on Forests 1873; see also Jacobs 1957).

As Chairman of the Forest Board, Goyder supervised the selection of almost all the sites of the modern forest reserves of South Australia (Figure 7) and was frequently consulted on similar matters by the Governments of the adjacent Colonies. He is also repeatedly credited with the idea of introducing the Californian tree, *Pinus radiata* ('Monterey Pine'), which now produces the most important commercial timber in southern Australia and New Zealand, but this point is by no means established. Certainly, Goyder encouraged its scientific trials in South Australia and recommended its wider use in his 1873 Report, but the species probably arrived in Victoria with the Californian miners during the 'fifties. Ferdinand Mueller and the Victorian Committee of 1865 had already recommended the introduction of a rich variety of exotics, including the plantation of pines and cypresses from California and Oregon in lowland and coastal regions (Report on Forests 1865). It is true, however, that for some years the overriding concern of Victoria's few conservation-oriented parliamentarians was for the control of clearing operations in the much more extensive *natural* forests of that Colony, and South Australia did indeed take an early lead in the large-scale plantation of *Pinus radiata* and other exotics, attempting to follow established European methods of sustained-yield management.

The problems of semi-aridity, rainfall variability and inadequate natural water storages were pressing hard upon the South Australians. On 21 August 1871 Lieutenant-Colonel Sankey of the Royal Engineers provided a brief and outspoken report on Adelaide's alarming water shortage, chastising the colonials for their comparative lack of reliable gauging devices and suggesting that the population of the city should be limited to about 240,000—an extremely bold notion for the time and place. Subsequently, the useful discussion sparked off by this controversial statement appears to have been stifled by over-confident expectations stemming from a misperception of the relationship between afforestation and rainfall potential, but there were at least increasing fears that the Creator may have forgotten a thing or two in designing the Australian Eden. The mixed reception of Sankey's report

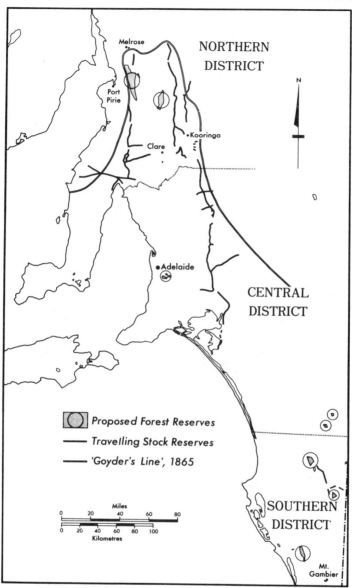

7   Goyder and the South Australian Landscape

South Australia's Surveyor-General G. W. Goyder was a man of considerable historical and geographical vision. The South Australian landscape bore the massive imprint of his major management decisions during his energetic tenure and for long after his departure. This map illustrates his celebrated 'line of reliable rainfall' and his strategic proposals for travelling stock reserves and forest reserves, contentious recommendations which profoundly influenced Government policy. As Williams (1974: 178-210) recently illustrated, Goyder was also a major figure in the development of modern drainage schemes in South Australia.

was unfortunate, for there is no denying that he had more than a little useful homework to support him: there were certainly echoes of important Indian and South African experience, for example, and some particularly significant praise for the emerging policy in Victoria. With this latter exception, he argued, Australians were still undervaluing their most precious natural resource, and therefore what was urgently required was

> the proper assertion of the public right to all streams throughout the country, and the desirability of at once, if possible, taking the most effectual measures to stop anything approaching to their permanent alienation.
> Nothing may at a future time lead to graver complications than the alienation to private individuals of permanent rights of this character. This need not in any way interfere with the disposal of water supplies to private individuals or companies, for various industries and uses, or short leases, renewable under defined restrictions, somewhat in the way already effected in Victoria in connection with mining (Report on Water 1871).

Australia's engrossing forestry debate during the 'seventies was liveliest in these two Colonies and although they should not be overstated, there were important differences in emphasis between the South Australian and Victorian interpretations. Broad ecological and utilitarian arguments were promoted in each Colony, but in the initial phases the Victorians were rather less concerned with the climatological issues and produced a more penetrating analysis of their own situation which was directed towards a practical and wider-ranging management policy, championed by Mueller and well publicized in the metropolitan dailies.

The untiring efforts of Ferdinand Mueller were rewarded in 1871 when he was made an hereditary baron by the King of Wurtemburg, and for many of his fellow-colonists the impressive new title became yet another piece in the complex mosaic of this eccentric figure. There was a stubborn streak in the man and also more than a trace of bitterness, born of, or nurtured by, his experience of personal sacrifice and lonely endeavour in Australia, and for some years leading up to this treasured recognition of his accomplishments and international standing he had pursued an almost desperate search for acceptance which was not always productive of mature and useful judgements. Today it might be said that he 'published too much too quickly' and that as a professional seeking to establish the bona fides of his scientific role in the civil service, his 'public relations' style frequently left much to be desired. Against this must be placed his unchallenged local supremacy in several fields, which meant that his opinion was very frequently sought, and the established guarantee of a prompt, honest and courageous response to every situation in which the Baron perceived an opportunity to inject a more scientific attitude into contemporary thinking. Occasionally, his enthusiasm for the promotion of eucalyptus plantations throughout the world dangerously overstepped the mark. In 1866 for example, Mueller had been engaged as a Commissioner of the Melbourne International Exhibition. He contributed a lengthy essay on the economic value of many indigenous plants and there was good sense in his remarks on the potentials for regional planning schemes which stressed the complementarity of recent techniques of afforestation and

8   Baron von Mueller (1825-96)

irrigation, but this was clouded to some extent by the boldness of another claim:

> ... in the Australian vegetation we probably possess the means of obliterating the rainless regions of the globe, to spread at last woods over our deserts, and thereby to mitigate the distressing droughts, and to annihilate even that occasionally dry heat evolved by the sun's rays from the naked ground throughout

extensive regions of the interior (Mueller 1866; quoted in Daley 1924: 42).

For over forty years Mueller was indeed actively engaged in distributing seeds throughout Australia and internationally, and in his capacity as long-standing Vice-President of the Victorian Acclimatization Society (originally founded by Edward Wilson) he played a leading role in local projects of all kinds. Arising from several of his papers presented to this Society, Mueller eventually published *The Select Extra-Tropical Plants* in 1871, a fine example of his passionate advocacy of national botanical research for utilitarian purposes. The book ran to at least eight editions before his death and was also translated into French, German and Spanish. But for a deeper appreciation of the man himself and of his broader contribution to the philosophy and practice of conservation and resource management, the smaller, possibly more relaxed and certainly less celebrated pieces must also be consulted.

Take one example: 'Forest Culture in its Relation to Industrial Pursuits', a lecture delivered on 22 June 1871 at the Industrial and Technological Museum in Melbourne (Mueller 1876). This was a very rambling address, pulling in local and overseas examples with great display and too little order, yet there was also political, economic and scientific punch in much of what he said. In addition, Mueller provided the modern researcher with a rare and early glimpse of his own conservational philosophy, remarkably advanced for the Australia of his day.

> The inhabitable space of the globe is not likely to increase, except through forces which would initiate a new organic creation, or at all events bring the present phase in the world's history to a close; but while the area of land does not increase, mankind, in spite of deadly plagues, of the horrors of warfare, and of uncountable oppressions and miseries, which more extended education and the highest standard of morals can only reduce or subdue—mankind, in spite of all this, increases numerically so rapidly, that before long more space must be gained for its very existence. Where can we look for the needful space? Is it in the tropic zones, with their humid heat and depressing action on our energies? Or is it in the frigid zone, which sustains but a limited number of forms of organism? Or is it rather in the temperate and particularly *our* warm temperate zone, that we have to offer the means of subsistence to our fellow-men, closely located as they in future must be? But this formation of dense and at the same time also thriving settlements, how is it to be carried out, unless indeed we place not merely our soil at the disposal of our coming brethren, but offer with this soil also the indispensable requisites of vigorous industrial life, among which requisites the easy and inexpensive access to a sufficiency of wood stands well-nigh foremost (p. 60).

And again, for the very heart of the conservation ethic:

> What is vitality, and what mortal will measure the share of delight enjoyed by any organism? Why should even the life of a plant be expended cruelly and wastefully, especially if, perhaps, this very plant stood already in youthful elegance, while yet the diprotodon (a wombat the size of a buffalo) was roaming over the forest ridges encircling Port Phillip Bay—when those forest ridges on the very place of this city were still clothed in their full natal garb . . . that individual life, whatever it may be, which we so often so thoughtlessly and so ruthlessly destroy, but which we never can restore, should be respected. Is it not as if the sinking tree was speaking imploringly to us, and when falling wished to convey

to us its sadness and its grief? (p. 94)

There were also said to be *aesthetic*, as well as *utilitarian* and *ethical* arguments for forest conservation.

Contrast the magnificence of a dense forest, before the destructive hand of man defaced it, with the cheerless aspect of wide landscapes, devoid of wooded scenery—only open plains or treeless ridges bounding the horizon. The silent grandeur and solitude of a virgin forest inspires us almost with awe, much more so than even the broad expanse of the ocean. It conveys also involuntarily to our mind a feeling as if we were brought more closely before that Divine Power by whom the worlds without end were created, and before whom the proudest human work must sink into utter insignificance. No settlement, however princely —no city, however great its splendour, brilliant its arts, or enchanting its pleasures —can arouse those sentiments of veneration which, among all the grand works of nature, an undisturbed noble forest-region is most apt to call forth (p. 95).

So these three dominating arguments, too often depicted as almost separate, and occasionally conflicting, streams of thought in the history of the conservation movement in the United States of America, were clearly perceived by Baron von Mueller as the essential, interdependent props of his own credo. In the same lecture he praised the work of Marsh very generously and, with an eye to practical considerations, pointed to the successes of the European and Indian 'Conservators' in afforestation and sustained-yield practices, yet emphasized that the complexity of Australian conditions demanded the development of entirely new systems of management: 'trees might be sold by numbers, at certain sizes, with saving of the youthful trees, or the wood might be removed by the square mile, with a view of replanting', as in parts of Europe and India, but the introduction of special controls was urgently required to investigate and regulate the destructive local techniques of ringing and bark-stripping (p. 52). Approximately 25 per cent of the area of Victoria should be maintained under some type of forest cover, and he approved of the idea of local Forest Boards, provided the members of local Roads Boards and Shire Councils were excluded: 'The predilections of a member of a municipality will often be in [timber-using] building operations and kindred subjects, while for [tree-] culture processes he may have neither inclination nor experience' (p. 53). On the other hand, for some unaccountable reason he did not object to the employment of the Mining Boards in this capacity. The remainder of the lecture was given over to an oddly deterministic argument concerning the happy longevity of the forest dweller, which he ascribed to 'remoteness', 'freedom' and 'the bracing pureness' of the air, and a further public reminder of Mueller's untiring efforts in the dissemination of plants and seeds to all parts of Australia and overseas during his controversial supervision of the Botanic Gardens: 'Although I may have incurred the displeasure of a few of the less thoughtful of my fellow-citizens, who wished the slender means of my young establishments appropriated for the ephemeral glory of floral displays, and who wished to sacrifice lasting progress to unproductive gaiety' (p. 93). Yet his closing statement was as fine an expression of conservational beliefs as anyone could hope for; it became indeed a favoured quotation among his admiring followers.

I regard the forest as an heritage given to us by nature, not for spoil or to devastate, but to be wisely used, reverently honoured, and carefully maintained. I regard the forests as a gift, intrusted to any of us only for transient care during a short space of time, to be surrendered to posterity again as an unimpaired property, with increased riches and augmented blessings, to pass as a sacred patrimony from generation to generation (p. 96).

Although given to the occasional rush of blood, the Baron was seldom so extravagantly rhetorical as this; yet the mood of Victoria's conservationists was reasonably well captured in his address. The whole subject had become inextricably linked with an optimistic view of man's ability to 'improve' his environment which at the same time displayed self-righteous indignation towards politicians and others, 'blind to Nature's light', who permitted or indulged in wanton destruction or dangerously short-term policies of exploitation. The opposing argument that the aggressive expansion of settlement and the growth of a flourishing timber industry were themselves supports or even expressions of a most desired form of improvement was apparently dismissed. Yet as Mueller's own efforts testify, the acclimatization of plants, animals, birds, insects or fish was scarcely ever queried as a management goal which was incompatible with conservational interests. The members of the acclimatization societies were in fact the most ardent promoters of a disjointed view of conservation which achieved only partial and temporary successes at this time.

Australia was of course a wonderful challenge for these ambitious organizations. They took as their models the British and European societies and proudly traced their own lineage to Bacon's *New Atlantis*. But the special circumstances of the New World insisted that their charters be re-written: 'attention should not only be directed to the introduction of living animals and plants foreign to the soil, but also to adopt efficient and energetic means for the preservation, domestication, and rearing [of] those indigenous to the colony' (Bennett 1862: 5). Similarly, special care was to be taken that scientists should not dominate the societies, whose members should include 'landholders, squatters, agriculturalists, breeders of stock, as well as the public generally' (Bennett 1862: 5). In fact the Australian societies were inevitably *élitist* bodies, frequently well-meaning but not always well-informed, even though they did include several eminent scientists. Those who proclaimed that 'The great Creator "gave man dominion over the fish of the sea, and over the fowl of the air, and over every living thing that moveth upon the earth", for his use, benefit, and study; not to lay waste and destroy for mere wantonness' (Bennett 1862: 40) were often the busiest of hunters, to whom the preservation of native animals was seen from a totally anthropocentric view—for were they not 'all forming good food' and even the unfortunate bandicoot 'only to be compared to sucking-pig in flavour' (Bennett 1862: 19)? Whatever the mixture of motives, the acclimatization societies at their worst made gigantic and notorious errors, and at their best greatly assisted the establishment of agriculture and rural industry. In the 'seventies, long before the colonial governments chose to make a direct and committed entry into the field via specially-created resource management agencies, these voluntary bodies were generally very active and influential.

1871 also promised to be a good year, for example, for the conservation and acclimatization campaign of Edward Wilson and the Melbourne *Argus*. Following Mueller's public lecture by little more than week, a letter in the correspondence columns of that paper again raised the issue of forest reservation and plantation, and the writer's urgent appeal for support in this 'truly national work' is worth recording.

> The true interests of the country find an advocate in you, so I make bold to ask your assistance in this good work. Our legislators, I fear, with very few exceptions, are too much intent on the loaves and fishes of the present day to allow time for the consideration of what would be an enduring and living testimony of their patriotism . . . (*Argus*, 1 July 1871).

James McPherson Grant's new *Selection Act* for Victoria had come into force on 1 February 1870 and it soon showed its improvement on its predecessors by placing some thousands of new settlers on the land. By 30 June 1872 there were 19,420 selections for 1,916,860 acres and the resultant pressure on timber resources for domestic fuel, fencing and building materials, as well as widespread clearing for cultivation and grazing paddocks, mounted to alarming proportions and captured the attention of the metropolitan and country newspapers. As Ministers of Lands, Grant and his successors commonly had to deal with petitions from established settlers of every rank requesting the preservation of valued patches of local woodland against the rushing tide of settlement. Both the *Age* and the *Argus* reflected and heightened public anxiety focussed on the perceived microclimatic connection between water supply and forest cover. The wholesale destruction of trees was sometimes vividly portrayed as a direct threat to the survival of the new country townships, which required an assured supply from local reservoirs to sustain them in their growing function as service centres for the frontier districts. In fact, every pioneer selector and his family then depended on natural springs and watercourses, with which even Victoria was relatively poorly endowed. The most practical recommendations emerging from this publicity called for the proclamation of local forest or woodland reserves scattered through all parts of the Colony to decrease the dangers of drought and to provide carefully regulated supplies of timber. An appeal was also made for an investigation of the possibilities of an increased provision of alternative supplies from other Colonies, particularly from the much-vaunted Jarrah forests of Western Australia (*Age* and *Argus*, various dates 1871; especially *Argus*, 7 July and *Age*, 14 July).

The Expert and the Public 1871-78

A Royal Commission convened in August 1871 to consider these matters for the Victorian Parliament, and also to report on the best means of making more of the opportunities for land-use experimentation inherent in the opening up of so much territory in varied ecological regions. An extensive range of 'novel industries' had been mooted for the Colony since the first efforts in acclimatization and the notion had provided an attractive ingredient in the grandiose but largely unsuccessful schemes of some of the earlier Lands Ministers (Powell 1970a: 102-4), but there was sufficient optimism in official circles during the early 'seventies to encourage renewed efforts in this field. The Commissioners' terms of reference nicely captured the controlling utilitarian motivation, although they also hinted at a continuing underlying concern for aesthetic and ecological considerations. The most important task however was

> to consider and report how far it may be practicable to introduce into this country branches of industry which are known to be common and profitable among the farming population of continental Europe, to specify which of such industries are most suitable to our soil, climate, and circumstances, and to report on the best means of promoting their introduction into Victoria, and how far the labor of persons at the disposal of the State may be advantageously used for that purpose; and to further consider and report on the best means of promoting the culture, extension, and preservation of State Forests in Victoria and the introduction of such foreign trees as may be suitable to the climate and useful for industrial purposes (Report 1871).

Smyth, Hodgkinson and Mueller were perhaps the most interesting scientific members of the fourteen-man Commission, which was chaired by Judge Samuel Henry Bindon; far less is known about the other members, apart from Paul de Castella, a leading expert in wines and horticulture, and Dr John Ignatius Bleasdale, chosen to express the support of the Acclimatization Society. Most interest was shown in 'wine, [olive] oil, dried fruits, silk, tobacco, opium, perfumes, dyes and the like, which the climate of Victoria is capable of yielding in perfection, [and which] belong to the most valuable and profitable class of commodities that can be sent to market in any part of the world' (*Age*, 3 August 1871; cf. Bleasdale 1871). The need for experimental State nurseries and an efficient official distribution of introduced seed-stock was another familiar topic covered by the Commission. But an interesting and hitherto neglected side-effect of these developments for improved rural education was suggested in the final submission: the intensive work demanded by the new crops would be 'highly beneficial in training the young of both sexes in the habits of frugality and care, which so essentially mark the rural population of those countries where such industries exist' (Report 1871).

The same rhetoric flooded the exhaustive debates on land disposal in each of the Australian Colonies. A seemingly irresistible image—blurred, yet tantalizing—excited each of these young parliaments. It was essentially a beckoning image of the future society they hoped to create, a society founded on a 'sturdy peasant proprietary', the 'family farm', an 'industrious yeomanry' and ' independent freeholders'. In all of this, British and American origins and continuing influences are readily apparent, but modifications were introduced from time to time to incorporate new scientific appraisals or wild speculations concerning the Australian environment. These modifications were derived essentially from the evolving local situation—from the experiences of success, failure and plain survival; from the lingering misperceptions, and the changing aspirations, of the people themselves. In 1871 the image-makers were conjuring another illusion to add to the confusion. There had been a good deal of discussion over the climatic similarities between Mediterranean Europe and southern Australia during the previous decade: indeed, Victoria in particular had been successfully promoted by medical writers as a healing refuge for 'the struma-saturated races of Europe', far superior to the French and Italian Rivieras as a resort for consumptives (Powell 1973a), and Bindon's Commission was apparently set on adding another touch of Arcadia to complete the flavour.

At the first meeting of the Commission (1 August 1871) Bindon actually proposed that an outline map of Europe be prepared to guide the public and his colleagues—it was important that the map should show 'at a glance the part of Europe favored, if he might use the expression, with an Australian climate [!]. This would strike many an eye, and teach what we desired' (*Age*, 2 August 1871). The Commissioners conducted a little field-work and dispatched a questionnaire to shire and borough councils, agricultural societies and a number of 'well-informed colonists', requesting an account of any local experience they may have gained in the cultivation and processing of the 'novel' crops, and their advice on the 'best method of apprenticing, or otherwise bringing up to advantage, for industrial purposes, the destitute or orphan boys or girls who are maintained at the expense of the State' (Report 1871). On the whole the response to this unashamedly utilitarian document was very enthusiastic (*Age* and *Argus*, from August through to October 1871) and reflected the current confidence in Victoria's 'singular' prospect of becoming a richly varied agricultural region, untroubled by the climatic extremes and uncertainties which plagued other parts of the world. And there was an interesting mixture of smugness and righteousness in the *Age's* commentary.

> . . . it is only a small climate belt of the earth's surface that is capable of yielding these products. They require a peculiarly exceptional climate to bring them to perfection—one where there is no excess of heat nor extreme of cold, where the rainfall is moderate, and unclouded sunshine is constant and uninterrupted throughout the year. Victoria and the regions of Australia immediately adjoining, in common with the South of Europe and a small portion of Western Asia, enjoy this happy climate. It would argue us then but a barbarous people if we did not study to turn this grand advantage of our adopted country to good account (*Age*, 3 August 1871).

Was this final remark a new twist, even a mild challenge, to Marsh's arresting thesis? Marsh's historical summary was often taken out of context by contemporaries who believed that he had totally ascribed the rise and fall of ancient and modern civilizations to the environmental attitudes which characterized their development. Both the *Age* and the Commission exuded an ultimate confidence in man which Marsh himself obviously shared. There is at least one interesting American parallel here: only four years earlier, in direct response to the public reception of *Man and Nature*, a special Commission appointed by the Wisconsin legislature presented a *Report on the Disastrous Effects of the Destruction of Forest Trees Now Going on so Rapidly in the State of Wisconsin*, and its preamble certainly found a responsive chord in Australia (for example in von Mueller 1876).

> Both past history and present experience show that a country destitute of forests as well as one entirely covered with them is only suited to the condition of a barbarous or semi-barbarous people. Deprive a people of the comforts and conveniences derived directly or indirectly from forest products, and they soon revert

to barbarism. It is only where a due proportion between the cultivated land and the forests is maintained that man can attain and enjoy his highest civilization (Carstensen 1958: 9).

Agricultural settlement had rapidly expanded since its inception on the rolling prairies and 'oak openings' of southern Wisconsin in the 1830s. By the late 'fifties and early 'sixties the threat to the valuable pine and hardwood forests of the northern part of the State provoked considerable controversy, but Marsh's book offered a sound ecological and economic case which quickened the search for a new settlement policy to conserve the forests. In southern Australia there were similar tensions, less clearly defined, between 'developmental' and 'preservationist' interests. These were also investigated by select committees of experts, as in Wisconsin. The authorities quoted in the final submissions of these 'consultants' were fairly similar in each country and the same arguments were used, even the same words and phrases. Allowing for the strength of local needs and peculiarities in regional environments, their recommendations were also substantially in accord. The ideals of 'efficiency' and 'rational development' were thus given an important early hearing in Australia and North America within about six years of the first appearance of *Man and Nature*.

The formal title of the first Victorian committee was actually the Royal Commission on 'Foreign Industries and Forests'. It called for 'prompt and decisive action...to put an end to the wasteful practices hitherto incidental to the felling of trees and the stripping of bark in the Forests of Victoria', and recommended the establishment of tree nurseries near the principal country railway stations to assist the development of future State plantations and the introduction of small private plantations, via special land regulations, on allotments which were still under lease or credit-purchase from the Government. The number of State forests should be increased; some should be set aside in the Western District and on the North-western Plains to discover the best means of afforestation there; and the recent decision to create local Forest Boards, after the fashion of the local Lands Boards, was approved (Report 1871).

Hays (1972) has illustrated that the thrust of 'modernization', of which conservationist forces were part, resulted in increasing the tension between centralizing and decentralizing forces in different geographical contexts— within the administration of cities, regions and States, and at the national level, for example. The implementation of evolving principles of natural resource management in the United States greatly assisted in the injection of 'system, expertise, centralized direction and manipulation—and the activation of tension between centralizing and decentralizing forces' (Hays 1972: new preface). Further research may disclose that this judgement is also generally applicable to Australia before 1914 but it is vital to point out that the processes identified by Hays probably demand the insertion of the adjective 'reciprocal' to describe their true functioning here. In other words, the tensions between the primate capitals and the subordinate provincial towns, or between the inhabitants of town and country, and different types of land-use enterprise, and individuals, groups and bureaucracies, also discouraged some forms of innovation and/or their spatial diffusion, and worked against the local adaptation of well-proven imported notions of resource management. In part, the failure of Australians to introduce some enlightened and well-publicized concepts of forest management can be set down to the operation of these forces—which, stripped to its essentials, probably means no more than that the mass of the people, or at least the most influential of them, did not share the concern of the conservationists.

Commercial interests were blamed for the worst destruction in Victoria's forests. A recurring complaint, first raised in the 'sixties, was that the timber-getters were taking 'only the prime parts of the trees they fell, leaving large quantities of timber to go to waste, and rendering the forest liable to injury from extensive conflagrations, owing to the incumbrance of the ground by so much felled and abandoned wood' (Forest Conservancy Papers 1874; cf. Marsh 1964: 233-5). In the mining districts thousands of young trees were felled every year to provide material for props, and so intense was the competition between the sawmill operators that large areas were felled simply 'to prevent a rival mill-owner from obtaining them, or to block up the access of the rival mill-owner to some coveted patch of fine timber'. By the early 'seventies the evils of this confused situation had been greatly exacerbated by the continuation of a ridiculous annual licensing system which charged between £12 and £15 for permission to erect and maintain a mill, £10 for each log carriage, £5 for each man employed in felling; similarly, splitters at one time paid £1 per annum and suppliers of firewood only ten shillings. In 1873-74, despite the introduction of more stringent methods of collection, these trifling sums provided a total revenue of less than £4,500.

> It is probable that no more effectual method of legalizing the destruction of timber could have been devised than this indiscriminate use of licenses, except the barbarous practice of ringing or girdling trees by selectors and others in densely timbered forest.

> A license at ten shillings or one pound per quarter is a legal instrument giving authority to any person to cut any quantity of timber he pleases, and, virtually, from any Crown Land he pleases (Forest Conservancy Papers 1874).

There were only three official Forest 'Caretakers' (at various times also referred to as 'Inspectors', 'Conservators' and 'Rangers') at the Victoria, Cape Otway and Bullarook forests; another two men were 'chiefly so employed' in similar duties in other reserves and the remainder of the work was said to be under the supervision of the 'Crown Lands Bailiff', a most intriguing and in some respects very powerful position, centrally placed in the hierarchy of the Lands Department (Powell 1973b). It was forcefully argued that the problem was not simply to increase staff, but to give the whole management programme a logical, scientific basis, yet the early polarization of applied forestry and private enterprise already seemed assured and Australia's forests were the losers. With good reason, the foresters bitterly complained that each of their proposals had been 'looked upon as an interference with the self-created and long apparently recognized rights of the woodcutters, and resulted in public meetings and representatives of grievances to the department and to the Minister'. In Australia, as in North America, the lumber industry provided the most dramatic example of resource exploitation in the latter half of the nineteenth century. Low prices for forest

land (or cheap licenses), a good demand for timber and the small amount
of capital required, encouraged many individuals and companies to enter the
field. Hays' observations could indeed be safely borrowed and applied to
Australia:

> The industry was highly mobile; lumbermen rapidly cut and abandoned lands,
> and moved on to new areas. Facing the uncertainties of a high degree of com-
> petition, timber operators could not, with profit, utilize fully their resources.
> Few cut more than the most valuable trees; they left second-grade timber as
> waste (Hays 1972: 27).

In response to these conditions, strong leadership emerged from the public
and private sectors to ensure better management for the forests of the United
States, but in Australia the relentless efforts of independent conservationists
and several gifted scientists in public service found much less support.

Victoria's *Papers Relating to Forest Conservancy* were presented to Parliament in 1874 when the second edition of Marsh's book appeared in Britain
and America. They constituted an impressive *cri de coeur*, detailing the current
situation and drawing upon relevant material from the other Australasian
Colonies, India, the United States, Britain and several European countries,
to hammer home the same old points. The first local Forest Board had been
gazetted on 5 September 1873 for the protection and restoration of forests
in the Ballarat district and the appointment of other regional boards soon
followed, but the system quickly proved itself a hopeless failure. The representatives of competing shire councils bickered constantly at board meetings, local people challenged or ignored the boards' authority and the boards
questioned the authority of the bureaucrats in Melbourne. The bureaucrats
in turn charged that their detractors were guilty of condoning or participating
in various types of corruption, castigated them for their obsession with the
revenue potential of the forests and generally argued that the abuses inherent
in the system of local control were leading towards an intolerable attitude
of irresponsibility on the part of the boards towards their appointed role as
the stewards of vital resources, which in reality belonged to *all* the people of
Victoria. The *Australasian* had also smelled a rat or two: 'Can it be that the
evil has been surmounted by the appointment of a couple of local boards of
management, or was the cry raised simply with a view to secure the transfer
of the state property to certain individuals?' (*Australasian*, 8 November
1873). A central co-ordinating board was established on 6 March 1874 under
Smyth and Hodgkinson, and although the latter resigned five days later there
was at least some improvement in the monitoring of timber exploitation in
each region. This system was described by W. E. Ivey, Secretary of the Central State Forest Board, in the Victorian section of the 1874 Papers.

The chief objective of Ivey's report was to demonstrate conclusively that
the Colony's timber was being shamefully and dangerously wasted, but,
in addition, his detailed exposition clearly illustrates that the concept of
sustained-yield management was quite well understood at this early date
in local professional circles. It was somehow calculated that in the most
valuable forests the ratio of timber used to timber wasted was about 1:8 and
this led to the far-sighted demand—which was not only Muellerian and desperate, but also revolutionary and unattainable in those circumstances—

that a charge should be made *for each tree felled*, to put an end to the 'selfish indifference to the wants of future generations displayed by timber cutters', some of whom might then be persuaded to 'occupy themselves with more profit to the community in general by following other avocations than by destroying, for a pitiful wage, what should be preserved as the inheritance of future generations' (Forest Conservancy Papers 1874). And indeed the Victorian public, particularly the rising number of urban residents just beginning to show some political muscle, was obviously being deprived of an important source of revenue, while individual settlers in wooded areas were said to be cashing in to the extent of charging up to seven shillings a week for the privilege of cutting timber on their own lands, between seven and ten shillings for each mining prop taken out, so much for each railway sleeper, and so on.

Another small but important digression might now be permitted. There has commonly been an unfortunate but inevitable nationalistic bias to recent writings on environmental history—inevitable, because it has so often emerged from a fear for the future of one's own community, from confusion and suspicion about certain values and attitudes which appear entrenched in that community, which has led to a search for the historical roots of the present predicament to identify causes and trends; to reorientate, start again. But it is important to stress once more that this very natural preoccupation should not be allowed to obscure the pervasive impact of new forms of scholarship, especially in science and technology, which transcended national boundaries. The debate over forest conservation illustrates further that however isolated Australia was from the rest of the world in a physical sense, Australians were far less removed from the world of scholarship, especially in technology and the applied sciences. The links with relevant American research and practical experience are plain enough, but in the field of forest conservation there were also much older, European traditions upon which Australians could draw, particularly through their membership of that most unique of loose spatial assemblages, the British Empire.

There must have been countless individuals who chose to use (or were required to use) the great variety of physical and cultural environments of the Empire for all kinds of comparative research, or as a special type of employment field for administrative experience, and even as a complicated career ladder, moving from one country to another with an envied facility made possible and profitable by the unifying focus of British influence and the dominance of London, which functioned as the central hub. There have been many invaluable works describing the impact of the emergence of natural resource management policies on the accelerating 'modernization' of the Western World. Undoubtedly there is more to come, particularly when the recent extension of the field to embrace the built environment of the city and region is more widely accepted, and the interpretation of the Australian experience obviously requires these perspectives. But the question of scale is fundamental. It is not difficult, for example, to establish a case for the renowned Indian Civil Service as one of the most powerful and multifacetted bureaucratic institutions in any part of the world, at any time, with a prestige and influence extending far beyond the Indian subcontinent. Certainly for Australia and also for New Zealand, with which my own research has occasionally been involved, the wider imperial context provided a reservoir of professional people and ideas for environmental management which cannot be dismissed lightly. In the evolution of ideas for the conservation of forests, and possibly to a similar extent in water management, British experience in India offered impressive models which attracted great interest throughout the Empire. From the very early appointment of a Conservator in 1806 forestry languished in British India until the arrival of Dietrich Brandis, an impressive German administrator, in 1856. Brandis was appointed first Inspector-General of Forests to the Government of India in April 1864 and brilliant progress was made in all forms of forest conservation and plantation under his guidance. Before his retirement in 1883 he had also established an elaborate technical training programme and a sophisticated system of regional supervision; his subordinates often moved to senior staff positions in newer administrations in other parts of Asia and they were regularly sought for short-term secondment to British territories elsewhere (Ribbentrop 1900). It is therefore not surprising to find that in 1874 Victorian foresters chose to include in their *Papers* an eloquent statement by N. A. Dalzell, Conservator of Forests for the Bombay Presidency.

> It has been said that to pursue the progress of man step by step in the destruction of forests would be to write the history of civilization, as man is developed only at the expense of forest vegetation. Hence an endeavour has been made to establish it as a maxim that civilization is antagonistic to the conservation of forests. When this sentiment, however, is analysed, it will appear pretty evident that it is more distinguished for brevity than for truth; for it is in civilized countries, such as Germany and France, that the conservation of forests is considered of vital importance to the progress and well-being of man, and that without forests these would become, like Asia Minor (the cradle of the human race) a country of ruined cities.

> It is only in the first step of civilization that man is the enemy of forests. When the savage hunter begins to be dissatisfied with the precarious produce of the chase, and to perceive the advantages of a settled abode and a regular supply of food, he cuts down the trees which formerly sheltered him, and 'establishes a clearing'. The pioneers of the so-called civilization may come from a country already civilized . . . but their acts and objects are the same as those of the savage, and a man cannot but feel that in becoming a pioneer of the so-called civilization in a new country, he has gone back, for a time at least, into a state of semi-barbarism (Forest Conservancy Papers 1874).

This was mainly a restatement of an established version of the utilitarian argument for conservation which linked it with anthropocentric concepts of 'progress'. But in putting the ecological case, Dalzell seems to have functioned very well indeed in the time-honoured role of 'overseas expert' which we have come to expect (and sometimes endure) in this country.

> We now know that a forest is not merely an aggregate of trees, but an embodiment of life, subject to disease, old age, and death, and that in their living functions they influence the physical character of a country, and are connected with important changes in the economical, commercial, and artificial relations of the population; that they enter into mutual relations of cause and effect, with many physical phenomena which affect the productiveness and agricultural interests of a country. This knowledge has been of slow growth and has had to

combat with much ignorance and prejudice, and whatever good ground may have been discovered for despising scientific theories, the facts collected together are too numerous and too authentic not to carry with them the fullest conviction (Forest Conservancy Papers 1874).

Yet there were no prizes for addressing the colonial *cognoscenti*, and the rape of the Victorian forests continued. The situation was only a little better in South Australia, which was already concentrating on afforestation, and the Governments of New South Wales, Tasmania and Queensland, which were more comparable to Victoria in their endowment of extensive tracts of natural forest, were not greatly pressed beyond the introduction of some loose and unimaginative regulations, including the reservation and subsequent underfinanced, impotent administration of a few special areas of high commercial value (Jacobs 1957; Rule 1967: 56-69). Apparently the best advice available, which was very good indeed, was not widely known or understood; but it may also have been rejected or somehow challenged, diluted—or perhaps it was simply down graded, when placed by the colonists in the full perspective of the contemporary setting of rapid settlement expansion.

*

The natural bush of Australia was fast disappearing over extensive areas of the south-eastern crescent. What then of the celebrated bush ethos? It was then gaining strength in the same regions; yet even in later years, it offered very little protection for the diminishing wilderness. The point has often been made, however, that the aesthetic evocation of the bush was concerned with rural Australia *in its entirety*, not solely or even largely with the true wilderness areas, and if we are to continue the search for social-scientific explanations it will be more constructive to narrow the lens and consider instead a type of 'agrarian myth' which was incorporated into the bush ethos. It is particularly instructive to analyse the implications for several aspects of resource management of the most arresting manifestation of the myth, the vaguely-defined but immensely useful political symbol of the 'yeoman' farmer.

6 Official and Popular Appraisals in Resource Management

In 1860 an angry mob stormed Parliament House in Melbourne, demanding 'a vote, a rifle and a farm'. This was the sequel to a long series of public meetings calling for the unlocking of the public lands, then held in temporary licences by the big pastoralists. Throughout Australia similar movements were building, and the land issue was always tightly intertwined with the demand for political and social reform. Victoria received the major input of British Chartists, Irish rebels and other radical elements, and it was these newcomers, together with the city *bourgeoisie*, who initiated the land reform movement (Baker 1958: Serle 1963; Powell 1970a). They borrowed much of their rhetoric from Feargus O'Connor and other leading British Chartists, whose scheme for 'land colonies' based on small holdings of less than five acres had been pursued with great enthusiasm (Armytage 1958; MacAskill 1962). The Chartists had found that 'land for the people' provided a tangible and comprehensible goal and a valuable rallying pont: 'The land belongs to the people. It is the people's heritage. Kings, princes, lords and citizens have stolen it from the people'. Man is after all a symbol-using animal, and for the struggling masses in the urban slums the vision evoked by the fiery oratory at each rally was probably far more than an escape to independent comfort and dignity, even though they may not have shared all of the political ambitions of the leaders. As presented to the British proletariat the dimunutive holdings were the epitome of comfort and the 'just reward for honest toil', and a form of secure, unpretentious, 'cosy' self-sufficiency appeared to be an aim in itself. Australians were soon enticed by a similar but far more attractive lure in the form of a mythical figure, the independent freeholder, who lived with his family on a small, intensively cultivated farm, which he carefully tended until it was duly inherited by his equally stable and industrious offspring. Despite the ambiguities inherent in the term (Powell 1968b, vol. 1: 28-9), this symbolic character was almost invariably entitled the 'yeoman' farmer.

Management Implications of the Yeoman Myth

Social anthropologists have indicated that myth and its associated ritual may begin by satisfying a set of identical or closely related needs of individuals or small groups, and that conditions can be so altered as to make some types of obsessive behaviour or fantasy generally congenial, in which cases the 'private' ritual is socialized by a much wider group (Kluckhohn 1966). Though it was obviously assisted by the complex British inheritance at all levels of society, the local political utility of the 'yeoman' symbol was supremely important in bringing about the diffusion and adoption of the agrarian myth. Between 1860 and the mid-'eighties a series of *Land Selection Acts* was

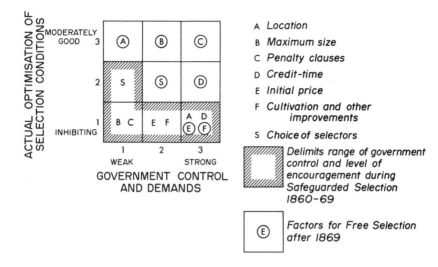

A *Location*
B *Maximum size*
C *Penalty clauses*
D *Credit-time*
E *Initial price*
F *Cultivation and other improvements*
S *Choice of selectors*

ACTUAL OPTIMISATION OF SELECTION CONDITIONS

MODERATELY GOOD 3

INHIBITING 1

WEAK   STRONG

GOVERNMENT CONTROL
AND DEMANDS

Delimits range of government control and level of encouragement during *Safeguarded Selection 1860–69*

Factors for Free Selection after 1869

9   Degree of Legislative Support for Pioneer Settlement in Victoria, 1860-80

The diagram is a subjective interpretation of the positive and negative ranges of Government influence, in terms of the seven factors listed. A major break in the pattern occurred with the introduction of 'Free Selection' in 1869, as the matrix illustrates. At no time, however, was the Government doing much to assist the pioneer settler; nor did it succeed in guiding the settlement process as the legislation intended. In short, the selector had to make his own way for the most part, yet the legislative structure was still an important part of his decision-environment. This situation is discussed in detail in Powell 1970a: 59-172.

passed in each of the Australian Colonies to facilitate the settlement of small farmers on the public domain (Roberts 1968). The leading land reformers were usually aspiring or practising politicians who made little attempt to assess the real potential of the land for intensive settlement and the squatters could justifiably complain of the incompetence of their opponents: 'whose knowledge of laws and ideal of a country has been founded in the culture of a cabbage garden or flower pot of a city suburb'. There was of course rather more to it than this. Imbued with very British tastes in landscape, colonial politicians appear to have cherished an image of a landscape with small fields, carefully tilled, 'softening the horizon' or yielding 'a pleasantly settled aspect', *and* they were held fast by a political and philosophical ideal for which the small freeholder was the symbol.

The functioning of this motivating image was exhibited in the efforts of each of the colonial governments to mould the cultural geography of its territory. Survey systems varied regionally and from Colony to Colony, and they were repeatedly modified, but the important point is that for a long period, permanent settlement was expected to advance according to the blueprints laid down by the official survey plans—land could not be sold without some form of prior survey, and this gave the State the opportunity to control the pace, direction and detailed pattern of settlement expansion (Figure 9). The ritual was most rigidly prescribed in Victoria and South Australia, where an effort was made to organize the land in such a way that it conformed to a rudimentary appraisal of quality, so that the farm blocks varied in size and sometimes in shape. In the same Colonies, township plans were carefully drawn up to provide well designed local centres for the densely-packed rural population which was anticipated (Williams 1966a; Powell 1970b). Even when the stipulation of pre-sale survey was removed the maximum size of new holdings permitted under the law remained very low (usually ranging between 320 and 640 acres), considering the difficulties of Australian conditions. So it was never expected that the 'yeoman' class envisaged by the politicians would be brought into existence by the legislation alone; it would create itself, by dint of sacrifice and manly endeavour, but it would be founded on the opportunities presented by the State in the form of small holdings. Parliamentary debates, newspaper campaigns, official emigrants' guides and the like all suggest that the idealism which assisted in spawning the land legislation assumed that the independent Australian farm, like the homestead in the United States, would be a home for the pioneer's lifetime, to be devotedly tended and passed on to his children in due course. Consequently, the official regulations included severe penalties for non-residence and neglect. Yet in both continents mobility was a prominent feature of rural settlement, conditioned by the existence of open territory, the type of economy practised and a generally commercial, unsentimental attitude towards the land.

To some degree, Queensland and Western Australia devised their own, more rational versions of controlled expansion, but these were overshadowed by developments in the older and more populous southern Colonies. As successive *Land Acts* gained only local successes in their stated objectives and vast areas were freeholded by speculators and the sitting pastoral tenants, it was increasingly argued that the small grazing property, or at least the practice of mixed farming on a moderate-sized holding, was the only realistic form of land-use. And the price demanded for the land was quite as unreasonable, especially when the meagre resources of the potential settler are considered: for a standard 320-acre farm in Victoria in the mid-1860s, a total investment of £1,000 was required in short time, and a third of this outlay was directed merely to the purchase. Credit facilities were gradually introduced to improve this situation, but the traditionalists continued to hold strongly to other principles which were also central to the yeoman symbolism. The hallowed tenet of intensive cultivation, for example, was for them the ultimate test of the *bona fides* of the settler. Perhaps a furrowed acre or two and a bristling field of stooked corn made the most pleasant or tangible change which they were capable of acknowledging, and anything resembling a continuation of the despised and 'wasteful' pastoral economy was usually rejected out of hand: 'Let a man take his 320 acres, at a shilling a year if you like; but let him remain on the land; make him cultivate it, because, if he does not cultivate it, it may be very reasonably assumed that he does not want it' (*Victorian Parliamentary Debates* 1869: 956).

With the exception of premium locations near the towns, cultivation was not a paying proposition and until the development of refrigerated shipping

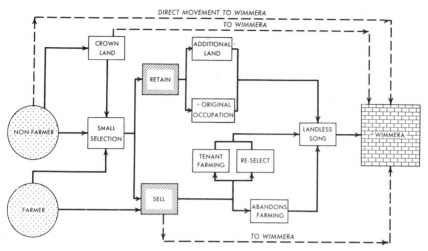

10 Settlement Mobility as a Response to Opportunities and Restrictions,
1860-80

The example is taken from Victoria's Western District—an 'old' frontier, unsuccessfully opened to pioneer settlement in the 'sixties when speculators and the incumbent pastoralists easily managed to hold or take most of the region. The Wimmera was not opened until improved legislation was introduced encouraging and to some extent protecting *bona fide* settlement. The diagram illustrates the decision-routes available to farmers and non-farmers in the old frontier. The range of alternatives open to them obviously depended upon their financial and family circumstances. It is perfectly conceivable that in these conditions individual 'resource managers' (farmers) holding adjacent parcels of land which were to all appearances similar in their basic potential might use those resources (the farms) completely differently, since the men occupied different positions along the decision-paths. Farmer A, in other words, might have decided to maximize his returns as rapidly as possible in order to finance himself on a direct move to the Wimmera, and may have chosen highly exploitative techniques to do so; he was also anxious to sell his land as soon as possible. His neighbour B might have 'arrived' at his destination, completed the circuit, so to speak, and may be more likely to maximize over a long term. Although the two farms were otherwise identical in this hypothetical case, their styles of management might differ profoundly. For a time, there was certainly a high level of local migration within and then beyond the region, and this was associated with a high turnover of owners and tenants.

Land was the fundamental resource, and its management was open to many interpretations at every level. Throughout Australia designs for the disposal of the public lands were intended to bring needed revenue and to provide for major social and political changes; the pioneer settlers made what they could of these designs and the contemporary economies and landscapes were in some measure the products of the interplay between popular and official appraisals of the social and physical environment (Powell 1970a).

in the 'eighties, dairy farming suffered under the same handicap. It was normally essential for the pioneer to raise sheep, but this was hardly possible on the small acreage permitted under the law. In the general process of 'adaptation', each new *Land Act* contributed something towards the learning sequence and since this was in large measure a 'controlled' situation (that is, in comparison to settlement evolution in the United States), the characteristic official-popular dichotomy is of fundamental significance to any analysis of the management of the public lands. Whereas the official viewpoint was obscured by a recurring mirage and blinkered by an abiding ignorance of Australian conditions, the 'man on the land' worked within a legislative as well as a physical and economic environment, and he sought his own solutions to achieve a viable working unit—in spite of the deficiencies of the law, and frequently in defiance of it. Until the last quarter of the nineteenth century neither markets, railways, nor port development were properly studied by any of the colonial governments, and the agricultural research and education so vitally needed was largely ignored. Contemporary North Americans tended to regard the most pleasing and distinctive aspect of their economic life to be the 'climate of opportunity' which would yield wealth and security in just proportion to a man's diligence. Similarly, Midwestern farmers were advised to 'root, hoe or die' and Horace Greeley, a champion of yeoman farming, believed in 'manly self-reliance and a spirit that asks help of no man and no treasury' (cf. Smith 1950; Robbins 1964). Yet Australians could claim that American soil was richer, cheaper and more abundant, and they desperately required the positive support of their Governments. Without this assistance, various settlement techniques developed as spontaneous folk contributions to the emerging cultural geography of the frontier regions; some of the legislative controls and settlement responses developed in Victoria are illustrated in Figures 9 and 10.

South Australia was from the outset consciously designed to be different from the other Colonies. Intensive cultivation was encouraged and protected, and by the 1860s a vigorous 'yeomanry' was supplying grain to the rest of Australia. Government policy in Adelaide had maintained the basic Wakefieldian concepts, insisting also upon a regional separation of squatters and farmers and thereby avoiding much of the crippling social and political competition which characterized the management of the public domain in the neighbouring territories. George Goyder was the chief architect and promoter of the 'parkland town' (Figure 11) and several exercises in regional planning. But his most renowned and durable memorial resulted from his definition, in 1865, of a northern limit of reliable rainfall approximating the ten-inch isohyet, originally intended to guide the Government in its implementation of drought relief for pastoralists, but quickly endorsed as the 'official' frontier for agricultural settlement (Figure 7). Exhilarated by the success of the northward expansion of intensive farming in a succession of good years, popular demand grew for the abandonment of this arbitrary limit. Petitions were presented for the opening of the northern country, pointing to the proven tradition of empirical testing by actual settlers: 'The question of the suitability or otherwise of this land for agriculture should not rest on the dictum of one individual; it being notorious that much of the land now under culture and growing good crops, has been formerly pronounced totally unsuitable for that purpose' (Meinig 1970: 53). 'Goyder's Line' was widely ridiculed as 'the most absurd thing known in squatters' ingenuity' and the Government relented under popular demand. In 1874 a

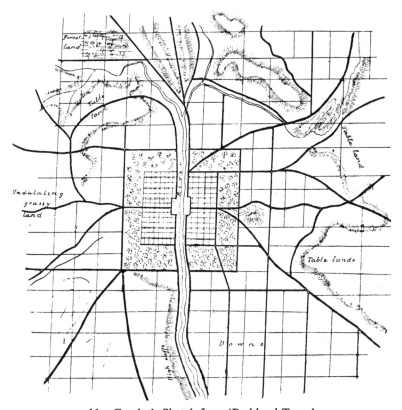

11   Goyder's Sketch for a 'Parkland Town'

Goyder provided this rough sketch to guide his subordinate officers in the preparation of town plans in the frontier districts (*S.A. Parliamentary Papers* 1864, No. 36). It became the basic model for the rest of the century: between 1865 and 1909, of the total of 218 Government Townships surveyed, 179 had full or partial parkland designs (Williams 1966b).

new *Land Act* opened the whole of the Colony to farming settlement; the authorities no longer presumed to be the sole judges of land quality, no longer attempted to separate the good from the bad.

Settlement moved north, very frequently employing the 'parkland town' principle, and wheat yields were at first excellent, supported by unusually good rains which actually caused some local flooding and revived the old folk idea that 'rain follows the plough'. The rural press seized the idea and in an inebriation of optimism the Minister of Agriculture decided to give it his own blessing. As the eager settlers penetrated into even drier territory Schomburgk and other scientists were roused to stress again the necessity for extensive afforestation as a safeguard against drought, but the country editors discovered this an even more popular and useful theme, for it could be publicized as 'authoritative support' for their own wild predictions—provided they ignored the inherent contradiction in their continued en-

couragement of a form of development which appeared to be set on removing the existing sparse tree cover, or skilfully wove science and con-
fortable folk-myth together in an appeal for a comprehensive plan for settlement, afforestation and the local reservation of patches of the original
vegetation (Meinig 1970: 57-71).

The ancient idea that forests influence the amount and distribution of
precipitation has long been the basis of action programmes in many parts
of the world. In the United States, the *Timber Culture Act* of 1873 was
launched in the belief that if pioneer settlers were encouraged to plant trees
in the open country of the Great Plains and in the prairie States, the drought
hazard would be removed (Thornthwaite 1936: 209; Brown 1948: 417-9;
Meinig 1954; Robbins 1964: 217-37; Hibbard 1965: 411-70; Kollmorgen and
Kollmorgen 1973). Only a few years later in South Australia, Goyder appointed
John Ednie Brown, an energetic Scottish forester with American experience,
as the Colony's first Conservator of Forests. Brown's credentials were im-
peccable: he was a distinguished member of the Scottish Arboricultural
Society, a gold medallist of the Highland and Agricultural Society of Scotland for his detailed reports on *The Forests of California* and *The Forests of
the Eastern States of America*, a prize essayist of the Scottish Arboricultural
Society for two useful works on *Extensive Planting* and *The Trees of America*,
and author of an emigrants' guide to Canada and its resources. His practical
talents and undoubted dedication might have combined with Goyder's unique geographical and historical vision to put South Australia in the forefront
of contemporary forest management and regional land-use planning, but
within two years of Brown's arrival he was at odds with his Surveyor-
General over a fundamental question of interpretation and the breach was
never healed.

Brown chose to present the case for forest conservation almost entirely
in terms of its ecological significance. In addition to its 'amenity' value the
tree cover was said to have a direct and indirect influence over climate
through its provision of shelter, soil, fertilization, a reduced evaporation
rate and a guarantee against sudden flooding, and also by means of its
potential for increasing humidity, attracting rain clouds, 'equalising' rainfall
variability, and generally 'purifying' the atmosphere (Report 1879). But some
of Schomburgk's earlier statements were repeated and vastly extended in
Brown's massive claim that the disturbing aridity of the interior of the
Colony was due entirely to its comparative lack of trees. Although Goyder
refuted this at once, in a thoroughly researched and balanced exposition
resembling the guarded review compiled by Marsh in 1864, the Conservator's arguments were then of course far more acceptable to the South
Australian public, and under conditions of apparent boom, the political
advantages of extending settlement still further into the dry north proved
too strong to resist. Forestry was to provide the mythic yeoman with a little
insurance.

In nineteenth-century Britain the application of the theories and findings
of the flourishing physical sciences to the infant social sciences led to such
extreme forms of environmental determinism as those expressed in H. T.
Buckle's (1821-62) *History of Civilization*, and the equally materialistic but
far more valuable explanations of human and social evolution in the works

of W. Bagehot (1826-77) and Herbert Spencer (1820-1903). The few surviving statements of the unrepentant South Australian Conservator appear to reflect similar views in his own naive fashion and there was, in addition to that implicit faith in systematic material improvement which motivated Brown's contemporaries, a genuine religious interest which was surely quite as central as materialism to nineteenth-century thought, especially in Australia. So, in the second edition of *A Practical Treatise on Tree Culture*, Brown offered a brave rehashing of Jefferson's 'yeomanry' argument with, perhaps, a little borrowing from the earlier Victorian reports already discussed.

> It is now generally admitted by all the enlightened people that trees play a very important part in the general prosperity of any country, and that, by the amount of attention paid by its inhabitants to their cultivation, so may the physical and intellectual standard of the people be estimated. As our surroundings become physically more perfect, so in the same ratio do we become morally better (Brown 1881: vii).

And there is nothing to suggest that he did not believe most of this himself. In the same meticulous little manual, which was really of inestimable value to the pioneer settler, nurseryman and professional forester, he also promoted afforestation for reasons that can only be labelled 'un-commercial', though he would claim that they were still fully 'applied': 'In an ornamental point of view, then, trees are a necessity of our life; they instruct the mind in the work of the Creator, and they elevate the soul to things noble and cultivated' (Brown 1881: 14).

The clash between the two powerful personalities of Brown and Goyder restricted the activities of South Australia's Forestry Board and it was abolished in 1882 when its executive functions passed to the Conservator. In fairness it must be said that Brown was highly successful with many planting experiments in all parts of South Australia and that the average colonist was almost certainly oblivious to the heated controversy which deeply divided these leading public servants and their supporters. The present point of interest is, however, that so much more might have been achieved, so much damage and hardship saved, had the partnership endured.

The Ring-barking Controversy

The abnormally wet seasons of the early 'seventies were a great spur to pioneer wheat farmers, but they hit the high country pastoralists of Victoria and New South Wales very hard indeed (cf. Hancock 1972: 107-30). Foot rot and liver fluke decimated many flocks and in 1873 William Farrer, better known later for his experimentation with new wheat strains, joined other scientists and livestock farmers in advocating ring-barking as the cheapest and most efficient method of combating the disease—especially via an improvement in the quality of the native grassland after the removal of the 'competitor', the subsequent increase in light and so on. The idea was rapidly accepted and was soon widely credited with the 'sweetening' of pastures and the eradication of 'the fluke', but ring-barking was usually indiscriminately employed and its rapid diffusion to drier districts is not easily condoned.

Fortunately for much of eastern Victoria, especially where gold-mining still continued, there was sufficient interest in preserving local timber reserves to curb the practice. Even so, the destruction of the major protective cover within some regions characterized by a high variability in relative relief led inevitably to severe landslips and gulleying.

Ring-barking had long been practised in the Australian Colonies, but its extension in the 'seventies caused great alarm in some quarters, especially among scientists who still held to the belief that the forests were the principal causative agent in precipitation and moisture retention. One most interesting group of clergymen protested against all forms of haphazard clearing on both scientific and religious grounds: they rejected evolutionary theory and retained their faith in the destiny of 'Man, to whom the dominion of this lower world is given', yet they pursued an almost pantheistic form of nature worship. Endowed with a comfortable understanding of Paleyism, often familiar with the scientific and other literature of America and the Empire, and commonly favoured by their calling with opportunities for travel and regular field excursions, they were frequently avid botanical and geological 'collectors' and faithful supporters of the local scientific societies. Some, like the Jesuit J. T. Woods, whose pastoral duties had permitted extensive palaeontological research in South Australia, New South Wales, Tasmania and Queensland, claimed to have found considerable evidence in the records of Australian tertiary geology to support the anti-Darwinists. Others were increasingly drawn to the investigation of the changing world immediately around them, which they found equally disturbing and challenging. One of the most prominent of these was Rev. William B. Clarke, who studied at Cambridge under the great field geologist Adam Sedgwick and spent his formative years in Britain at a time when geology was beginning to shake off its theological trappings to mature into a fully-fledged inductive and observational science. From the time of his arrival in New South Wales in 1839 Clarke was as disturbed as any other good geologist of the time over the great question of reconciling *Genesis* with the growing accumulation of scientific argument, but he was already deeply influenced by Lyell's *Principles* and remained far more receptive to new ideas than most of the contemporary Australian clergy. By the mid-'seventies he had built a distinguished reputation and his timely Vice-Presidential address to the Royal Society of New South Wales in 1876 still makes interesting reading. Its title was 'Effects of Forest Vegetation on Climate'—by then a familiar theme, but it was quite exhaustively treated and given greater force by Clarke's individualistic presentation. His objective was to illustrate that 'civilisation has destructive as well as conservative tendencies' and he deliberately emphasized aesthetic considerations and the inevitability of mankind's own degradation with the destruction of the God-given forests.

> I would not dwell on the influence upon scenery of improperly conducted clearings. A consideration of that kind can hardly enter into the mind of a person who can deliberately leave acres of unfelled timber, bare of foliage, barkless, and broken by the winds, such as might be enumerated by the score in some of the once most beautiful tracts in the counties of Cumberland and Camden; nor is it necessary to point out the array of giants of the forest that stud the summit of the Dividing Range at the back of Heidelberg, in Victoria, or examples

of landscape scenery partly ruined by the ravages of insects. It may be true that the custom of *ring-barking* trees is productive, for a time, of some extra growth of grass; but to say nothing of the deprivation of shade to flocks and herds, or of waste of timber, as in the cedar districts of our eastern coast rivers by the ruthless and wilful wielders of the axe, who leave upon the ground to decay in ignominy some of the finest and most noble of our trees, I cannot help expressing great surprise that gentlemen who in general character and condition of life are far above the hungry and uneducated selector or wood-splitter can allow ring-barking in places where grass can never grow, and where nature embellished the rocks with woods. Such I have seen to be the case in many a spot far away from those before alluded to. It is a questionable policy that some of such clearings should have been permitted, and till the 'woods and forests' have been taken under the protection of Government, many a district of rich timber will continue to be foolishly destroyed, and many a scene of sylvan beauty will be desecrated (W. B. Clarke 1876: 180).

Clarke quoted liberally from *Man and Nature* and from a number of recent British geographical publications which had applied Marsh's arguments to the occurrence of drought and the advance of the desert in Russia, India and Africa (for example, Wilson 1865; Markham 1866; Bidie 1869). He was also a great admirer of Baron von Mueller and strongly declared his agreement with the Baron's recent eloquent appeals for forest conservation. While in other lands the eucalypts were regarded as the 'Trees of the Future', they were 'suffered to stand [as] ghastly monuments of the covetousness of Australians' in the 'great Australian Garden' where they had been planted by the 'All-Wise Creator' (W. B. Clarke 1876: 213). Yet Australians too had to face the facts, bear the cross, of droughts and threatening deserts; it was therefore incumbent upon them to discover Nature's 'alleviations' which 'defy the wisdom of man to parallel'.

We may thus be led to study the mysteries of the visible creation with humility as to what we cannot discern, and with hopefulness as to what, by well-tempered zeal and proper direction of what we may be permitted to discover, our Sciences will finally attain.

If, by a just employment of observation, we can arrive at any positive means of counteracting the adverse, or employing the friendly forces of Nature to our advantage, it is not only permitted us to do so, but it is our duty to do it, for the good of mankind; and it is not beneath the aim of rational and accountable beings to seek guidance as to the planting of a wilderness or the clearing of a jungle, if either be necessary, by inquiry as to the facts which may be obtainable by experience, and accepted as warnings or encouragements (W. B. Clarke 1876: 187).

Clarke's predispositions caused him to exaggerate the climatic influence of the forest and he was chided for his sermon by Charles Moore, the Director of Sydney's Botanic Gardens; yet his anthropocentrism was very similar to that of Marsh and represented a sizable body of informed opinion. Similarly the Rev. Dr William Woolls, a leading amateur botanist in New South Wales, returned to the 'murderous practice of ring barking' in his *Lectures on the Vegetable Kingdom* and stressed that there were fundamental dangers to the very health of the colonists: 'if you destroy, without any reservation, the gum trees, which in many places are necessary for the purification of the atmosphere, you will add to the amount of low fever, dysentery, and ague' (Woolls 1879: 91-2). This was a reference to the neo-classical 'miasmatic' theory of disease which was widely held until the end of century, and concerned the supposed facility of native forests to counteract the 'miasmatic vapours' by their fragrance, open texture and water-retaining properties (cf. Thompson 1970; Powell 1973a).

The unfortunate divisions in scientific opinion were gradually closed and in the 'eighties renewed efforts were made by this small group to examine and influence every facet of resource management. For the bulk of the people, the burning issue of the day was still the disposal of the public domain. Fortunately for our present analysis, however, the change in orientation which this now requires is assisted by the availability of an excellent source of material for the elucidation of some important contemporary attitudes.

Yeomen, Bureaucrats and the Environment

John Ednie Brown's arrival in South Australia roughly coincided with the initial stages of a most interesting type of confrontation between the official and popular appraisals of settlement expansion and environmental change—Victoria's Royal Commission on Crown Lands, which was held over a period of twelve months in Melbourne and a variety of country centres, beginning in June 1878 (Powell 1973b). The published Reports and Minutes of Evidence of this Commission provide one of the richest of all contemporary sources for an exhaustive investigation of changing approaches towards resource management, for they record many of the detailed views of administrators, pioneer settlers, legislators, merchants, financiers, country tradesmen and others who were involved in this multi-facetted process. Much of the material was naturally concerned with local critiques of the management of the disposal of public domain for small-scale settlement, demonstrating the need for greatly improved credit facilities, Government-sponsored research and the relaxation of the clauses insisting on cultivation and residence. The evidence also pointed to the increasing demand for larger blocks to continue the trend towards more rational, mixed farming pursuits and the innumerable deficiencies of a semi-centralized administration which had shown conclusively that it was incapable of managing vital inter- and intra-regional development. And indeed, in many cases the shire councillors and other local worthies (unreasonably blind to the honoured precepts of modern locational theory?) had obviously deliberately moulded the cultural landscapes of their own little worlds to suit themselves (so that the magical theory in this instance provides only marginal assistance for today's bewildered researcher).

Harassed witnesses were frequently called upon by the Commission to prove their own credentials as *bona fide* 'yeomen', or to declare their allegiance to the current official programme, which was 'copied from the American system to settle a yeomanry class upon the land' (Powell 1973b: 173). During one melodramatic but engrossing episode in the proceedings, an attempt was actually made to challenge the Commissioners by calling in a solicitor to discuss the definition of the term: 'I came to tell as an expert what is the meaning of the word "yeoman". It is a legal word, and I think you do not know that'. Predictably, the Chairman indignantly refused to give him a hearing: the resilience of the image, and its potency, depended on the very ambiguity of the term; it would never do to dilute it (Powell 1973b: 243-4).

Settlement in Victoria was then advancing on every front into wooded regions—the Otway Hills, the scrubby plains of the Mallee in the north-west, the foot-hills and ranges of the Eastern Highlands—and the Commissioners were made acutely aware of the special characteristics of those areas. Much of the evidence illustrated the economic and ecological costs of the current methods of clearing; there was no clear consensus on these matters, but the employment of *indiscriminate* ring-barking techniques was usually condemned, the destructive practice of felling rather than lopping certain trees for emergency fodder was drawn to the Commissioners' attention, and there was some support for the idea of reserving sizable areas or belts of forest for timber supplies and climatic purposes. The practice of sowing introduced British grasses was rapidly increasing, with the prior experience of the Western District's highly successful pastoral freeholdings as an impressive guide. While the pioneer selectors still had to be content with whatever stock they could quickly obtain, the established men in the Western District were then developing lucrative stud properties and were preparing to promote and sustain a major revolution in the improvement of Australia's flocks and herds. In the north-east, the big pastoralists had established the utilization of the high plains for summer grazing as a normal part of their management system and many smaller men were beginning to follow their example, or wished to do so. For the north-west, it was made clear that a great deal had been accomplished in the management of natural fodder resources from the various bushes and dwarf eucalypti, and rotational fallowing and other dry-farming techniques were relatively well advanced on a number of properties. The Commission eventually compiled the first detailed inventory of the Mallee and advocated an intelligent scheme for its future development, based upon the recognition of a fundamental shortage of natural water supplies and the efficacy of an intra-regional partitioning which had been more or less established by the settlement process itself, distinguishing the special resource characteristics of the 'fringe' and 'interior' (Powell 1970a: 211-7; 1973b).

As a contemporary guide to decision making, Victoria's Royal Commission on Crown Lands was badly handled and deserved most of the criticism it received in the metropolitan and country newspapers. For the modern student, on the other hand, it is simply and primarily a valuable human document which records a wide range of views that are too often completely beyond our reach. Commissioners and witnesses alike tried to press home their own ideas, but the recorded dialogue exposes some new developments in the official-popular interplay which still dominated Australian resource management. Consider, for example, the fact that as settlement advanced into the more difficult regions another element in the yeoman symbolism, the freehold principle, was subjected to closer scrutiny. With the useful public domain apparently swiftly diminishing, there was a rising demand in the older Colonies for the resumption of the great pastoral runs—and, to a lesser extent, for the introduction of a closely-policed system of leaseholds which would bring in a continuous revenue to the colonial treasuries. The movement was definitely an indigenous response, based upon the economic arguments and bookish research of local scholars and politicians, but it obviously gained articulation and direction from the United States, in the form of Henry George's quasi-messianic 'single-tax' philosophy, and later from Britain, where the associated principles of land nationalization were popularized by Alfred Russell Wallace. In Victoria the movement was strongly based in the metropolis and it strengthened the distinctions between town and country.

Some of the Commissioners tried to explain and promote the concept of leases to witnesses in 1878-79 and, although they were usually rebuffed in every area of proven agricultural quality, there was good local support for the idea of 'grazing leases' on the high plains and in the Mallee. Later, it was successfully argued in the metropolitan press and by urban members in the Victorian Parliament that the introduction of leases for new settlement in these regions would preserve the public interest by giving a breathing space for empirical testing to proceed, at the same time permitting the Government to introduce various caveats into the conditions of the leases to ensure good management, including the conservation of water and timber. Detailed land classification, another associated principle in the continuing sophistication of official policy, was similarly deliberately floated by the Commissioners, but it must be said that this idea had also emerged spontaneously in several regions of Victoria.

*

In 1870, for the first time, native-born Australians outnumbered the immigrants; by 1880 two-thirds of the population were Australian-born and they had begun to claim their inheritance. During that decade and for most of the period before the First World War, they were deeply influenced in what they chose to make of that inheritance by a simple utilitarian dream, and the loftier ideals which the ecological scientists W. B. Clarke, Mueller and Woolls had associated with the 'contemplation' of Australian nature were certainly not widely shared. Yet it is fairly clear from the evidence of contemporary painting and creative writing that the aesthetic appraisal of the environment was also moving towards a more satisfactory level of 'accommodation'; indeed, Nash's ecological and aesthetic 'streams' were also beginning to run strongly through Australian society, each with the capacity to sustain and replenish the other. The chief focus of conservational interest and activity was the forest cover, then under great pressure from pioneer settlers and commercial interests. Additional foci emerged in the succeeding decade, with increasing emphasis upon land classification, land taxes, and especially upon water storage, reticulation and irrigation, to reform, consolidate, rationalize or intensify the promiscuous regional development of the settlement net as it came to be judged an inefficient spatial organization for the type of society and economy then envisaged.

'The Australian forests are funereal, secret, stern. Their solitude is desolation. They seem to stifle, in their black gorges, a story of sullen despair.' So Marcus Clarke introduced Adam Lindsay Gordon's *Sea Spray and Smoke Drift* in 1876. But he wrote also of 'the strange scribblings of nature learning how to write', and of how 'the dweller in the wilderness acknowledged the subtle charm of this fantastic land of monstrosities'. The paradoxes of Australia were being unravelled by the techniques of natural science and obviously, unlike their immigrant forbears, the growing numbers of native-born colonists need be neither disturbed nor dismayed by the local scene: 'The phantasmagoria of that wild dreamland called the Bush interprets itself, and the Poet of our desolation begins to comprehend why free Esau loved his heritage of desert sand better than all the bountiful richness of Egypt' (M. Clarke 1876). The mass of the people were still easily intoxicated by the opportunity of new lands and their exploitative attitudes continued to threaten the environment they were learning to accept as a home, but there were signs that the frontiers were already being reached, and urban radicals were already striving to dilute the heady brew by removing one of its prime ingredients, the right of freehold. Utilitarian motives in the 'sixties and 'seventies had been sufficiently pervasive to encourage some general progress towards conservational practices, but the emergence of a true conversation ethic demanded far more public concern, far more understanding, than the Australians had yet developed for their environment. And it required, possibly, some social or political mechanism to bring about the convergence of all three streams, ecological, aesthetic and utilitarian. No such mechanism occurred.

IV Seducers and Guardians: a Colonial Coming of Age, 1880–1914

BETWEEN 1880 and 1914 settlement and land-use patterns in Australia continued to be fashioned by activities based upon the extensive production of raw materials and food-stuffs, functionally linked with the maturing British economy. But the special dependency of Australia in this relationship can be overstated, for within the general framework established by the British connection local individuals and groups had abundant opportunity for interpretation and creative expression. British investment was certainly vital in sustaining important phases of expansion and its removal or reduction was a severe handicap, but most of the critical decisions in capital formation and in the general orientation of the economy were taken in Australia for Australians, and these decisions were influenced very heavily by strictly local socio-political conditions (Butlin 1964). For the boom period of the 'eighties, the subsequent depression and readjustment of the 'nineties, and the early experience of Federation before 1914, no aspect of the changing management of Australia's resources can be understood without careful analysis of the interaction between various indigenous and imported influences—including regional and nationalistic sentiment, the development and adaptation of technological innovations, the transplantation and modification of certain British and American perspectives on 'modernization' and 'efficiency', and the pivotal roles of prominent groups and individuals.

7 Ethos and Aesthetics

BY mid-century, conventional aesthetic description in Australia had established the terms 'mysterious', 'melancholy' and 'grotesque'; the few good Australian artists simply identified with their landscape and concentrated upon these essential features. Increasing local patronage eventually offered a liberation from the need to cater for British sensitivities, yet much of the best work followed the lead of the popular romanticism then in vogue in Britain and North America. The artists William Strutt and W. S. Gill, for example, produced a pictorial record of the perils and adventures of frontier life—the camp under the stars, hunting, bushfires and the entire gold-mining pageant. But the representation of the Australian landscape for its own sake (as opposed to its being a back-drop for people and events) continued to pose problems, and some artists chose to focus upon the settled fringes of the continent, where in comparative comfort they managed to reproduce something approaching the true Australian colours. It was not until the 'eighties—that is, after a century had elapsed since the landing of the First Fleet, and when over two-thirds of the population was Australian-born—that a distinctive national style of painting really developed. Native-born artists were by that time well-supported by the development of an illustrated press and at Heidelberg, near Melbourne, Tom Roberts and his friends experimented with some impressionistic treatments. From the aggressive Heidelberg school there emerged a succession of new paintings which were alive with typically antipodean colours. Put differently, the traditional *cognitive dissonance* between the perceived environment and the equally perceptual 'thought model' looked like being resolved at last, and with the break made the Australian landscape was apparently due for a fresh and uninhibited artistic exploration. In the twentieth century Australian paintings and painters have won some international approval and, despite a lingering inferiority complex about home-made products and a general Philistinism in the attitude to 'culture', the Australian public recognizes and generally accepts (though it does not yet sufficiently value) the qualities of landscape which have been evoked.

Another landmark in the aesthetic appreciation of the Australian landscape was the publication of three anthologies of Australian poetry in the late 'eighties (Sladen 1888a, 1888b, 1888c). The best-known selections were the works of Henry Kendall and Adam Lindsay Gordon, both of whom are still firm favourites with Australian readers. Kendall's work had been snapped up as a 'useful product' by a society which positively desired the arrival of 'an *Australian* poet'. Distilling the varied literary imagery which preceded his own contributions, he offered a subjective and emotional view of an Australia sharply divided between Eden and the land of Cain, but his evocation of mountain scenery was admirable, his frequently interlinked imagery of the mountain forest (shade, coolness and water) was readily accepted by the Australians, and his descriptions of the interior were quite as familiar,

100

especially with their solitary figures rooted in a threatening and unrelieved desolation (Wright 1965). But Kendall's local supremacy was short-lived in comparison with that of Gordon, who was regarded as Australia's leading poet from his death in 1870 until the early 1930s. Gordon's poems were probably mediocre by any standard except one: they were exceedingly well received by the mass of the people, and their stronghold was unchallenged in city and country until the arrival of the present generation of readers. Brian Elliott believes that Gordon's success can be explained by his simple articulation of the contemporary, common attitude to landscape (Elliott 1967: 74-99). From another viewpoint, it might also be said that Gordon thereby elevated the status of the Australian environment in the minds of his readers by increasing their interest in the landscape and assisting their identification with it. A basic ingredient in his very finest descriptions is the fresh perception of the effect of light in Australia, notably the nuances of dawn and sunset, and in this respect Gordon's achievement predates the painters of the *plein air* Heidelberg school. As Elliott and others have illustrated, Gordon responded very warmly to Australian fauna and flora and conveyed such realistic impressions of bushfires, droughts and desert scenery that these features were invested with heightened interest, in so far as they were also accepted as *actual* conditions, not merely (in contrast to Kendall) as symbolic vehicles of expression. Gordon offered fleeting glimpses of broad vistas, rather than detailed reconstructions of his immediate surroundings, and this element of perspective is of course eminently suited to the vast plains of Australia. The themes of light, colour, movement and perspective were constantly repeated in a series of simple poems and, once he was 'discovered', Gordon was seen as the very type of the young colonial poet. His public found a daredevil sportsman who had been a mounted trooper in bush-ranging days, a most successful amateur rider in Australian racing circles, a capable boxer, a mysterious character who had led a short, sad and eventful life, ending in suicide. City and country people who read little else contentedly feasted on Gordon fare, and 'Gordon cults' emerged among the toughest of outback settlers and migratory workers (Green 1961; Elliott 1967; Serle 1973).

Increasingly, Australians looked inwards to 'the bush'—the whole area beyond the cities—not outwards to Britain. They were indeed frequently challenged with a basic problem of choice by their creative artists: the City or the Country, which in essence was 'Vice or Virtue', and became best known as 'Sydney or the Bush'. In eighteenth-century America, Thomas Jefferson had proclaimed:

> Those who labour in the earth were the chosen people of God . . . the proportion which the aggregate of the other classes of citizens bears in any state to that of its husbandmen, is the proportion of its unsound to its healthy parts, and is a good enough barometer whereby to measure the degree of corruption.

And in similar fashion, country life in Australia became the mystic symbol of a chance for *regeneration*. In severe contrast to earlier interpretations, the bush was now conjured for city man as a lost Eden. Yet the manner in which it was evoked also suggested very strongly that true purification could only be obtained through a ritual of hardships endured in solitary communion with Australian nature. Gordon himself was no apologist for the bush, but his work drew wide attention to various aspects of Australian country life. As yet, the city had no champions. Towards the turn of the century, writers of the 'bush ballads' took much of their inspiration from Gordon, Kipling and Bret Harte, and they were encouraged by the patronage of the *Bulletin*, a vigorously nationalistic journal. Literary historians do not see the balladists as the instigators of a new movement to celebrate the Australian bush, but rather as the people's spokesmen: the ballads were simple in the extreme and catered for the current popular taste, which the writers manifestly shared. In part, they built upon a heritage of oral communication which had been developing slowly in the lonely outposts of rural Australia, a tradition based upon the bush song —a close relative of the frontier verse and songs of the United States, and like them, a New World variety of the European folk ballad. Ward (1958) and others have shown that the bush song was masculine, anti-authority, often Irish in derivation and a raw product of largely illiterate pioneers. Pastoral workers and nomadic labourers of all types provided the words, the audience and much of the music. But the bush ballad was ultra-democratic, choosing to extol the virtues of *all* types of country people, rather than to concentrate invariably upon attacking authority or favouring bush-rangers and the like; it was a more civilized product, intended for recitation rather than for song and, since it was written down, the true record remains for modern scrutiny. From the 'nineties to the depression of the mid-1930s the bush ballad retained its attraction for the Australian people (Dutton 1964; Wright 1965; Serle 1973).

It must be agreed that the bush ballad has a special place in the Australian repertoire. As Elliott (1967: 150) has pointed out, every examination of the drive towards self expression must consider the 'vulgar aesthetic of native impulse': the ballads promoted the idea of the 'uniquely Australian' charac-ter of the 'heroic' inland, discarded the coastal regions and formed a bridge between the inspired few, who had been struggling towards an interpretation of the environment for so long, and the mass of the people, for whom they provided an unusually meaningful type of 'pop culture'. In this sense they contributed handsomely towards the 'bush ethos' which was nurtured during the growth of nationalistic sentiment in the latter part of the nineteenth cen-tury. The inland was portrayed as strange, merciless and 'fatally beckoning': viewed as a whole the dominant theme had indeed become the landscape, with man now held as a constant, set within it. Yet the great appeal of the ballads is due partly to the fact that they were usually anecdotal, employing a simple narrative style which was an excellent medium for the time. This characteristic was exemplified in the work of A.B.(Banjo) Paterson, a reg-ular contributor to the *Bulletin*. 'Clancy of the Overflow', the healthiest survivor of Paterson's numerous productions, has been assessed by Elliott as 'pure, consummate cliché', but even in the sophisticated 1970s it can claim an admiring readership. Paterson's type of 'noble frontiersman' offered a two-fold symbol for the romantic imagination of the nineteenth century in Britain, America and Australia—an escape from urbanization and indus-trialization, to some degree a compensation and justification for the evils inherent in the process of imperialist expansion; yet in addition, as Ward (1958) has also shown, the same motif assisted the polarization of patriotic nationalism. In 'Clancy', Paterson contrasted the free life of the truly Australian frontiersman, who enjoyed 'the vision splendid of the sunlit plains extended', with the restricted city dwellers 'with their eager eyes and greedy, and their stunted forms and weedy/ For townsfolk have no time to grow, they have no time to waste'. And if this 'challenge' to the one-third of the Australian population then living in the coastal cities became somewhat threadbare, it was only because it was thrown down repeatedly to the succeeding two or three generations.

There is an obvious parallel to all of this in the evocation of the Canadian North. A recurrent theme in the literature of that country in the latter half of the nineteenth century was that Canada's unique character derived from her northern location, her heritage of Northern European races and her severe northern climate—the 'Advantages of Northerness' were in fact compared with the symbol of the West for the United States. The northern image was reinforced and sustained in novels, poetry, travellers' tales and in the works of scientific exploration, and it was further defined and disseminated by the nationalist 'Group of Seven' in Canadian art in the early decades of the present century (Berger 1966). But the comparison between Canada and Australia should not be overstated. Even the romantic appeal of the 'outback'—the most remote parts of the 'bush'—is quite different in intensity from Canada's northern myth, especially if we consider the extreme form of environmental determinism occasionally embodied in the latter and the fact that nationalism in Australia did not have to compete with any neighbouring 'big brother'. Also, many Australians became greatly roused by the ideals of unionism and socialism, by 'future images' of the good *society* as well as by the evocation of a romanticized *physical* environment, and towards the end of the century they were prepared to state confidently a new nationalistic objective: 'free from the wrongs of North and Past/ The land that belongs to you' (Turner 1964: 32).

It is at first sight very difficult to reconcile the glowing optimism of creative workers in the 'nineties, for the country was then gripped by a severe economic depression. A great deal of this optimism must have been related to the Australians' increasingly acute awareness of their international isolation during the latter half of the nineteenth century, which seems to have determined them to 'turn to account the freedom it gave them by building up something like an earthly paradise for the common man' (Palmer 1971: 1), and another part of the explanation lies in the marriage of socialist politics to the bush ethos. The foundation of the attractively innocent ideology of the young Labor Parties forming at this time was in fact the celebrated egalitarianism of the bush—Australia was a country of working men, and organized labour could make it their own utopia. 'Mateship' became an enduring title of this ideal, which was eventually acted out in some interesting settlement innovations, and it attracted the radical intellectuals of the day as much as the workers (Sutcliffe 1921; Fitzpatrick 1941; Gollan 1960). It has been said that unlike many of his European counterparts, the Australian intellectual felt a responsibility to (not necessarily *for*) the workers, who were seen as the creators of the nation's individuality, ethos and wealth. Yet the socialist poet Bernard O'Dowd—a disciple of Walt Whitman—warned that as physical poverty was overcome a new class division might arise, showing intellectual, artistic and spiritual gluttony among the new castes, and so writers of this persuasion deliberately set out to create a literature which spoke of, for, and to the common man (Turner 1964).

Surprisingly, the cities, where so much of the new radicalism was born, were largely ignored in this movement and the life of the bush retained its strong attraction. But the reason for this rejection was now slightly different: 'It was also that these writers were beginning to sense that, while in the bush loneliness had a natural origin and was offset by human community, in the new centres of industry the weave of common life and purpose was somehow destroyed and loneliness was absolute' (Turner 1964: 44). The *Bulletin* published an interminable round of short stories during this period and, significantly, these bush 'yarns' were received enthusiastically in the cities. A. H. Davis ('Steele Rudd') presented a series of sketches dealing humorously with the life of a pioneer farmer and his family; Henry Lawson wrote of the experiences of a drifting bush-worker; and both were eclipsed, in 1903, by Joseph Furphy ('Tom Collins'), who became the first author to produce a good and recognizably Australian novel, *Such is Life*. For the purposes of the present discussion it could be said that this signified the culmination, in the early years of the present century, of the primary struggle with the local landscape: a few urban poets and authors did emerge, but after a dull interlude the major thrust for creative artists in general was towards international approval and universal truths. And in the process some of O'Dowd's worst fears were realized (Serle 1973: 89-118).

8 A Regional Overview of Resource Appraisal and Management

THE 'eighties were naive and supremely confident years in which a host of writers, artists and politicians were seduced by a type of utopianism which envisaged Australia peopled by a chosen race (usually white), morally and materially superior to the Old World and destined to emulate the progress of the United States (Clark 1963: 153-78: Serle 1973: 60-88). One peculiar feature of this vigorous nationalistic promotion was the contrast between the literary vogue and occasional political symbolism of 'outbackery', with its emphasis on independence and 'mateship', and the parallel development, stemming from the same optimism, of a form of 'colonial socialism' which welcomed and even demanded widespread Government intervention. A mixed economic system evolved, in which massive overseas borrowing for public works encouraged dangerous hyper-activity in the field of private speculation. Australia's public debt grew from about £66 million in 1881 to £155 million in 1891—from about £10 to nearly £50 a head—and despite some reckless accounting, the tyrannical control of distance was at last boldly challenged. Almost 75 per cent of the public debt was spent on railway construction and there were over 10,000 miles of line in operation in 1890, a tenfold increase in twenty years; nearly 40,000 miles of telegraph were opened in the 'eighties, and telephone exchanges were established in each of the capital cities (Butlin 1964; Shaw 1969).

Agricultural Development

(i) The traditional grazing industry made good use of the improved credit and transport facilities to breed better stock, increase flock sizes and generally improve grazing capacities. For the most part the native fauna was still deemed to be 'more destructive than useful' and its selective eradication had become accepted official policy for the grazing regions: the estimated number of kangaroos and wallabies killed in New South Wales in 1885-86 was almost 1.4 millions, one-fifth of the assumed population (Coghlan 1887: 120-1). Australian pastoralists had been slower than their American counterparts in adopting barbed and plain wire fencing, but new credit and tenure arrangements in the 'eighties greatly assisted in the rapid diffusion of this innovation. In central Queensland and the dry interior of New South Wales and South Australia the discovery and exploitation of extensive artesian basins further increased the potential for greater intensification, and in the higher rainfall regions such as Victoria's Western District, the well-established grazing freeholds consolidated their reputations for stud-breeding by confident investments in water storages, elaborate subdivisioning and management research. The cumulative benefits of all these efforts were obvious enough: the sheep population of Australia increased

12   Advertisements for Agricultural Machinery (from the *Leader Supplement*, 1894)

from 42 millions in 1872 to about 106 millions in 1892. What the industry still lacked, however, was the ability to adjust to drought, and the concurrence in the 'nineties of dry seasons, rabbit plagues and the economic depression proved that far too many holdings, especially in the outback, had become over-financed and over-grazed. They never regained the high stocking rates of 1891 (for a general discussion of these themes, see Kiddle 1961: 283-400; Heathcote 1965; Jeans 1972: 271-94).

(ii) Refrigeration and related technical advances in dairy farming were important innovations with obvious spatial repercussions, as Williams (1975) and others have emphasized. Australian cattle, previously accepted in the export market for their skins and tallow alone, found a new value. In direct response there was an increase in the cattle population of Queensland, from about three millions in 1880 to nearly seven millions in 1896. Similar increases were recorded elsewhere and New South Wales and Victoria commenced significant exports of frozen mutton, but marketing, transportation and breeding problems effectively postponed the chief regional impacts for another decade. Refrigeration machinery, the Babcock testing machine and the cream separator made it practicable for butter to be made in the 'eighties under factory conditions and thereby provided a highly suitable addition to the limited repertoire of the small 'yeoman' farmer, whose mythical virtues were still being preached by political idealists (Figure 12). Promoted by new land legislation, railway construction and Government-sponsored research, the axe rang with new purpose in the Victorian hill country, parts of Tasmania, and throughout the coastal belt of northern New South Wales and southern Queensland. In close association with all of these developments the various colonial governments gradually repurchased many of the great estates and intensified the rural settlement pattern according to the new design, while other estates were offered for private sale and sub-division, or were remodelled to take tenant farmers (Roberts 1968; Waterson 1968; Powell 1970a; Williams 1974).

(iii) Between 1880 and 1900 the area under cultivation in Australia almost doubled, to 8,750,000 acres. This was principally due to the migration of wheat growing from the leached soils of the coastal regions to an extensive subhumid inland area of calcareous clays and loams, assisted by the trial and error development in South Australia of early maturing strains of wheat to minimize the effects of the summer drought. Subsequently, in western New South Wales, William Farrer produced a number of successful new strains by the application of more scientific cross-breeding techniques, although his major achievement came from 'Federation' wheat after the turn of the century. Novel implements were developed by the pioneer farmers themselves, or by the highly-valued bush blacksmiths, to clear, cultivate and harvest. This also reduced the chronic labour shortage, but the new regions were less fertile and the new wheat strains normally lower-yielding than those favoured before, so that increasingly larger areas were required to rest the land, while at the same time maintaining good returns to repay the investment in mechanization. From the time they turned the first sod on the wheat frontier, and even before their arrival in some cases, pioneer settlers were hungrily searching for more land than was generally allowed under the cautious, confused, innocently idealistic or unnecessarily complicated land laws.

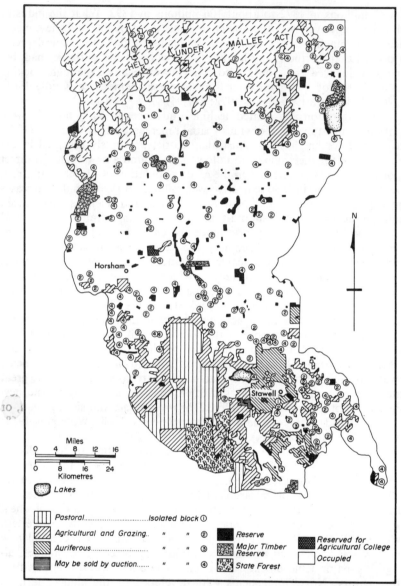

13   Land Classification in the 'Eighties: Borung County, Victoria

Although the principle of detailed land classification was of course an important step towards conservational regional planning, in fact it was mainly concerned with 'forward planning' of a sort—providing an inventory of the remaining public land to guide its best disposal. In addition, these detailed maps often took several years to complete.

In South Australia a widespread drought shook the confidence of the wheat farmers beyond Goyder's Line and some of them appealed in vain for Government assistance: as a Commissioner of Crown Lands reasonably pointed out: 'After considerable pressure this land was resumed from the squatter, and placed on the market for selection. It was not fair then to charge the Government for mistakes the men themselves had made with their eyes open' (*Port Augusta Dispatch*, 30 December 1881, quoted in Meinig 1970: 85). Rain did not follow the plough, after all, and the frontier advance was stalled and then repelled. Yet the lessons learned from defeat in those 'marginal lands', and elsewhere the retreat to more conservative agricultural practices and better-adapted modes of legislative control, particularly the wider use of leasing systems and land classification, have been generally acknowledged as enduring folk contributions to environmental awareness in their respective areas. For all of these reasons, it can be said that the wheat belt which emerged in the south-east of the continent at this time was very largely the product of a peculiarly Australian agricultural revolution (Figure 13).

(iv) Through most of these years Australia remained a divided country. Even the remarkable expansion of the railways resulted in a riot of different gauges and a loose set of more or less discrete systems based upon each of the port-capitals, with a few trunk lines connecting Melbourne, Sydney, Brisbane and Adelaide (Rimmer 1975). But one common feature in the 'nineties was the concentration of heavy unemployment in the previously booming cities, and in part the general response was also broadly similar: a return to the old panacea, 'Back to the Land'. Following their earlier introduction in New Zealand, 'Village Settlements' of landless and unemployed families were scattered through the bush. In South Australia and Victoria some of the most successful of these were founded on co-operative, occasionally communistic principles, notably in and near the irrigation districts along the Murray River where exciting prospects had been disclosed by the efforts of the enterprising Chaffey brothers from California. Contemporary observers hoped for 'a frugal and contented peasantry, with a "fowl in the pot" and a little money in the Government savings bank', but the new villagers occasionally had loftier ideals and proudly gave their co-operative endeavours such addresses as 'Energy', 'Perseverance', 'Star of Hope', 'Advance' and 'Enterprise'. As the crisis lifted, the majority of the settlements were disbanded, but a few more 'novel industries' had been given a trial, a few more lessons had been learned about the Australian environment. The rural landscape still bears the imprint of the experiments (Powell 1973c).

(v) Another development common to all of the Colonies, but especially important in the oldest group, was the increasing impact of Government-sponsored scientific and technological research upon agricultural progress. The modification or 'improvement' of native soils is central to the Australian story and obviously requires highly specialized historical studies for every part of the country. For the broader contribution of contemporary scientific research, it could be said that South Australia and Victoria led the way with major discoveries in soil physics and chemistry, applied botanical, chemical and biological studies, and the establishment of agricultural colleges and experimental farms. The benefits of superphosphate, shallow ploughing, new rotational practices, seed-pickling and more efficient harvesting techniques were gradually demonstrated. Weekly journals such as the *Leader* and the *Australasian* provided an excellent specialized service in explaining these and other innovations, also advertising the full range of new equipment and generally providing a useful forum for the discussion of rural affairs. They did not always contact the average pioneer farmer directly, perhaps, but definitely reached the local agricultural societies and the individual 'leaders' involved in the complex sociological processes associated with the diffusion, adoption and rejection of innovations—as Bogue (1963) has shown in far more detail for the American Corn Belt. But this was obviously insufficient for a country with such heavy investments in an agricultural future, and it was left to some of the senior researchers to take every opportunity to promote the cause.

In the 'nineties urgent appeals were made for the establishment of sound ecological principles which would guide the future development of the country along conservational lines. Common-sense frameworks were required, it was insisted, to distinguish Australia's basic 'faunal regions' and to determine a 'rational popular nomenclature' of native and introduced plants—simple but appropriate divisions and descriptive terms which could be easily understood by all (Hedley 1894; Holtze 1894). Some progress was made in each of these areas, but the familiar and misleading British terminology proved to be a major stumbling-block for some time and most scientists and technologists were apparently fast giving up the battle, if they ever recognized it as such, for they had developed a marked tendency to restrict their communication to members of their own species. The 'scientific attitude' born of this incestuous relationship was challenged by a few outstanding characters, and not the least of these was Rev. Thomas Blackburn, who told the public and his scientific colleagues alike to stop their arrogant meddling in the affairs of nature. '*Man's* powers are so out of proportion to the powers of all other living things', Blackburn warned, that he seemed be to making a habit of disturbing nature: he waged war on particular plants and animals without pausing to consider their significance in the broader ecosystem upon which he too was dependent and, for sheer practical reasons, intensive studies of the Australian environment were therefore required to reduce the risk factor. A sounder knowledge of ecological relationships was also claimed to be essential for those well-meaning scientists in the public service who were engaged in removing 'pests', whether introduced or native to Australia. In the twentieth century, Blackburn's brave prophecy regarding improved methods of 'biological control' had a better chance, though profound errors still resulted from misinterpretations or incomplete preparatory research. His suggestion was that the safest and most efficient form of control over introduced pests was to bring in to the new environment 'the particular influence that in its natural environments was hostile to its holding an excess of power beyond what nature intended to wield' (Blackburn 1894). Initially, this was far easier to say than to do; subsequently, the method became a favoured ploy and was even over-used, with some disastrous consequences.

As the new century began, a number of perceptive observers stressed the singular importance of improving the means of communicating the findings of the scientists and technicians to the Australian public.

How is the agriculture of a country to be brought under the control of science? This, at present, is not a question of agriculture, but rather a problem in practical psychology. It is certainly a question of getting new ideas into the minds of men. Some may call it a question of technical education, but it is much more than that. It is a matter of getting a whole nation to feel the gravity of these facts, and of rousing the people into action (Pearson 1900: 27).

It could be argued that the subsequent activities of the Council for Scientific and Industrial Research (C.S.I.R.), founded in 1926, and of its powerful and prestigious successor the Commonwealth Scientific and Industrial Research Organization (C.S.I.R.O., 1949), represented a consummation of the visionary schemes for the future dominion of science which had attracted major researchers and administrators in Australia during the late nineteenth century. But A. N. Pearson, Victoria's official 'Chemist for Agriculture' quoted above, was one of several prominent public servants who were at that time vitally concerned that their fellow scientists should be made aware that their growing separation from the rest of the community posed an obvious threat to the realization of their dreams of future leadership. Pearson and his colleagues called for the deliberate harnessing of public energies in the pursuit ·of practical scientific goals. Specifically, they emphasized the need for more experimental farms and improved public access to them, systematic official sampling and analysis of farm produce coupled with the supply of free and expert advice, the institution of soil and climate surveys for *every farm* and the provision of books, pamphlets and travelling lecturers to dispense agricultural and horticultural information (Pearson 1900: cf. *Year Book* 1905). With the unfortunate but understandable exception of the notion of the basic local environmental surveys, most of these recommendations were accepted and incorporated in some form into official policy throughout Australia during the first decade of this century.

Urban and Industrial Australia

(i) Most of these developments served to emphasize the dominance of the south-eastern crescent, but the discovery of new mining fields greatly benefited the 'peripheral' areas and removed or alleviated the worst effects of the depression in the 'nineties. This was especially true of the discoveries of gold in Western Australia, boosted later by the opening of tin, copper and coal mines; representative government was soon granted and Perth's population increased tenfold. Similarly, the first mining leases at Broken Hill in the interior of New South Wales were pegged in 1883 and the population had soared to 20,000 by 1890 when the now famous Broken Hill Proprietary Company produced £3,500,000 of silver, lead and zinc. In Tasmania, Mt Lyell and Mt Zeehan yielded prodigiously silver, lead, zinc and environmental catastrophe, and enlivened the flagging economy of the island.

(ii) A marked structural reorientation towards commercial and industrial specialization was accelerated during the 'eighties, and this trend was firmly associated with a preference for urban locations, especially for the six capitals (Urlich Cloher 1975). By 1891 almost two-thirds of the population were located in concentrations of 500 people or more, despite the impressive growth of the agricultural sector. Melbourne and Sydney, the two largest centres, were comparable products of liberalism and secularism, but Melbourne had a much stronger radical intellectual tradition and staunchly supported

Victoria's policy of Protectionism, whereas Sydney espoused Free Trade. They were unchallenged in their own regions but vigorously competed for over-all commercial leadership and for the wheat and wool trade of the Riverina district, midway between them. Brisbane grew rapidly in the 'eighties, but had to share its developing hinterland with a number of smaller sugar ports, and Perth's major development occurred after the turn of the century. Adelaide's relatively slow growth reflected a general levelling-off in the South Australian economy, and Hobart had to share a small hinterland of apparently limited potential with Launceston. The problems of urban management were therefore most acute in Melbourne and Sydney, yet neither was blessed with an enlightened planning scheme.

(iii)   One of the most pronounced geographical features of this formative period was the transition from the pedestrian to the public transport city. Under sustained boom conditions and boosted by speculative pressures, residential construction became the leading private investment field and brought about a dramatic transformation in the internal structure of the Australian city, beginning in Melbourne and Sydney. The most attractive and tangible expression of the simple utilitarian dream indulged by the great majority of Australians—including those who spurned, or were denied or disenchanted with, the agrarian ideal of a yeoman's freehold—had become the single-storey, detached or semi-detached family house set in its own garden, and the resultant suburban sprawl was matched only by the Californian experience. The boom reached its hysterical climax in Melbourne, where the spread of the city over one hundred square miles was stimulated by the comprehensive undercover influence of land speculators on the Victorian Government (Davison 1969). Decisions on the construction of the railway system were usually determined by haphazard concessions to local interests: in 1884, for example, 1,170 miles of track in sixty-five new lines were authorized under the famous 'Octopus Act', in which the Government casually and openly abandoned strict economic calculation as the basis for its suburban lines policy (Rimmer 1975). At first the Government Railways deliberately concentrated upon the promotion of the middle-class passenger traffic from the outer suburban areas, and private companies were permitted to 'develop' the inner areas for workers' residences, supported by privately-owned horse and cable tramways. Later, however, there was some mutually destructive interpenetration of the two systems which accelerated the urban sprawl by providing an unusually cheap, varied and intensive commuter system. The financial crashes of the 'nineties were in no small measure brought about by the artificiality of Melbourne's boom, exemplified in the parochial, short-term planning of the public transport systems. Roads, water and sewerage followed as elaborations of the patterns drawn so brazenly by the private developers and railway promoters, and the various local authorities within the expanding city were obliged to borrow heavily to provide these services (Cannon 1966, 1972).

(iv)   The renowned egalitarianism of Australian life was (and unfortunately is) often exaggerated, but it is true enough that visitors to the booming Australian cities were frequently astonished by the common juxtaposition of mansions and workers' cottages and the apparent lack of any marked social differentiation between the expanding suburbs. This was for a time especially noticeable in 'Marvellous Melbourne', where the flat to gently rolling topography served to stress the general homogeneity of the townscape. But it would never have done for that rising parasitic class of land agents which continues to monitor and manipulate space and society to great effect in the 1970s. With the connivance and even vigorous support of local councillors and members of parliament, real estate companies successfully marketed the image of 'prestigious', 'salubrious' and 'panoramic' seaside and hilly sites wherever they occurred—noting always the therapeutic qualities of plain 'fresh air', pointing out the dangers of the 'noxious vapours' in the lower areas away from the coast and repeatedly quoting suburban mortality statistics without regard for demographic, occupational or other variations. Similarly, as if by common consent, the existence of an elementary and easily visible 'line' was highlighted long before intensive development occurred as an obvious, almost God-given 'boundary' between residential areas of higher and lower social status: perhaps in lieu of a wider range of topographical 'cues', the Yarra River was made by this process to play a very crucial role in the spatial evolution of the city. Initially promoted by a few leading agents, the line of the river became increasingly reified with successive days and months of frantic land transactions and this procedure helped to fashion odd confrontations of suburban 'opposites' across the river frontier—the plush and pretentious residences of Toorak, Kew and South Yarra on one side, facing the workers' houses in the polluted industrial districts of Burnley, Collingwood and South Richmond (Davison 1969).

Wilderness and Amenity

(i)   The reservation of large urban parks was an important feature in the earliest plans of each of the major cities and the idea was repeated in many country townships. Increasing urbanization, improved transportation and the growing interest in outdoor recreation in Australia did not produce the same degree of pressure for non-urban parks as occurred so impressively in the United States: in both countries the mass of the population was still engrossed in the plain business of making a living, but the Australian population was much smaller and still possessed vast empty areas which had not yet received the inspired and devoted championship of talented and influential individuals and groups which dominated the parkland movement in the United States. Even so, several important reservations were made throughout Australia before 1914 and the political processes and general motivation behind these decisions showed some similarity to the far more complex developments in North America. Improved health and recreation were very frequently cited as 'civilizing' or 'modernizing' arguments in support of the parks, but the preservation of 'wilderness' areas of outstanding natural beauty and/or of considerable scientific interest may have been closer to the hearts of the majority of the original proposers. This judgement may be a little unkind; whatever the common origins in *élitist* urban and scientific groups, there was no significant national organization for parkland reservation during this period and the decisions made for each political unit therefore require separate and detailed consideration, beyond our present scope, before any firm opinion can be expressed. A very brief and imperfect sketch may serve to complete this general review.

(ii)   In New South Wales one of the earliest of these historic but comparatively uncontroversial reservations concerned an area of 5,000 acres in the Jenolan Caves district in the Blue Mountains in October 1866. The caves were only discovered a decade or so earlier and the legislation was intended to protect 'a source of delight and instruction to succeeding generations and excite the admiration of tourists from all parts of the world'; similar reserves were later proclaimed in this vicinity. In 1879, only seven years after the Yellowstone proclamation which produced the world's first truly 'national' park in the United States, 18,000 acres south of Port Hacking were set aside for the 'rest and recreation' of Sydneysiders, and the New South Wales Government later enlarged this 'Royal Park' or 'National Park' to 36,000 acres. But the historical significance of the creation of Australia's first great park escaped the notice of most contemporary observers and has continued to elude generations of scholars who have been preoccupied with other interpretations of the Australian experience.. A preliminary and perhaps superficial view suggests that the decision was quickly and rather easily reached, yet failed to provoke much public debate, even though it may have been associated with secretive, high-level efforts to freeze some local coal deposits (Bardwell 1974). In 1891—once again, apparently, without intensive lobbying or campaigning—an additional 35,000 acres were reserved for similar purposes in the Ku-ring-gai district, and whatever the original motivations of the first decision makers, the ensuing administration of each of these parks was fundamentally and almost entirely pointed towards public amenity, producing lasting modifications in the flora, fauna and topography.

(iii)   South Australian and Tasmanian reservations during this period were also made with the minimum of fuss, without substantially altering the course of public policy and the pace and direction of development. The Royal Society of Tasmania had unsuccessfully urged the proclamation of flora and fauna reserves from the late 'forties, but after the formation in 1904 of the Tasmanian Field Naturalists Club and the Royal Australian Ornithological Union the naturalists found it more profitable, at least in the short term, to tag their own goals on to the islanders' rising demand for outdoor recreation, and particularly the economic attractions of the tourist trade. A National Park Association was formed in 1913 with the support of the scientific and naturalists' associations, the major city councils and, notably, the Australian Natives' Association. This led in 1915 to the *Scenery Preservation Act* and the formation of the Scenery Preservation Board, the first central authority in any Australian State to concentrate solely upon the control of public parks and reserves. Samuel Dixon and his supporters in the Field Naturalists' section of the Royal Society of South Australia gained an earlier success when they protested against the plans to subdivide the Government Farm at Belair, and in 1891 the area was designated as a 'national recreation and pleasure ground'. Although the field naturalists managed thereafter to exert some influence over Government policy, they were conspicuously less successful in their appeals for a comprehensive system of plant and animal reserves. At the end of our period the official emphasis was still firmly set upon the protection of popular recreation interests in and around the 'resorts' in the hilly areas near Adelaide and this was incorporated into the *National Plea-*

sure Resorts Act of 1914. The case for fauna and flora reserves gained a better hearing after the First World War.

(iv) In Western Australia some equally good efforts, led especially by B. H. Woodward the Director of the Western Australian Museum, Governor Sir William Robinson, the Premier Sir John Forrest and, from afar, Baron von Mueller, were thwarted by the developmental urge and particularly by the exceptions made for mining interests and pioneer settlement in most of the reservations. The best known of the early champions of national parks and nature reserves in Queensland was Robert Collins, a pastoralist from the McPherson Ranges, with some American experience. He was at first unable to gain the type of influential support which was then promising so much in Western Australia, but the situation improved after his election to Queensland's Legislative Assembly in 1896. Direct and indirect advantages for tourism were stressed once more by Collins and others, especially after the passing of the *State Forests and National Parks Act* of 1906. The first so-called 'national' park was proclaimed in 1908 at Witches Falls on the Tambourine, on land that was judged, significantly, 'unfit for any other purpose'. In the same year, however, the Bunya Mountain Park was proclaimed, embracing important Aboriginal territory and affording some crucial protection for the giant Bunya pines.

(v) In Victoria, too, the leading roles in the promotion of parkland reservation were taken by prominent individuals and amateur and professional organizations based in the cities. But there was certainly no national parks *movement* properly so-called, and indeed the term 'national' was itself too frequently misapplied throughout Australia to projects which were strictly local in their initiation, subsequent control and orientation. Some harmony was achieved from time to time following the more general perception of a few well-defined issues; on these occasions good progress was made, but for the most part a relatively unproductive disunity prevailed. Major organizations included the Field Naturalists' Club of Victoria, the Australian Natives' Association, the Royal Society of Victoria, a small and evanescent National Parks Association, the Victorian branch of the Royal Geographical Society of Australasia, the Acclimatization Society of Victoria, the Royal Ornithological Union and a variety of minor walking and touring associations. Among the better-known of the individual workers were Sir Walter Baldwin Spencer, the Professor of Biology at Melbourne University from 1887 to 1919; Edmund Fitzgibbon, Melbourne's Town Clerk from 1854 to 1890 and Chairman of the Melbourne and Metropolitan Board of Works for twelve years from 1891; James Smith, a noted journalist and compiler of the three-volume *Cyclopoedia of Victoria*; J. L. Dow, J. M. Mackey and other Lands Ministers; and, naturally, Baron von Mueller. By 1911 approximately 176,000 acres were reserved in nine distinct areas in all major regions of Victoria— possibly half of the total area included in all the parkland proposals known to have been made to Parliament (Bardwell 1974).

*

The pressures for development did not always exclude or oppose those interpretations of conservation which called simply for the 'wise and fullest use' of the Australian environment. This was especially true of much of the agricultural sector and to a lesser extent of the cities, whereas the mining industry remained highly exploitative in itself, yet also gave useful support to some forms of timber conservation. But with a few slight exceptions in the nascent park movements, strictly *preservationist* arguments tended to find little favour in any quarter and the minority voice calling for the elevation of conservationist principles above all other considerations must have been muffled by the growth imperative and by the continued separate existence of a bewildering number of distinct conservation-orientated societies sprinkled around each of the capital cities. From the 'seventies at least, positive moves had been made towards Australia-wide co-ordination by some far-sighted individuals and the economic crisis of the 'nineties strengthened the motives for national union among conservationists, as it did in many other spheres (Robinson 1975). The Commonwealth of Australia was born on 1 January 1901 and although Federation had achieved very little in terms of direct impact on resource management by the end of our period, a few important initiatives had at least been taken towards the sytematization of local efforts and the instigation of nation-wide research. The following parts of this section are therefore focussed upon the continuing endeavours of scientists and interested laymen to improve and preserve the natural environment of each Colony (or, after 1901, each State). They also explore in particular the impact of what might be very loosely but conveniently termed an increasing sense of 'national identity' and the further progress of the ideal of 'professional commitment' to community services in the changing management of the natural resources of forests and water, and the built environment of the Australian city. As far as possible, for continuity and economy, attention will be concentrated on Victoria.

9 Forestry, Economics and Politics

THE several advantages of scientific forestry were well appreciated by individuals and groups in all parts of Australia during the 'eighties, but the introduction of sound management principles had to compete with rising speculation and the passion for settlement expansion. In one sense, it also had to compete with the persuasive appeal of water resource management, which attracted an increasing amount of scientific and political attention. Australian forestry did not fulfil the promise it displayed in the 'seventies, despite the continuing efforts of gifted individuals. In the United States Gifford Pinchot emerged towards the end of the century to make forest management the spearhead of the American conservation movement (Pinchot 1947; Huth 1957). The most exciting events in Australia, the driest of continents, were in the field of water managment, but the successes and frustrations of forest management do require a brief summary here to balance the picture.

The moves towards land classification in the mid-'eighties (Figure 13) were clearly beneficial to conservational management of any description, but the necessary base maps frequently took years to complete and they were quickly outdated in the endemic intrigue and locational mobility which characterized the expansion process. John Ednie Brown continued his useful work in South Australia before moving to New South Wales as Director-General of Forests in 1889 when he succeeded the Inspector of Forests John Duff and the poet Henry Kendall, Duff's predecessor, who had received his 'gift position' from Premier Sir Henry Parkes in 1881. Kendall's love for the bush was complemented to some extent by his limited but useful experience in the timber business, but he achieved very little during his short tenure. Duff's modest efforts had been thwarted by grazing and agricultural interests and by a lack of political support, and Brown's appointment promised much more. There were then about 5.5 million acres in 862 forest reserves and a rough inventory and 'end-use' classification of the most favoured timber species had been established (Coghlan 1887: 102-9). Brown concentrated upon improving the valuable Murray redgum forests, but also continued valiantly to promote afforestation to alleviate the climate of the dry inland plains and for various reasons failed to persuade the New South Wales authorities to experiment with *Pinus radiata*; he left in 1892 and subsequently became Western Australia's first Conservator of Forests. In general terms it could be said that scientific forestry was not vigorously pursued before 1910 in Western Australia, Tasmania or Queensland, even though each had developed extensive interests in timber production. Elsewhere, the depression of the 'nineties, a widespread drought from 1900 to 1910 and a series of unrelenting, devastating rabbit plagues, combined to stultify the efforts of Australia's best foresters.

George Perrin, Alone

Victoria's Conservator of Forests, George S. Perrin, did his utmost to improve the status and effectiveness of his small division, which was tucked away in a corner of the monolithic Lands Department—an organization which was said by a later Conservator to be hostile or unaccommodating towards forestry, since it was committed 'to open all lands to settlers as quickly and as freely as possible' (Mackay 1903). Perrin's first annual report was a mixture of passionate protest and concise judgement for forward planning. More qualified foresters were urgently required to assist the overworked two-dozen men he had to administer the entire Colony. The traditional grazing rights of commonage in the State forests should be abolished and the general public should be denied open access: the forests should indeed be fenced. And, while he admitted that the ecology of the native forests was in part fire-dependent, new legislation for fire prevention should be enacted and far more firebreaks should be employed (Report 1890). Gifford Pinchot was only graduating from Yale when Perrin, about whom so much less is known, took up his appointment in Victoria. It is therefore important to record this spirited bid for forestry's leadership in the conservation field, which deserved far better reward from Perrin's contemporaries. In his proposed scheme of management, each forester would mark the trees which were available for sale and would ensure that the sawmillers purchased *entire* trees in every case (cf. von Mueller's earlier arguments). Similarly, the wasteful process of allowing monthly licensing over undetermined areas would be replaced by an annual licence system determined on a base of 1,000 acres, together with a strict limitation on the number of men employed and a charge for the licensing of each employee. These controls are clearly recognizable to the modern forester, but for the Australian community of the time they were quite advanced. New South Wales had had mixed success with similar but less elaborate programmes (Coghlan 1887: 115-19), but the significant models were in all probability the Indian, German and French systems. Certainly Perrin's scheme promised more efficiency than the current Victorian practice,which permitted a massive invasion of the bush over a short cutting season. Sustained-yield management would be further guaranteed by compelling the miller to clear his allotted area completely before moving on to another; the cleared area was then to be declared forbidden territory for between five and twenty years according to local conditions, until its restoration by replanting or natural regeneration. Opposition was clearly anticipated, but Perrin was prepared to stand fast.

> The saw-miller, with the timber-getter generally, must recognise the importance of forest conservation on systematic lines. Therefore the necessity for a radical change of existing conditions is self-evident over a system which is wasteful, does not provide for the future, is opposed to common-sense, and therefore should be abolished (Report 1890).

He also challenged the mining companies to face up to the impending crisis and support all measures to avert it. Instead of leaving the solution to the Government, they should realize that they were partly responsible and accept the introduction of stringent controls which would curb their activities.

[The miner] must be prepared for sacrifices; he must submit to see the forest lands properly fenced and placed under strict supervision; he must give up his old ideas as to his rights to timber; he must recognize no rights save those of the Crown; he must submit to being heavily fined if he should transgress the forest laws; he must assist the forest officers in their work by moral and active support. If he does all this, there is a certainty of a regular supply of timber being available for his use (Report 1890).

This repeated Perrin's earlier evidence to the Gold Mining Commission, in which he had appealed for the establishment and strict protection of a forest cover over one-fifth of the entire area of Victoria. In reply, the *Argus* (7 June 1890) had already commented that 'Experts are prone to give way to enthusiasm, with the result that good schemes are made to appear too formidable for adoption' and that Perrin 'should have resisted the temptation to subordinate the practical to the ideal'. But the newspaper decided to alter its stance a little after the Conservator's official statement was tabled, offering the unnecessssary caution that 'as his reforms must touch vested interests more or less severely, it is better to proceed slowly' (*Argus*, 22 October 1890). Yet it still rejected the proposed system of royalites.

In principle no doubt it may be right to make all saw-millers pay a prescribed price for each tree felled, but there are some practical considerations which have to be taken into account. The State does not wish to make a direct profit out of its timber. It is willing to dispose of trees as it disposes of coal or gold— in such a manner as to promote general prosperity. The only reasonable stipulation should be that there must be sufficient revenue from licenses to enable a staff of inspectors and rangers to be maintained as is necessary to protect the forests and prevent spoliation. So long as the department [can] pay expenses the community will be satisfied. But the imposition of a royalty would not only be unnecessary for purposes of conservation, but would directly tend to increase the price of timber. The saw-miller would charge the royalty to the timber merchant, the timber merchant to the builder, and the builder to the house-owner. Besides, if the market is disturbed in this way there will certainly be a stronger demand for timber from other colonies than now exists, and our saw-millers will claim additional protection (*Argus,* 22 October 1890).

Speculation, manipulation and nepotism had been widely indulged throughout Victorian society (Cannon 1966, 1972; Serle 1971) and neither of the leading metropolitan newspapers were removed from these powerful influences, but it was perhaps particularly unfortunate that the *Argus*, an early champion of forest conservation before the death of the radical Edward Wilson in 1878, should dilute its support at such a critical point. Conservation was then faring much better in North America. Its scientific, aesthetic and utilitarian arguments were more clearly and frequently enunciated, and they were actually winning strong support for forestry from those same 'vested interests' which the *Argus* was so reluctant to challenge in Victoria (Hays 1972).

During the 1890s the organized forestry movement in the United States, which had established a much stronger *national* base than the fragmented Australian movement, made the same decision to shift the emphasis from the objective of saving trees from destruction to the promotion of planned, long-range or sustained-yield management. The purists still demanded total

14 Australia Tempted: the Boom Years (from the *Melbourne Punch*)

preservation, but the National Parks movement siphoned off some of these dissenters; on the other hand, most of the prominent lumbermen were either ignorant of the philosophy or regarded it as an impractical dream. Then Gifford Pinchot, who had studied advanced forestry principles in France and Germany, returned to the United States to become the leading figure in American forestry. In 1898 he was made Chief of the Division of Forestry, later the Bureau of Forestry within the Department of Agriculture, and his remarkable successes in educating the public and the timber industry about the management of scientific forestry for utilitarian purposes brought sweeping changes in official conservation policy. In addition, his commanding personality and great conviction attracted many enthusiastic followers and eventually won the financial and political support of the powerful timber companies. The earlier efforts of the unfortunate Perrin were far less successful for a number of reasons, including interminable bureaucratic wranglings, personality clashes, real and perceived economic troubles and the lack of any strong popular support. There was of course some sympathetic response within the scientific fraternity, which was beginning to establish good coordination on a national basis, particularly after the founding of the Australasian Association for the Advancement of Science in 1886. Yet several of the most respected individuals in that illustrious institution had clearly become rather more interested in the ecological and aesthetic arguments which supported the preservationist cause.

The Baron and Others, 1890-1900

Senior members of the A.A.A.S. were deeply conscious of its dual role: to provide a much-needed forum for scientists scattered throughout Australia and New Zealand, while at the same time continuing the 'dissemination of useful knowledge' for wider consumption, but at a much grander level than was ever permitted to the previous learned societies. So the aged and venerable Baron von Mueller, in his inaugural Presidential Address to the Melbourne conference, chose to communicate once more his view of the public duty of the professional scientist, this time with a flourishing, confident pride in achievement:

> how powerful and trusty an influence by this widely spreading and annually refreshed organization can be exercised on the public mind, to speed progress, particularly of utilitarian tendency, in a telling and in an impressive manner . . . Irrespective of carrying on original research, worthy of a country of juvenile freshness, it is our duty more especially to instil the flow of information from so manifold sources near us in such a manner that new growth for further developments may arise through that limpid course in all possible directions (von Mueller 1890: 2-3).

Without putting too fine a point on it, Perrin's ambitious proposals appear to have been labelled 'technological' and 'administrative' rather than strictly 'scientific'. Although von Mueller probably endorsed the proposals, he simply chose to speak of other things in his introduction to the Melbourne conference, to grasp the opportunity to discuss other matters which he now found more important or more attractive. Above all, his 1890 address displayed a continued mellowing towards the aesthetic viewpoint and there were surely echoes here of von Mueller's lonely treks in the Australian wilderness, when the earnest young botanist had enjoyed a unique experience of communion with nature.

> Choice areas, not necessarily very extensive, should be reserved in every great country for some maintenance of the original vegetation, and therewith for the preservation of animal life concomitant to particular plants. Where the endemic riches are greatest, there also the danger is more imminent of these being swept out of existence, unless timely measures are adopted for the reservation of some sequestered spot, to which rural occupations should never be allowed to have any access with their disturbing influence on primeval harmonies. Such spots should be proclaimed for all times the people's inalienable property, and every inhabitant or visitor of the locality should consider himself the co-preserver of such areas, so as to aid in preventing accidental invasion or casual ignition or intentional spoliation [sic]. Furthermore, to such places of security should be transferred plants and animals of exceptional rarity occurring near these seclusions. 'Floral commons', thus established, would soon be amongst the most attractive features, not only for pleasure excursionists, but also for travellers from abroad, and would afford future generations in various territories some idea of the wondrous natural beauty of vegetable and animal life in its once unique loveliness, pristine grace and unimpared freedom. Measures like these once initiated would earn enduring gratitude, and would find imitation in all countries, and particularly in those where nature has scattered its floral gifts most prodigiously over the territorial expanse. Under intelligent supervision such places, through restricted concessions, might be made to yield a greater income than accruable through ordinary rural occupation. Who would not plead in this case? as our Field Naturalists' club has indeed so fervently done already. More and more of rarities are commencing to succumb and to be made unrestorable, and scarcely a spot seems safe on the face of the globe against the defacing hand of man! (von Mueller 1890: 10).

Australia's forests, ever close to his heart, were also included in this historic address, which may one day be judged our first great appeal for conservation on a national scale. But there was no mention of timber resources, *per se*.

> May also the forests be pleaded for here in this assembly? It should be a fixed plan in national economy anywhere, to maintain masses of forest-vegetation near sources of rivers, and to establish some broad arboreous bordering on streams, where it does not extensively exist, as much calculated to reduce sweeping water-volumes by soakage and mechanical retention. For this purpose, nut-trees, cork-oaks, basket-willows and other trees, prominently utilitarian, could be chosen.

> ... Should some one in opulence desire to build up for himself one of the most lasting of monuments, it would be by the bequest of an isolated, primeval forest, ever untouchable for the free enjoyment of the orderly portion of the public (von Mueller 1890: 11).

At the same conference Frederick Turner, official botanist to the Department of Agriculture in New South Wales, broadened the scope of the appeal to national sentiment by delivering an excellent paper which called for the retention and deliberate diffusion of native grasses.

... a new era seems to have dawned upon Australia. By establishing departments of agriculture throughout the colonies, we may reasonably expect most valuable results to accrue therefrom, and if these are assisted by the patriotic exertions of private individuals, much of the prejudice at present existing with regard to the value of our native pasture-plants may be consigned to oblivion...

The comparative merits of our native fodder-plants and grasses should form a part of the curriculum of the national education. If there were placed in all country State schools an enlarged drawing of each species that is peculiar to the district the school was situated in, with its botanical and common name, together with a short popular description and analysis, it might form a lasting impression upon the young mind, and would most probably lead to valuable results in after-years (Turner 1890: 586).

When the A.A.A.S. convened at Adelaide three years later, Walter Gill, Brown's successor, spoke bitterly of the deforestation of South Australia and, like Perrin before him, insisted that the foresters should be armed with vastly increased powers to remedy the situation. Graziers and cultivators were at best negligent and at their worst, their activities were said to rival the wasteful destruction wrought by the timber industry. Gill's foresters were working diligently to try to ensure that the industry was permitted to take only the natural interest, not the capital, of the native forests, but they were repeatedly thwarted.

When this system [of scientific forestry] is adhered to timber felling never degenerates into timber slaughtering, but the pity of it all is that under existing conditions when an experienced forester in a State forest in these colonies decides that enough timber has been cut and decides to reserve the rest the timber-getter gets up a memorial and secures the aid of the local Parliamentary representative, who depicts in moving tones to the central authorities the tragic circumstances of hardship under which the timber-getter is placed in being prevented from getting timber, which is of course, in his opinion, abundant, and the result is that the faithful servant of the State takes a 'back seat' as the reward of his disinterested service, while the sawyer or splitter gratifies his own self-interest at the State's expense (Gill 1894: 528).

Gill had inherited a good system of plantations, but they had been ravaged by drought and rabbit invasions and he was unable to persuade his Government to release additional funds to support their protection and extension. Undoubtedly this also influenced his embittered attack before the A.A.A.S. Conference and it may have encouraged him to look forward to the emergence of a higher political authority—a Federal Parliament, presumably, though this is not made clear—which could purge the whole issue of its maddening parochialism.

The remedy will be found when every individual member of an intelligent democracy shall, after careful study of the deplorable tale which the history of forest devastation has to tell, take warning by the ruinous experience of other nations, and recognize the fact that the forests of a country are not the property of the first man who chances to grab them, be he sawmiller or farmer, blocker [the holder of a small allotment] or squatter; that they are national property, productive of national benefits, and should, therefore, be legislated for on such a broad national basis as to ensure the wise preservation for posterity of an equal share of similar advantages to those we have ourselves derived from them (Gill 1894: 536).

Forestry does not appear to have been considered very seriously, however, in the conventions leading up to Federation, and although the reasons for this are still obscure it has been suggested that it can scarcely have improved management conditions, since the Commonwealth Government was eventually given a range of powers 'which vitally affect the conduct of forestry operations by the States, without implied responsibility for the health of the industry' (Jacobs 1957: 136).

Fighting for Recognition, 1901-14

Forest Bills were introduced into the Victorian Parliament in 1879, 1881, 1887 and 1892, but none became law. Berthold Ribbentrop, the Inspector-General of the Indian Forest Service, was invited to comment on the state of Victorian forests in 1895 and a Royal Commission was appointed two years later. Its final report was not presented until 1901 when it advised among other things that high standards could not be established or maintained until the forest reserves were declared inalienable by Act of Parliament, and not before the control and administration of the forests were removed from 'political interference' and vested in an independent Conservancy Board (following British, German and American practice). But Perrin died in December 1900 and the Government was cautioned that his successor 'should be a strong man, because he must ever be the buffer between certain conflicting interests, and between political influences and the best interests of the state, which, unfortunately, do not always run along parallel lines' (*Argus*, 25 April 1901). Although it claimed that: 'From the commencement, there has been no real power attached to the office of conservator, and therefore no real responsibility' and that Perrin had suffered the humiliation of being treated 'as a subordinate officer of the Lands Department', yet the Royal Commission pressed for the triennial appointment of a three-man Conservancy Board responsible to Parliament for the centralized administration of forest policy and the management of forestry personnel. While the Government took its time digesting the Commissioners' report, Perrin himself was not replaced. In the interim, water management, which was originally conceived to be inextricably linked with the management of the tree cover, had in a sense been dislodged from its true environmental setting and was attracting almost exclusive official attention as a quasi-independent resource in its own right. Due perhaps to the comparative absence of local opposition, the centralized mode of control unsuccessfully proposed for forestry was implemented fairly rapidly in the development and administration of Victoria's water resources. And forestry was left stranded in the tangled mesh of bureaucracy.

> Just now we are really without a policy at all. Forests have been a sort of shuttlecock, [moved] to and fro between [the] Minister of Mines and [the] Minister of Lands. Neither Minister has had the conservation and improvement of forests as the immediate purpose of his office. The persuasion used towards him was always persuasion to destroy. Mining men wanted the timber, without much regard for posterity. When a Minister of Lands had control he was constantly asked to excise some block for selection. 'This is a forest', he would urge. 'Forest be hanged', the importunate member would reply, 'I want it for

one of my constituents' (*Argus,* 7 August 1907).

The history of our forest administration is from first to last one of shameful neglect, of almost criminal indifference to the public interest. The control of forests has been tossed from the Department of Lands to the Department of Agriculture; from the Agriculture to the Mines, from the Mines to the Lands; then back again to the Agriculture and the Mines, and so on. Each department in turn has played the part of a careless stepfather to the unfortunate intruder, with the usual consequences; and Parliament has been as erratic in its treatment of the forests as the various departments have been in their control (*Age,* 14 August 1907).

At last, the *Forest Act* of 1907 introduced most of the principles enunciated in the 1901 report and H. Mackay, the new Conservator, eventually achieved modest but hard-won successes in the management of native hardwood forests and important new plantations. Indeed, whatever its problems, Victoria probably had a better record than any other Australian State during the difficult period 1890 to 1910, and this was mainly due to the determination and skill of its Conservators and their handful of colleagues.

The succeeding decade showed more progress: the first Interstate Forestry Conference was held in 1911, the University of Adelaide established a degree course in forestry and Victoria established a Forestry School—another of George Perrin's ideas—at the old mining township of Creswick. In 1914 the British Association for the Advancement of Science convened a special conference in Australia and it was decided to present the visitors to Victoria with a lavish *Handbook* describing the State. One of these visitors was D. E. (later Sir David) Hutchins, a leading forester with wide experience in the Empire, who encountered some of Mackay's operations in the field and was treated, in addition, to a careful account of the progress of Victoria in the *Handbook*. There he read of Mackay's own code, repeated verbatim from a fiery statement in the official *Year Book* for 1903.

> The true aim of forestry is the preservation of the forests of a country by wise use. In practice, it embraces a knowledge of rocks and soils, the food of the plant life which covers them; of botany, the knowledge of vegetable living bodies; of chemistry, the science which reveals the nature and properties of bodies; and of sylviculture, the rational treatment and working of forest areas, so as to maintain them in a timber-yielding condition. It includes also planting and sowing where Nature has clothed the surface of a country with niggard hand, or where, by the action of man or the ravages of fire or tempest, areas have been denuded of tree vegetation and rendered unprofitable. But the primary function of the forester in a newly-settled country is to maintain and increase the sylvan wealth with which Nature has clothed hill, valley, and plain, by regulating and correcting wasteful or inferior growth, while at the same time carefully restricting the yearly output of timber and other produce to such quantity as the forest can safely yield without deterioration (Mackay 1914: 310; see also Mackay 1903: 411).

Mackay had success as well as frustration to report in 1914 but he made it abundantly clear that there had been no profound change in the attitude of the Victorian public.

> As settlement creeps up from the plains denudation of tree cover goes on apace. The American wood-lot, the strip or belt of live timber which is so marked a

feature on farms in the North-eastern States and even in Quebec and Ontario, is scarcely ever seen in Victoria. Here the axe is set to every tree, and often not a shrub is left for shelter or cover. In summer the cattle and sheep vainly seek restful shade. The dam or creek has no screen from the fierce rays of the sun. Evaporation quickly empties the stock supply, which under dense canopy might well outlast any ordinary summer. Around the homesteads may be seen a few sickly pines, keeping the air from the living rooms, and ruining the soil of the small garden enclosures, but the stockyards and outbuilding are left un-sheltered. Often on bleak winter evenings dairy cattle may be seen shivering near naked homesteads, vainly trying to escape from the driving rain, while in the paddock hard by native trees, which would have afforded warmth and shelter, stand leafless and dead. What this neglect of shelter means to the dairyman in shrinkage of milk supply is only now being realized. Even in sheep paddocks the same neglect of cover commonly prevails (Mackay 1914: 331.)

*

Obviously the *cognitive* element of the public attitude towards the tree cover had changed very little, despite the great progress made by the educated *élite* and the professional experts—the economic, aesthetic and ecological functions of the tree cover were still insufficiently known or accepted. In the *affective* component there was still hostility, or at least indifference. Of the associated *behavioural* component it could be said that far more pioneer settlers had been moving into heavily-wooded regions than ever before in the nation's history, that in general the long-term environmental consequences of this invasion were unsuspected or misperceived, and that the very nature of this drawn-out 'encounter' situation probably reinforced existing negative attitudes. The pioneers in these difficult districts were naturally preoccupied with the urgent tasks of clearing, building and fencing, and generally with establishing a viable productive system as rapidly as possible. Some major bushfires around the turn of the century, in part a direct result of the new settlers' ignorance and carelessness, only strengthened their resolve to make their homes more secure from the threatening wilderness. But Mackay's dreary picture also describes much of the *present* rural land-scape and it is disturbing to reflect that the work of men of his commitment and ability, including the best efforts of his predecessors Goyder, Brown, Perrin and others, had failed to persuade Australians to adopt more con-servational attitudes towards their native tree cover. And certainly, if foresters had held a unique opportunity to influence public opinion on environmental quality, that time was gone forever.

Yet the local authorities did choose to accord greater respect to their distinguished visitor Mr Hutchins; he was soon invited to report on the forests of each State and this became the basis of a new move towards an Australia-wide management policy (Hutchins 1916). Professional forestry was given a boost by Hutchins' activities, and afforestation and the manage-ment of Government reserves for climatic and timber purposes soon showed considerable progress. But it proved to be particularly difficult to check the exploitative instincts of private enterprise, a problem which continued to be aggravated by the lack of popular and political support.

10 Water Management:
the Victorian Experience

ENTERPRISING landowners were irrigating on a small scale in various parts of Victoria during the 'fifties, and it was already recognized by professional scientists at that time that the intermittent and unreliable flow of most of the Colony's streams would demand the construction of storage basins to conserve winter flow. On the dry Northern Plains, pastoralists had commonly modified the available watercourses by constructing weirs and dams and by dredging the 'chains of ponds' which were their most pronounced natural characteristics, and there were moves in the 'sixties to persuade the Government to improve the natural supply by building local systems of channels across the plains. In 1871 Benjamin Hawkins Dods, an energetic Scotsman with skill and imagination in hydraulic engineering, founded the Grand Victorian North-Western Canal, Irrigation, Traffic and Motor Power Company. This was an ambitious and controversial project, involving the construction of a channel from Murchison on the Goulburn River to run westerly for more than 200 miles before turning south to enter the sea via the swampy lowlands around Portland; providing some fifteen million acres of the northern country with irrigation water in summer, drainage in winter and a cheap line of transportation for the increased production. The cost was estimated at £5 million stirling and the Victorian Parliament was requested to supply a lease of three million acres of Crown land and to gazette a temporary reservation of the land along the proposed routes of the interconnecting channels. Possibly, it was also anticipated that the Government would feel persuaded to carry out the work itself, recouping the expenses of the promoters.

It was not a propitious time for such a visionary plan: the good seasons continued until the mid-'seventies and small scale wheat and sheep farming appeared to be quite successful without Government support on the fringe of the Mallee-Wimmera country. Dods and his colleagues were scorned as confidence tricksters by the metropolitan press and a visiting irrigation expert from India ridiculed the proposal after a very fleeting examination. But there was abundant enthusiasm in the country districts and this rapidly grew when another Scot, Hugh McColl, elected to join Dods in spreading the gospel of irrigation. McColl was then widely respected in the Bendigo district for his efforts in securing water for domestic and mining purposes, principally by the construction of reservoirs (including a major share in the early preparations for the important Coliban scheme). As secretary to the company, McColl engaged in lively correspondence with a number of Californian contacts and became very familiar with the recent successes of public companies in developing irrigation in that State. He fully used his local influence and some earlier experience in journalism by addressing public meetings and contributing detailed articles on irrigation to the *Bendigo Advertiser* throughout the later 'seventies. Nothing came of Victoria's Grand Canal, but in 1880 McColl became member for Mandurang in the Legislative Assembly, where he was more successful in attracting Government support for the 'water question' in general (McColl 1917).

'The Sound Principle of Decentralization'

The crippling drought of 1877-81 eventually shook the Victorian Government from its apathy about the Northern Plains. In previous droughts only a small number of squatters were affected, but now there were thousands of small farmers and their families in dire distress, with only their votes to lift them out of misery. A Water Conservancy Board was appointed in 1880, consisting of George Gordon, formerly Chief Engineer of Water Supply, and Alexander Black, Assistant Surveyor-General, and this resulted in some intriguing management proposals for the Northern Plains—that the waters of each river should only be utilized in its own basin, and that weirs and dams be constructed on several major rivers so that floods and freshets could be directed down minor watercourses when the main streams would normally overflow. The northward advance of pioneer selectors had exposed the fundamental deficiencies of the natural resources of the plains to support a closely-settled farming population. Well-sinking and boring had met with very little success, stock were commonly driven forty miles to water during the parching summers and water was actually being carted and manhandled by struggling selectors over the stark landscape, frequently from a supply-point at a country railway station—for there were also 'water-trains'. Urgent relief was obviously required to improve stock and domestic supplies, and the competent reports of Gordon and Black were acted upon with little delay. Yet their insistence on avoiding more than the minimum of Government interference is also notable—and unusual, considering the genuine and widespread distress among so many who had selected under the 'liberal' land laws and who had yet to complete their credit payments to the Victorian Treasury: '...it being our decided opinion that the chief responsibility, as well as the management of such undertakings, shall rest with those directly benefited by them, because we greatly prefer the true English spirit of independent action and self-reliance to the enervating influence of Government interference' (Report 1880: 13).

Later, the enquiry was extended to cover irrigation as well as domestic and stock supplies, and this formed the substance of the final two (of the total of fourteen) reports. The enthusiasm for cure-all irrigation was then running very high and Gordon and Black decided it was time for a little sanity. With commendable restraint they reminded the Victorians that the entire irrigated area of Spain could be comfortably accommodated in that part of the Victorian county of Rodney then being boosted by McColl and his friends and that India's irrigated acreage, though more than that of all European countries combined, would scarcely exceed the comparatively empty area of the Victorian Mallee. Accordingly: 'We believe that too sanguine views of its profitableness [sic] are often entertained from an under-estimate of the cost and an over-estimate of the results, arising from a want of information or due consideration of the conditions essential to success...' (Report 1882: 10-11).

The first result was the *Water Conservation Act* of 1881, establishing Urban and Rural Waterworks Trusts to be administered after the fashion of the legislation of the 'sixties for the supply of the mining towns. Despite all the earlier experience of using local bodies to manage settlement expansion and native forests, the legislature was banking again on local control and initiative, even though it is true that the central Government in Melbourne retained an important role in decision making by means of its provision of supporting finance. The *Argus* warmly approved this 'sound principle of decentralization' (*Argus*, 19 October 1881), as opposed to the establishment of a new department of water supply, which 'would assuredly be more influenced by political pressure than by actual necessities and sound mercantile considerations, the outcomes being pecuniary loss and public demoralization'. Under the new Act the public would be guaranteed that all water management projects for the north 'will rest upon a truer appreciation of local requirements and of local ability to pay the cost of applying them' (*Argus*, 17 October 1881). But the likelihood that the Government would soon have to discover an equitable means of breaking the inevitable deadlocks between the various authorities was widely perceived and debated. Before the end of October 1881 there was a great deal of support for the notion of an appointed board of independent and impartial specialists to control all aspects of water conservation. Even the *Argus* warmly applauded this early effort to substitute the supposedly detached, rational, stable and efficient behaviour of the 'expert' for the ignorance of the politician, whose circumstances usually demanded the frequent exercise of other skills which were not always entirely compatible with the best principles of resource management.

> In our opinion it would be a great advantage if the whole working of the water supply scheme were entrusted to a non-political body . . . There is no reason why a Minister, who is never in office long enough to get a thorough grasp of affairs, should be burdened with the details of administration. It is utterly impossible for him to deal with technical matters half so well as a board of experts thoroughly acquainted with any given system (*Argus,* 24 October 1881).

The commitment to decentralization did succeed in harnessing some significant local energies. In July 1882 representatives of two northern shires (Echuca and Waranga) met at Goyder's Hotel in Melbourne to prepare their own comprehensive plan for water conservation *and irrigation* in the Goulburn Valley: the Goulburn was the best of the few good streams running entirely within Victoria. The engineer to the historic new Trust, which was formally constituted on 11 October 1882, was Stuart Murray. Gordon and Black had submitted their first cautionary report on irrigation on 22 September, but soon enlisted the support of Murray in the preparation of a second, more detailed report, which concerned the Goulburn scheme. A new *Water Conservation Act* was passed in 1883 to provide for Irrigation Trusts, but no financial undertaking was given by the central Government. The existing Water Trusts were proving more costly to support than their original estimates had suggested and the politicians were warned to guard the public purse more carefully: the proposals of the Irrigation Trusts 'should be required to pass through a thoroughly searching scientific and financial examination at the hands of the engineers as well as of Parliament itself', and it might be wiser in the first instance to finance a single experimental project in a region which was considered to offer 'either the most or the least favourable conditions' (*Age*, 15 October 1883). The new Act offered petitioners the chance of an official survey of any detailed scheme which claimed the support of a majority of local landowners. Plans might then be prepared and exhibited for public inspection and a second petition was required, signed by three-quarters of the landowners holding two-thirds of the land. After approval in Melbourne, finance had to be secured on the open market.

On economic as well as philosophical grounds, there was general approval for 'the great principle of self-help which the measure contains' (*Argus*, 26 October 1883). Understandably, uncertainties continued to surround the irrigation question and the old road of independent empirical testing, though signposted and graded just a little by the State, was still the preferred route. Irrigation in Australia

> must adapt itself to the peculiarities of soil, of climate, and of water supply, and these conditions can be found out only by trial. Under the bill now accepted these trials can be made. Without it they were not possible, but now rivers can be tapped and water can be carried over roads and properties as the farmer may require. No such powers existed before; they are conferred now. Any man, or half dozen men, or any parish of men, seeing water within their reach, can set to work to bring that water to their farms. They can work individually, or can form trusts, or can float companies. We believe that our farmers will do this, and that we shall have to chronicle such great successes as will win confidence, and will in due course secure the capital required for large head works and extensive designs (*Argus*, 26 October 1883).

Whatever its support in the metropolitan press, this cumbersome Act was really only a crude copy of recent Californian legislation and served mainly to confuse the Victorians. Then, in 1884, the second irrigation report of Messrs Gordon and Black sketched an alarming picture of crippling expenditures for the new legislative framework and threw a dark shadow across local ambitions.

Empirical testing was no substitute for sound engineering skills linked to agricultural economics. In fact, this traditionalist attitude at official and popular levels was encouraging the pioneer irrigators to favour the so-called 'low plain' country adjacent to the main river beds—areas which could be served by the most rudimentary of facilities, especially of course where braided streams were common and natural channels could be used to 'carry' the irrigation water. It took many years before the deficiencies of these areas were fully realized: the soils were not self-mulching, had relatively low levels of permeability, and were mainly suited to less intensive forms of irrigation farming such as the fattening of lambs on annual pastures. The most promising land types were found to consist of the coarse-textured deposits forming the 'high plain' country—mainly the shallow beds and levée-like deposits of ancient streams—and, to a lesser extent, the 'mid-level plain' formed from more varied deposits of the same or similar 'prior streams'. After the turn of the century both land types proved to be highly adapted to a wide range of crops and annual pastures (Rutherford 1974). Anticipating some of these findings by more than twenty years, the impatient Hugh McColl scornfully compared 'Gordon's Gutters' on the low plains with the bolder and more efficient American system of carrying the water on the higher land in long semi-surface canals, from which it could be widely distributed by elementary gravitation. Continuing his campaign for the speedy completion of a detailed hydrographic contour survey, he recommended the establishment of an experimental area in which invited American experts might demonstrate the latest techniques, and asked for a Royal Commission on the subject.

It will be conceded, I think, that the American people have earned a worldwide reputation for making the most of their opportunities. They certainly are not fools or crack-brained dreamers, and yet 'surface' canalization for irrigation purposes is making long and rapid strides in America. While successive Governments in this country have been hesitating, doubting and only talking about comprehensive water schemes, or at most issuing obstructive reports couched in meaningless generalities, the people of America are doing the work (McColl 1883).

Of Rights, Responsibilities and Progress

Public interest in water conservation and irrigation was then far too advanced for any Government to neglect and on 23 December 1884 a Royal Commission on Water Supply was at last appointed under the chairmanship of the rising young politician Alfred Deakin, at that time Minister of Water Supply, formerly an accomplished journalist with the *Age* and a brilliant lawyer (La Nauze 1965). The other Commissioners were members of parliament for the areas in question, leading engineers, and senior public servants representing the relevant departments; McColl, Black and R. L. J. Ellery were also on this powerful board, and Stuart Murray was appointed Secretary. Four impressive Reports were submitted, showing that irrigaton was not only a sound investment, but also vitally necessary to 'progress' if Victoria was to 'utilize her abundant natural advantages, bring her productiveness to the highest point, and secure to the agricultural population of her arid districts a permanent prosperity' (Report 1885: 56). The first and fourth Reports consisting of reviews of irrigation practices in Western America, and in Egypt and Italy, were produced in 1885 and 1887 respectively. The second progress report (1885) was prepared by J. D. Derry who accompanied Deakin on his tour of the Western United States, and concerned the engineering aspects of irrigation in that area; the third and vital report (1885) presented detailed recommendations for the introduction of irrigation into Victoria (Progress Reports 1885, 1887). Murray's contribution towards the engineering aspects of the third report was considerable and he was soon appointed Chief Engineer for Victorian Water Supply, a position he held from 1886 until 1908. It was the promise of marked innovations in legal and administrative practice, however, which made the recommendations of the third report so memorable and these can be largely ascribed to Deakin— though Hugh McColl, who died in April 1885, had undoubtedly greatly influenced the whole tenor of the momentous publications he was never to see.

Deakin had been particularly influenced by the superficial but useful comparisons to be drawn between Victoria and California.

> [California] is like Victoria—a new country, settled by the pick of the Anglo-Saxon race, attracted in the first instance by gold discoveries, and remaining after that excitement passed away to build up a new nation under the freest institutions and most favourable conditions of life. California is almost exactly the same age as our colony, and in soil also the two countries are not unlike. In both, water was first employed by miners, and in both agriculture has been a later development. The price of labour bears about the same relation in each to the price of commodities. Their products are similar, and in both the chief markets are found at a great distance (First Progress Report 1885: 11-12).

The Victorian party received considerable assistance from many American administrators, including Major John Wesley Powell the Director of the United States Geological Survey, N. H. Egleston of the Forestry Bureau, and Colonel Hinton and E. A. Carman of the Department of Agriculture; more specific technical advice and field guidance was provided by the State Engineers of California and Colorado. Drawing particularly upon the recorded experience of irrigation in the latter two States, and recalling the decisions made in Victoria under the Mining Statute of 1865 and the *Land Act* of 1869 regarding the supremacy of public ownership over private water interests, Deakin introduced a promising new framework for water management.

Deakin's special objective was to direct attention to this question of *water rights* and he emphasized the many legal difficulties which had obviously prevented the full utilization of water resources in the Western United States, calling attention to the marked advantage of a clause in Colorado's constitution which declared that all of the streams contained within the State's borders were *public property*. The *Irrigation Act* of 1886 prevented the establishment of further riparian rights and effectively nationalized Victoria's surface waters; it also authorized elected Trusts to construct strictly local irrigation works with Government loans and, with an eye to recent protests from established farmers in the Western District (*Leader*, 5 September 1885), provided for 'national' storages and headworks to be constructed by the central Government on the understanding that the determination of charges for water taken from these headworks would ensure the recovery of interest payments (East *et al*. 1958). Yet in the same year, against bitter opposition, a Waterworks Construction Encouragement Bill was passed to permit private enterprise to develop irrigation settlements in the Colony. The main point of this was to make the way clear for two young Canadian brothers, George and William B. Chaffey, who had encountered the Australian party during its tour of California: after some initial difficulties the Chaffeys succeeded in establishing the north-western irrigation colony of Mildura on the banks of the Murray, and Renmark, its companion settlement in South Australia. George Chaffey later returned to the United States to play a major role in the development of irrigation in California's Imperial Valley (Vincent 1887; Alexander 1928).

If irrigation could not bring the millenium; if it could not establish man's final and complete dominion over a hostile environment, or fulfil his sacred commission to 'improve' on nature, what could? Even Deakin allowed himself a little extravagance: irrigation would elevate the agricultural life to its correct and desired perfection by 'removing the element of risk, which robs it in bad seasons of most of its charms' and northern Victoria would be blessed with a contented community almost as numerous as the entire Victorian population of the mid-'eighties (First Progress Report 1885: 107-8). Irrigation was a right *and* a duty; if necessary it should also be promoted and accepted as a privilege.

If Victoria is to continue to progress in the settlement of her people upon the lands and the multiplication of her resources by the conquest of those areas hitherto regarded as worthless; if she is to utilize her abundant natural advantages, bring her productiveness to the highest point, and secure to the agricultural population of her arid districts a permanent prosperity, it must be by means of irrigation. No price, it may be said, is too high, unless, indeed, it implies the sapping of that spirit of independence and of that self-reliant energy and enterprise which have won her present position; for by these, and these alone, can she maintain it (First Progress Report 1885: 113).

Centralization and the 'Closer Settlement' Imperative

Irrigation was certainly destined to supply one of the most characteristically *Australian* of all the agricultural frontiers, though not in any of the ways that Deakin and his colleagues could have predicted. By the late 'eighties there were nearly ninety individual Trusts, and most were in financial difficulties. A *Relief Act* was passed in 1889 to write off 75 per cent of the Trusts' existing liabilities, and they struggled through the years of depression until further legislation was introduced in 1905 to attack the heart of the problem. Significantly, the architect of the new legislation was that practical and dedicated engineer in the public service, Stuart Murray, and the new mode of administration he advocated was clearly a reflection of the trained predispositions and rising aspirations of the powerful group of professional technicians to which he belonged. The duplication of 'official' services in the small worlds of the separate Colonies meant that each Government was bound to become the principal employer of several types of manpower. Furthermore, Australia's physical environment imposed particular tasks and offered some special opportunities for the engineer: this was no different from the situation encountered in most other countries of the New World, yet in many respects Australia may have had an older and stronger tradition of 'public works', as opposed to the high degree of influence exerted by private enterprise elsewhere. Before the turn of the century, some prominent engineers boasted that the achievements of their own profession offered a valid index to enable every society to assess its progress from the dark days of savagery: 'The standard of civilization, as well as the industry and wealth of a people, are measured by their engineering works' (Bell 1893: 199). This type of myopic innocence was quite widely shared, but fortunately it seldom persuaded other champions of technocracy to repeat the strange and rambling claims made by C. Napier Bell in his presidential address to the engineering and architecture section of the A.A.A.S.

Let these colonies not forget that wealth and greatness are measured by their engineering works, and if they would entertain the honourable ambition, once more popular than now, of being remembered to the distant ages of the future,

15   'After the Spree' (from the *Melbourne Punch*)

let them emulate those mighty peoples of the past who left imperishable records of their life in the ruins of their vast public works (Bell 1893: 199).

Social and political developments in the latter half of the nineteenth century increased the high level of bureaucratization in a number of occupations, for the Colonial Governments commonly chose to meet the problems of urban growth, railway expansion and so on by the increase of their own staffs. By the end of the century engineers—and surveyors, architects, hydrographers, draftsmen and other associated specialists—were already following the paths of a career cycle which had been suggested, even mapped out for them, by the previous activities of friends and relatives who were engaged in the public service. It is not surprising, therefore, that Victoria's irrigation 'problem' came to be widely conceptualized in the various government departments as an unusual example of the waste of good engineering by inexpert local administration. Stuart Murray's solution was to build a new management framework which would incorporate in every detail the engineers' ethic of efficiency and utility: it is still lauded as a major landmark in the evolution of the 'most socialized' of professions in Australia (Martin 1955; East *et al.* 1958; Corbett 1973).

Irrigation had not been successful under the Trust system. Landholders usually held large areas and showed no great enthusiasm for the intensive cultivation envisaged by the promoters and designers of the original schemes: 'When the seasons were good the landholders did not bother with the water. When seasons were bad there was insufficient water to do any good' (East *et al.* 1958: 37). There was inadequate conservation of water and yet at the same time a profusion of channels which could not be filled when the water was most needed. Neither the Trust Commissioners nor the landholders had any previous practical experience of irrigation, and the division of control between the local engineers and the Water Supply Department in Melbourne was another important factor, for whenever there were errors each disclaimed responsibility. In addition, these problems were exacerbated by two fundamental weaknesses: firstly, although the 1886 Act had prevented the establishment of *new* riparian rights, it did not define *existing* riparian rights; secondly, the local managers had shown an extreme reluctance—partially justified on political, legal and other grounds—to impose and recoup water charges which were sufficient to compel the landholders to adopt a more economical use of water. By 1904 the capital liability of the State for water supply undertakings was shown to be approaching £6 million. Increasing bitterness was expressed in the towns against the continuing 'imposition' of the country interests. Each of the Trusts was said to have played a lone hand: 'getting all the water it could and casting off whenever possible its liabilities to the State', while the urban taxpayers had been duped into supporting an inefficient and inequitable system. The Trusts 'used their political influence to have their debts to the State written down' (*Argus*, 8 September 1904). At this point, Murray was invited by George Swinburne, the Minister of Water Supply, to advise on the drafting of new legislation.

Once again there were established American models to guide, warn, justify or inspire the local professional. In the State of Wyoming an appointed senior engineer, after determining the amount of water available, decided the priorities between uses and users in each watershed, enforced them and had the power to grant new rights. The leading proponent of this concept was Elwood Mead, who introduced it successfully in Wyoming and then championed its wider use—with the increasing support of his fellow engineers, individually and through their professional institutions. After his appointment in 1898 as Chief of the Office of Irrigation Investigations in the United

States Department of Agriculture, Mead took the opportunity to market the idea at national and international levels (cf. Mead 1903). Similarly, Frederick Haynes Newell, chief hydrographer of the United States Geological Survey, developed the concept of a federal water development programme which encompassed power, navigation and flood control as well as irrigation, and so the modern principle of *multiple-purpose* water-use slowly gained strength. Australian scientists and technologists quickly became familiar with Newell, since he was also a very active voluntary worker in the dissemination of an extensive range of scientific information—serving, for example, as Secretary of the National Geographic Society in 1892-93 and 1897-99—and his promotional work *Irrigation in the United States* (1902) was well received.

Victoria's *Water Act* of 1905 abolished all of the Irrigation Trusts and introduced a new form of corporate body, the State Rivers and Water Supply Commission, to bring about efficient, *centralized* control throughout the State. Stuart Murray was the first Chairman of the Commission, which was to combine 'the authority of Government with the initiative of private enterprise' (East *et al.* 1958: 37). Common law principles relating to riparian rights were modified considerably under the same Act, which clearly defined the rights of the Crown and private individuals for the first time: the vital provision was that where any stream or lake formed the boundary or part of the boundary of an allotment of land, the bed and banks of the water body would always be deemed to have remained public property and not to have passed with the land on its purchase from the Crown. Murray's retirement from the Public Service was due in 1908 and, in a masterly stroke, the Victorian Government invited Elwood Mead himself to take the Chairmanship in 1907. He accepted, and for eight years Victoria enjoyed the services of one of the world's most experienced and innovative administrators in the field of water management (Baker 1951; East 1954; Rutherford 1974). Mead was then a leading opponent of the United States' recent programme for tighter federal control; he had preferred to foster private irrigation by providing expert technical assistance and by encouraging the States to develop a more rational water law (Hays 1972: 243-4). Newell and his colleagues had reacted to Mead's criticism very sharply and had tried to persuade President Theodore Roosevelt to abolish the Office of Irrigation Investigations. They were unsuccessful, but the bitter controversy probably influenced Mead's decision to accept the Victorian offer.

From his arrival Mead made full use of the considerable powers vested in his position. More than twenty years before, a simple cautionary note from the *Argus* had been passed over with little comment: 'The land may want water, but water needs men' (*Argus*, 13 December 1884). In 1905 the same principle reappeared in a more positive role, as the central prop in Mead's practical philosophy. He succeeded in convincing the Victorian Government not only that irrigation could never be justified as a mere side line on large holdings—the secret lay, he said, in the introduction of intensive settlement to make more and better use of the water—but also that a compulsory charge for water rights should be apportioned to every holding according to its size, to compel farmers in irrigation areas to take proper advantage of the resource, or make way for others who were prepared to do so (cf. Mead 1920).

The *Water Act* of 1909 introduced contentious new regulations along these lines; above all, landowners in irrigated districts were required henceforth to pay for the water allotted whether they used it or not. This action also led to a further extension of the Commission's power and responsibilities, for irrigation development was now seen to include the encouragement and support of 'closer settlement'. Eventually the Commission was authorized to purchase the land (if it had been alienated), survey and subdivide it, build the house, grade the slopes, finance the settlers and plan the townships. In fact, it became a most important regional planning authority with a high degree of independence, exuding in consequence a unique sense of self-esteem, which was and is very hard to shake.

Dramatic changes in policy followed Mead's appointment. The earlier and more primitive phase was dominated by the Victorian Government's hesitant efforts to encourage greater stability in selected regions of dryland farming by means of its support of locally-conceived 'Extensive' schemes on the low plains. The later period, under Mead's direction, was characterized by the Commission's own energetic promotion of elaborate 'Intensive' programmes on the more productive high plains. The Extensive (or 'Partial') irrigation schemes continued under a comparatively looser form of Government supervision, since they were usually dependent upon various combinations of irrigated and non-irrigated types of management, whereas the Intensive schemes relied completely upon the Commission's monopolistic control over the supply of irrigation water and the cultivation of those crops which could best repay the heavy outlay. Irrigation in New South Wales and South Australia, following the Victorian lead, displayed the same dichotomy.

Mead's contribution to the British Association for the Advancement of Science *Handbook* of 1914 was a discussion of irrigation practices in Victoria. Actually this was an advertisement for his Commission and a minor treatise on the benefits of combining irrigation and 'closer settlement' in which he passionately believed; a good example of the determination and confidence in 'development' with which he imbued his high office. The Commission had inherited several run-down schemes and Mead believed that his 'rational' policy of financial control was achieving good results against all difficulties. Only in recent years has the obvious question been raised with any consistency: intensive settlement as pursued so vigorously by the Commission could indeed pay for the water as the engineers required, but who was to pay for the settlement; was it a good long-term investment, considering Australia's other needs and other potentials?

> With irrigation, there is no dead season in the year, and there is scarcely a month when crops can not be seeded or harvested. With irrigation, two farm crops can be grown in the year, a wheat crop in the winter, and a maize crop in summer. With irrigation, from four to six cuttings of lucerne can be harvested in the year, and the dairyman can have green feed through the summer months and a continuous milking season. With irrigation, the orchards will produce everything from olives to apples; oranges, pears, and peaches grow on the same acre; all grow to perfection, and give an acreage return that enables men to make a comfortable living off 10 to 20 acres of land (Mead 1914: 258).

Densely-packed rural settlement supported by 'garden' cultivation of the sort envisaged by Mead had been a more reasonable social and economic ideal when Victoria functioned as an independent political unit, though even then there was a more complex array of management goals and problems, including many neglected regions and under-used resources. Furthermore, although the point can be overemphasized, the increasing preoccupation with the scarce resource of water may have led to an unbalanced development of vital technology—away from dry farming and scientific forestry, for instance. Mead's very appointment was in a sense another product of this premature focus, narrowed it still further, and for a time accentuated the local deviations in resource management technology. But there was no denying the continued Arcadian appeal in irrigation farming and Mead had done no more than to articulate a generally accepted contemporary view.

A 10-acre orange grove will bring a larger return than the 300-acre wheat field, and one acre of lucerne will fatten more sheep than 20 acres of native grass. Irrigation will, therefore, multiply the population, which would otherwise be supported on the land, 10 to 100 times, and give a corresponding increase in the value of products. Furthermore, an irrigation district is freed from the vicissitudes and losses that come with recurring years of drought, and a densely peopled area has better home conditions and more attractive social life than sparsely settled areas dependent on the scanty rainfall of the north (Mead 1914: 259).

The State Rivers and Water Supply Commission was clearly a major agent in transforming the landscape of large areas of Victoria, but its very existence may also have promoted or maintained an unfortunate attitude to the resource itself on the part of the users, which in turn gave them a special position within the community and increased their demand for more irrigation. The Commission could only enforce rates and charges which would meet annual maintenance and management costs, together with the recovery of interest payments, redemption on costs of works and the depreciation on perishable assets. With the increasing political power of a growing country population the collection of compulsory payments for water rights became a troublesome business—the Government of the day frequently refused to endorse the Commission's proposals for increases, even when costs where soaring. So the water users were secured against private owners' attempts at exploitation, but the Commission could not enforce charges which were sufficient to protect the general interests of the community as a whole, despite the corresponding increase in the local demand for more and more water rights. Irrigation added considerably of course to the value of the land it served, and indirectly to the value of the properties in the settlements serving or dependent upon the irrigation districts, yet rates were not levied on this 'unearned increment'—the unimproved capital value—until the late 1950s. The engineers' vision was simply the conversion of a vital resource to 'useful' purposes in the most efficient way they knew, and the consequences of the partial fulfilment of that vision are still reverberating. We are now beginning to realize that all preparatory cost-benefit analyses should be sufficiently comprehensive to incorporate the dynamic forces hitherto unsuspected or underestimated in traditional approaches, and that social and political factors, for example, must be evaluated as basic parameters, not as aberrations yielding the inevitable 'qualifications' to every finding.

The River Murray Agreement

Federation itself was another 'premature' idea, the dream of politicians, journalists, lawyers, bankers, economists and not a few scientists. According to one noted observer, the majority of the people were not ready for it.

> The changes effected in many of the colonies during the past ten years towards a real and an effective democracy, the uprise and present influence of Labour power in the Legislatures, and the gradual growth of a national sentiment out of a mere 'Colonial' feeling, all call for a longer lease of progress and more opportunities for a fuller and more complete development in the life of each state [*sic*] before Federation will become the needed complement of colonial evolution (Davitt 1898: 132).

There was a measure of truth in these remarks, but it is more important here to note that the debate on water management definitely assisted the movement towards political union in some circles and was a prominent feature during the early experience of Federation. This is best illustrated in the history of the River Murray Agreement which was ratified by the Parliaments of New South Wales, South Australia, Victoria and the Commonwealth in 1915—after a major Royal Commission and a long series of political and scientific conferences from the beginning of the century.

Interstate jealousies were deeply stirred by the recurrent droughts which gripped most of the continent. New South Wales and Victoria wanted the Murray for irrigation alone, and saw the dry seasons as ample justification or useful ammunition: 'We are too wise a people, and too practical a people, to permit these lessons to pass by us unheeded'. Although the desperate hunt for artesian basins might result in the discovery of a great 'subterranean inland sea' and fulfil the best hopes of its promoters, 'The momentous task now devolving on the Federal Government is to take occasion by the hand and make the use of our river waters wider yet' (*Age*, 15 December 1902). But the South Australians argued that any diminution in the volume of the great river would seriously affect water quality in the lakes at its coastal exit and reduce the potential of the Murray for steamer traffic. This last point gave an entrée for the Federal Government to try its hand (and, not incidentally, to throw some weight thereby behind the smallest of the three protagonists), since the *Constitution Act* granted the Commonwealth authorities jurisdiction over navigation. And although the 'reasonable use' of rivers for irrigation and water supply was recognized as one of the 'State's rights' under Clause 100, it was agreed that this section called for considerable definition.

Centralized and decentralized systems of administration were again in conflict over the management of a major resource. The South Australians were castigated for the exclusiveness of their mental map: 'The Murray, with its immense fan-like system of tributaries, looks to the South Australian eye as an ordination of nature for gathering the produce of central Australia and bringing it to South Australia for sale, coastwise distribution, or overseas shipment'. Victoria and New South Wales replied that the inland settlers themselves were already clamouring for railways and suggested that in any event, 'if we are driven to make a choice between production and transit, we ought unhesitatingly to declare for production ... In the utilisation of the Murray waters, however, it should be possible to combine all the uses' (*Argus*,

16 December 1902). The South Australians 'would see the productivity of the Upper Murray country shrivelled up in Famine, and the farmers driven off the soil before the drought'; why should Victorians be expected to stand for this?

> The great watershed of the Darling has poured its flood treasures down the river to a most wicked waste. The Goulburn drainage area of Victoria has done the same. The commonest of prudential reasons demands that this uneconomic recklessness shall cease . . . Australia owes it to herself not to fling away these treasures of the heavens. The most profitable use of her lands must always be her primary consideration. Their neglect must form a crowning offence against good government. The very river trade itself must depend largely on the relative productivity of the country beyond . . . River navigation, valuable as it may be, is quite of secondary importance as compared with the impounding of flood waters and their liberal distribution during the dry months of summer (*Age*, 29 December 1902).

So the case for the fullest possible use of the water had to be very forcefully presented to the politicians by their engineering advisers. After a number of painful bouts which exposed the fragility of the new Commonwealth and eventually underlined the increasing importance attached to 'expert' opinion, a common policy was agreed upon which acknowledged the good sense of the 'multiple purpose' principle (Eaton 1945; Harrison 1954). The River Murray Agreement provided for the construction of two large reservoirs and a variety of locks and weirs along over 1,000 miles of river, for the allocation of the water so regulated between the three States, and for the appointment of a River Murray Commission to arrange for the public works departments of the States to design, build and maintain the construction works under its direction. The Commission was to consist simply of a minister of the Commonwealth Government and one representative from each of the States concerned.

*

Each State has always been represented on this body by a leading engineer, the deputy of the Commonwealth Minister is almost always an engineer, and agreement on all decisions of major importance must be unanimous. In 1958 one of Victoria's most distinguished representatives on the River Murray Commission described it as a type of forerunner of the Tennessee Valley Authority and recorded his conviction 'that the successful reconciliation of conflicting interests has been possible only because all Commissioners were accustomed to dealing with problems as engineers rather than as defenders of parochial interests' (East *et al.* 1958: 38). The appointment of the Commission was certainly a major landmark in the evolution of the engineering profession in Australia and provided an honoured symbol of its status. But the activities of the 'R.M.C.' also became a prime target for those who would unfairly blame all of our environmental ills on the rise of modern technology, and of course it provides a most interesting challenge for social scientists, who are now identifying and promoting some new critiques of the conduct of environmental management.

11 The Response to Urbanization in Britain and North America

It is generally accepted that Britain inaugurated what has been called the 'Industrial Revolution' in the latter part of the eighteenth century. During the first half of the nineteenth century she also became the first nation to accomplish—some might prefer to say 'experience'—an urban transformation. This transformation rapidly gained momentum in the developing areas of the world and only in the last quarter of the century were the most perceptive social scientists beginning to come to grips with the phenomenon. Some of their interpretations focussed upon the growth of individual cities, but rather more attention was paid to the relationship between rural and urban populations; to the analysis of population growth, redistribution, and the process of concentration and agglomeration. At the end of the century the distinguished American scholar Adna Ferrin Weber concluded that urbanization was in fact the dominating feature of the age.

> That the most remarkable social phenomenon of the present century is the concentration of population in cities is a common observation, to which point is given by the foregoing comparison of two typical countries of different centuries. The Australia of today has the population of America of 1790; it is peopled by men of the same race; it is liberal and progressive and practical; it is a virgin country with undeveloped resources; it is, to an equal extent, politically and socially independent of European influence. But Australia is of the nineteenth, rather than of the eighteenth century; and that is the vital fact which explains the striking difference in the distribution of population brought about by the introductory comparison [that is, America in 1790, 3.14 per cent of its population in cities over 10,000; Australia in 1891, 33.2 per cent]. What is true of the Australia of 1891 is, in a greater or less degree, true of the other countries in the civilized world. The tendency towards concentration or agglomeration is all but universal in the Western World (Weber 1963: 1).

Educated Australians were made well aware of these processes. Apart from the evidence of the tangible modifications around them, they were also supplied with detailed commentaries by the statisticians appointed by the Colonial and State Governments, especially H. H. Hayter and his successors in Victoria and Timothy Coghlan in New South Wales. Clearly the responses to the profound changes wrought by increasing urbanization in the social and physical environment laid the foundations of more sophisticated forms of city management in Australia. Unfortunately it is still difficult to provide a succinct and balanced review of this vital but relatively unexplored theme. It is reasonable to suggest, however, that contemporary British and American developments were again highly influential, and that the equally significant contribution of prominent local groups and key personalities exhibited values and attitudes which were only partly derivative.

141

British Responses

One peculiarly striking feature of British society in the nineteenth century was its reluctance to accept urbanization as an inevitable product of its own prodigious energies. Writers and philosophers hated and feared the cities, which John Ruskin (1879) described as 'loathsome centres of fornication and covetousness—the smoke of their sins going up into the heaven like the furnace of Sodom and the pollution of it rolling and raging through the bones and souls of the peasant people around them'; they were 'spots of dreadful mildew, spreading by patches and blotches over the country they consume' (quoted in Pierson 1973: 878). Pierson (1973) and others have claimed that some of the anti-urban bias can be explained indirectly by the success of the landed aristocracy in accommodating to economic change, thereby retaining a good deal of its political and social pre-eminence. More importantly, the widespread dislike and distrust for urbanization arose from the impact made by economic and demographic changes upon older social and cultural forms: as the most obvious manifestation of these changes the large city became a dominating literary symbol, a focus for the expression of anger and hostility.

English Romanticism helped to perpetuate the myth of urban evil and rural goodness. The literature of evasion and regression failed to bring aesthetic perceptions to bear on the realities of the city, failed thereby to assist the urban inhabitants to come to terms with their changing world. On the other hand the Romantic ideology of flight was also closely associated with nineteenth-century emigration and with various land reform movements, including land nationalization, the provision of allotments for the poor, and the sporadic efforts of Socialists later in the century to implement the rustic vision in experimental rural communities designed to restore man to a harmony with nature and with his fellow beings. The alternative method for evaluating this social transformation was supplied by Utilitarianism, which stressed economic rationality, individual autonomy and the impersonality of social relationships, and generally assisted in the formulation of attitudes and values which affirmed many of the emerging characteristics of city life. The interest in city improvement stemming from this system of thought supported gradual and pragmatic change; quite as often, however, individual Utilitarian reformers were inclined towards Romanticism.

In the 'thirties and 'forties there were several major investigations of the urban environment which clarified and dramatized the highly complex and rapidly evolving situation and accelerated the pace of reform. Each new diagnosis persuaded influential members of society that the miserable plight of the masses was not only morally indefensible, but also embodied unimagined threats to the well-being and very existence of the more favoured sections of the community. The titles of these great reports are unfortunately more frequently quoted than their contents, which can still shake the modern reader, whatever his background and training might be: Dr J. P. Kay's *The Moral and Physical Condition of the Working Classes Employed in the Cotton Manufacture of Manchester* (1832); *The Health of Towns*, prepared in 1840 by a Select Committee of the House of Commons; and Edwin Chadwick's *The Sanitary Condition of the Labouring Population of Great Britain* (1842). As Ashworth (1954) has indicated, these reports suggested that crime and poverty, ill-health and poor housing, overcrowding and congestion, were all found together so commonly that some causal environmental relationship had to be assumed. A healthy workforce could be more productive and less dependent upon public and charitable organizations, and there was also the essential business of supervizing and maintaining urban property values, whether they were industrial or residential. Inevitably, the rights attached to property holding also imposed limitations upon the type and scope of reform which was attempted and called into question the abilities of existing organizational structures for municipal administration. 'Sanitary reform', above all the urgent provision of adequate sewerage facilities, was the special concern of Edwin Chadwick and his followers. Schoenwald (1973) recently added an intriguing psychological dimension to the standard interpretations of the work of these reformers: sanitary discipline prepared people for altered conduct, new and more ordered forms of behaviour which were necessary in an age of rapid urbanization. The water-closet and the sewer were therefore 'bringers of order' which emphasized and reinforced the restraints and controls required to maintain an industrialized society's functions of production and consumption: 'a society bent on order should put the body into order by putting order into the body' (Schoenwald 1973: 675). But the resistence to Chadwick's efforts to interfere with so intimate a human function was also based upon an ill-informed zeal for economy in municipal administration, linked with an honoured scale of priorities which afforded a very low ranking to sanitary improvement, far below the needs and achievements of commerce and industry. British urban society was certainly pressed into modernity in many different ways, yet it is indeed an interesting speculation that the long struggle for sanitary reform was due in part to what Schoenwald terms 'the immense weight of the old psychic ways'. This Freudian hypothesis may offer a rather more useful explanation of the motivations of the individual reformers, including Edwin Chadwick himself (cf. Finer 1952; Lewis 1952).

One of the best illustrations of a type of ambivalence in the British response is the rejection of the industrial city by a few leading representatives of the very class which had contributed so much to its creation. This was particularly marked in the North and Midlands after the middle of the century, when Akroyd, Cadbury, Crossley, Lever, Salt and others led the search for alternatives with their 'model' industrial villages and estates. But they were preceded in thought and action by Robert Owen and his early followers. The Owenite message was that man's character was moulded by his cultural and physical environment; that his irrationality and selfishness therefore resulted from an imperfect environment dominated by a divisive economic system which had depersonalized his relationships with his fellowmen. His model factory community at New Lanark was offered as a practical example to lead the search for 'harmony' and his numerous writings propounded, among other things, the benefits of a national, non-denominational education system. Owen's disciple John Minter Morgan also developed a scheme for self-supporting village communities, although in contrast he was particularly concerned to restore the established church to what he assumed to have been its central environmental influence. James Silk Buckingham borrowed from both Owen and Morgan in developing his concept of the model city of 'Victoria'—with a population of not more than 10,000 in an area of about one square mile, surrounded by 10,000 acres of agricultural land, with industrial sectors around the periphery of the built-up area, objectional trades isolated completely from the city proper, and the natural increase of the population to be accommodated in similar new settlements elsewhere. The model also prescribed an elaborate code of behaviour which insisted on the exclusion of tobacco, intoxicants and all weapons. It was never given practical expression, yet it proved immensely influential in the emergence of the town planning movement in Britain (Buckingham 1849; Ashworth 1954: 118-46).

The work of Ebenezer Howard and his 'Garden City Movement' was in this same tradition of Romanticism, qualified by a strong utilitarian or practical strain. Directly or indirectly, Howard's vision derived from Ruskin, Carlyle, William Morris, Tolstoy, Wakefield, J. S. Mill and Alfred Marshall, and his proposals for new settlements borrowed heavily from the schemes already outlined (Osborn 1946). In addition, he had lived for a time in the United States, where he was influenced by Mid-Western Quakers, the great Christian Scientist Cora Richmond, his own observation and participation in the establishment of new communities, and the changing environment of the city of Chicago. Together with his British contemporaries he was also deeply impressed by the work of Peter Kropotkin, by Henry George's *Progress and Poverty* (1882) and especially by Edward Bellamy's utopist portrait of communistic Boston in the year 2000, *Looking Backward* (1888). In October 1898 Howard published *Tomorrow: a Peaceful Path to Real Reform*, reissued in 1902 under the title *Garden Cities of Tomorrow*. According to some leading authorities, this classic statement did more than any other single book to launch and guide the modern town planning movement (Mumford 1946: 29).

Briefly, Howard's plan was to purchase an estate of 6,000 acres and to build a town occupying about 1,000 acres in the centre of the estate for no more than 30,000 people (Figure 16). A zone of public buildings was to be located in a park in the approximate centre of the town and a shopping arcade was to be built around this; the sizes of building lots and garden allotments were to be carefully controlled, industrial premises were to be placed on the periphery of the town, flanking a circular railway, and the remainder of the estate was to be retained for agricultural purposes with a population of some 2,000. Continued public ownership of the land was fundamental: the entire revenue from 'rate-rents' was to be applied in the first place to the payment of interest on the original purchase and the provision of a fund to pay off the principal and to support public works and maintenance costs; subsequently, this revenue was to service pension and insurance schemes for the residents. When the maximum population of 32,000 was approached, further expansion would be facilitated by immigration to adjacent areas and the repetition of the same process would lead ultimately to the creation of an attractive city-region, based upon a number of interconnected nuclei. The administration of each town was to be shared between the citizens in a most interesting fashion. The 'Municipal Groups' were those concerned with *public control*, including law, finance, inspection and assessment; *social purposes*, which incorporated music, libraries, schools, banks and recreation;

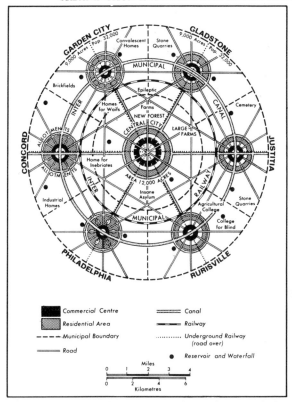

16   Ebenezer Howard's Design for a 'Group of Slumless, Smokeless Cities'
(after Howard 1898)

Howard's 'Garden City' design was frequently misinterpreted in its social, political and spatial aspects—not least in Australia, where a derivative of the original theory, the 'Garden Suburb', proved to be more acceptable. Howard was actually offering an attractive alternative system of separate but interacting settlements.

The New World might have offered a better proving ground for this and other novel solutions to the problems posed by rapid urbanization. Australians were certainly made aware of developments in Britain and North America and long before the end of the nineteenth century, urbanization appeared to be running beyond control in Australia, yet imaginative proposals for radical new designs were not forthcoming from the local professionals, despite the opportunities of 'a fair blank sheet'. The closest resemblance to Howard's scheme was, perhaps, that produced a little earlier by Rev. Horace Finn Tucker, working from similar principles and synthesizing a similar range of utopian plans, although Howard's masterpiece managed it much more effectively. Tucker's clumsy utopian novel *The New Arcadia* (1894) was an interesting feature of the 'Village Settlement' movement throughout Australia during the depression of the 'nineties. The movement assisted in the development of a large number of ephemeral settlements in the bush, which enabled thousands of poor and unemployed city families to obtain some respite for a few years. But this was a far cry from lasting 'decentralization' (Powell 1973c, 1973d).

and *engineering*, which performed a wide range of functions including roads, subways, sewers, rail and tramways, public parks and buildings, canals, drainage, irrigation and water supply, lighting and postal services. His 'Semi-Municipal', Pro-Municipal' and 'Co-operative and Individualistic Groups' included, respectively, those concerned in markets of various types; building societies, hospitals, churches and banks; and farmers, small holders, factories, clubs, dairies, laundries and small workshops. All were under the control of an elected and representative *Central Council*. If 'Planning is, in the final analysis, simply the effort to infuse activity with consistency and conscious purpose' (Altshuler 1969: 409), then Howard's idealistic scheme promised an extensive form of democratic participation which might have involved all sectors of society in the planning process (Howard 1898; Reissman 1964: 39-68).

Howard's vision appeared to offer something for virtually every idealist and 'anti-urbanist' of his day. Socialists were attracted by its evocation of co-operative endeavour, corporate life and communitarianism. Temperance reformers supported the notion of a town without a public house and those who dreamed of getting 'back to the land' saw the chance of a small holding. Some industrialists and financiers were persuaded of the opportunities for a sound investment linked with social duty. The idea of public ownership appealed to men and women who had rented land and houses all their lives. In the New World, as well as the Old, the attractive and practical restatement of the principle of comprehensive 'interpenetration' of town and country was possibly the most potent ingredient in Howard's very popular synthesis.

> There are in reality not only, as is so constantly assumed, two alternatives—town life and country life—but a third alternative, in which all the advantages of the most energetic and active town life, with all the beauty and delights of the country, may be secured in perfect combination; and the certainty of being able to live this life will be the magnet which will produce the effect for which we are all striving—the spontaneous movement of the people from our crowded cities to the bosom of our kindly mother earth, at once the source of life, of happiness, of wealth, and of power (Howard 1898: 7).

The Garden City Association was formed in 1899 and land was purchased in April 1903 at Letchworth, Hertfordshire, where the first experiment was initiated; the second project was commenced at Welwyn Garden City in 1919. But new towns were rare and costly, involving an element of risk, while rapid *suburban* expansion was an established part of ordinary commercial activity throughout Britain. With the first developments in the Hampstead 'Garden Suburb' in 1907 there emerged a prolific hybrid which borrowed from Howard's example to transform the chaotic suburban scene. During this period the British town planning movement made fair progress and established something like a professional base. In 1909 the vague and misnamed *Housing and Town Planning Act* was passed to guide authorities in the production of planning schemes for their suburban expansion, and a School of Civic Design was founded at Liverpool University; the inaugural meeting of the Town Planning Institution was eventually held in November 1913. It is significant, however, that the Institute's membership was drawn very largely from the powerful Royal Institute of British Architects, the Institution of

Civil Engineers and the Surveyors' Institution.

At this time, the planning movement clearly displayed an increasing sensitivity towards the condition of the physical environment but to some extent had lost sight of the relationship between the built environment and human experience, was less sensitive towards the needs and aspirations of a changing society. The freer and more open layout of the Garden City and Garden Suburb, well-adapted to topography and making full use of varied street patterns, public open space and recreational facilities, the encouragement of home gardening and so on, provided a tangible, comprehensible, attainable and apparently eminently desirable goal for progressive local authorities, and was enthusiastically endorsed by those professional bodies whose expertise was required. Too often, the adoption of low housing densities in commercially-based suburban developments was permitted to act as a force for social segregation, since the price of the land was well beyond the capacities of the lower income groups. Working-class housing was, in fact, better provided by piecemeal improvements sponsored periodically by various municipal bodies under the terms of the *Torrens Acts*, which enabled local authorities to force the landlord of an insanitary dwelling to demolish or repair it at his own expense, and the *Cross Acts*, under which local authorities could prepare redevelopment schemes for entire urban sectors. Without some more revolutionary changes—in the area of public ownership, especially —this useful legislation could seldom do more than maintain the wretched conditions of the mass of the people, but the little they did achieve was more than the influential supporters of the Garden City and Garden Suburb ideas seemed prepared to offer to the workers. The middle and lower-middle classes fared better, although this judgement too is open to interpretation. Critics protesting against 'the monotonous diffuseness of Garden Cities' and the crushing expense and boredom promised by the commuter belt, were ignored or branded as heretics, and in practice 'town planning' was grossly oversimplified to mean a system of control dominated by the architects, yielding low-density housing with gardens to the front and rear, set in tree-lined streets —concentrating upon 'the external appearance of things, not on the satisfaction of social needs' (Ashworth 1954: 194; for a general statement see Cherry 1970).

Howard's response to what he perceived to be an undesirable process of accelerating centralization had been to design an *alternative settlement system* which might generate sufficient attractive power to initiate and sustain an effective counteracting process of decentralization. His Garden City was particularly envisaged as a means of transferring occupations and jobs *out of London*, but this aspect of the scheme received very little attention until the era of 'new town' development after the Second World War. In its fullest expression, which would naturally have demanded a massive political and financial commitment, the design exhibited a far better understanding of the urbanization process, a much wider vision of the relationship, for example, between the city and its region, than the majority of Howard's professional contemporaries or the most earnest of his own followers ever contemplated.

The forces leading to the increasing urbanization of British society and to a lesser extent the development of city morphologies were allowed to continue with relatively minor checks and reorientations. Towards the end of our period, it is true, the biologist Patrick Geddes was calling for a better-informed and more positive intervention in these processes of environmental change. For Geddes, town planning demanded an understanding of 'civics', of the full range of activity in a town; architecture was therefore subordinate, and town planning as he conceived it had not yet emerged (Geddes 1904, 1915). The philosophy of this most original thinker was not rapidly accepted, but through his writing and teaching he soon established a remarkable international reputation.

The American Experience

The equally complex American response exhibited a number of special features which reflected important differences in the historical, cultural and physical environments, but the comparisons with the British experience should not be underestimated. It has been said that the basic dilemma of the modern American city is actually an intellectual crisis involving inherited images of the city which are either distorted or no longer applicable (Greer 1964). Whatever the problem—poverty, housing, pollution, transportation—its definition still depends upon the picture held of the city and of the type of life it should contain; a judgement on the city as an existing entity has been evoked, and the choice of action is dependent upon that judgement. Yet the intellectual crisis has endured beyond its recent recognition and elucidation by practical social scientists. As in Britain, the history of this crisis is not adequately shown in the simple symmetry of attitudes for and against the city. Ambivalence and confusion are also significant, and the changing management of the American urban environment has always been influenced by a variety of personal, class, ethnic and regional responses.

Between 1790 and 1900 the United States became nineteen times more populous, increased the number of her urban places about seventy-two times, attained the world's highest mean living standard, the highest rate of population growth, and probably the most blurred and socially-mobile society. As urbanization increased, so did the literary tendency to denigrate the American city, and the list of anti-urbanists included some impressive names: Adams, Dewey, Emerson, Hawthorne, Henry James, Jefferson, Melville, Poe, Sullivan and Frank Lloyd Wright. Walt Whitman, William James and the urban sociologist Robert Park spoke up for the city, but in general the verdict of the intellectuals was that it had subverted traditional American values (White and White 1962). From the early twentieth century professional city planners did their best to remove this legacy of fear; in the interim, successive waves of immigration accentuated the problem of congestion and ordinary city folk simply made what they could of their urban environment.

For many years the national urban 'policy', if it could be described as such, was merely commercial-expansionist, permitting any local standards and management practices which did not conflict with mercantile contracts or with the general democratic constitutions from which the city charters were derived. Yet most American cities were dominated by profit-minded oligarchies content to subordinate social and other environmental needs to the pursuit of growth: even in the best of the hundreds of 'proprietor' towns built between 1775 and 1906 there was a rapid collapse of planning controls, due mainly to the failure of the sponsors to anticipate or respond to the desires of residents and to control internal or peripheral growth. Private developers therefore chose to reject comprehensive planning and used instead an elementary and repetitive grid pattern which was normally cheap, quick and simple to prepare and describe, capable of a variety of uses and an excellent facility for rapid expansion. Very little provision was made for permanent open spaces or neighbourhood foci, public controls were usually only permissive, preferential location was accordingly allowed to the commercial-industrial functions because of their high ability to pay, and even before the motor car the needs of the pedestrian and resident were placed after those of high-speed traffic.

But the haphazard physical growth and social disorder accompanying the *laissez-faire* approach to American urbanization also stimulated increasing demands for amenity, systematic physical reorganization and social reform. Public gardens had appeared by the 1820s; 'naturalistic' suburbs and *cul-de-sacs* by the following decade; major city parks for passive recreation by the 1850s; boulevards and garden suburbs, decorative leisure-resorts and planned industrial communities by the 1870s; metropolitan park and playground systems for active recreation by the 'nineties; civic centres by the turn of the century. Yet there were always a few prominent reformers who resisted the claim that physical order was any guarantee of social order. In the 1830s, for example, Theodore Parker campaigned for a new 'industrial democracy' based on improved health standards, better working conditions and the provision of low-rent housing. Later, Henry George, Edward Bellamy, Henry Demarest Lloyd, several reformist mayors, the National Municipal League and just a few academics, variously promoted a radical reorganization of society and economy, including the democratization of local government, urban renewal, garden cities and the scientific analysis of the urbanization process. Towards the end of the nineteenth century and in the early years of the twentieth, although changing economic forces and transportation and construction technologies still played a dominant role, the social geography and physical structure of the American city were increasingly determined by this commitment to fundamental reform, and above all by the growing desire for a revitalization of the treasured sense of community which the reformers believed had been savagely eroded by the previous urbanization experience. The preferred territorial base and the selection of appropriate mechanisms for the reconstruction process varied between the extremes of the very small and distinctive 'neighbourhood' unit and the idea of a grand 'metropolitan' community spirit; in practice these ideas were neither mutually exclusive nor indeed restricted to individual cities or groups of cities (Tunnard and Reed 1955; Hancock 1967; Schmitt 1969).

Settlement houses and the institutionalized churches fought in Chicago and elsewhere for the establishment of neighbourhood parks and playgrounds, and for tenement reform and the development of social centres. In Cincinnati, local residents were organized to plan some of their own recreational facilities and health care; the emphasis in Rochester was on opening State schools after normal hours for community purposes. At the 'metropolitan' level, the concern was rather for redevelopment and especially the provision for new growth: the harnessing of the suburban thrust was regarded as the salvation of the urban community and, after the middle of the century, scores of cities cast their administrative nets over the surrounding satellite areas and established metropolitan police, port and park authorities to accommodate the sprawl. By the mid-'eighties, however, advocates of this metropolitan perspective had adopted some of the neighbourhood strategies to create new communities on the cities' peripheries. The garden suburb of Mariemont, Cincinnati, for example, was financed by a private philanthropist for the 'respectable working class' and, before the end of the century, George Pullman constructed an industrial suburb near Chicago in an effort to provide work, housing and community services—and also model citizens, it can be assumed.

Daniel H. Burnham's comprehensive plan for the development of metropolitan Chicago was far grander and made Chicago the pace-setter in the metropolitan planning movement. Burnham acted in 1893 as the chief architect of the Columbian Exposition, Chicago's World Fair. He was equally convinced that 'Beauty has always paid better than any other commodity' and that 'good citizenship is the prime object of city planning', and the activating symbol of his 'City Beautiful' exhibition made an immediate impact on citizen groups and urban administrators who visited the Fair. Between 1906 and 1909, in association with Edward H. Bennett, Burnham supervised the immensely influential *Plan of Chicago*, which established both a broad physical framework for future development and a series of proposals for immediate implementation. It is essential to note, however, that this powerful design was sponsored by the Commercial Club of Chicago and that from the outset it was based upon an acceptance of what might be called 'the metropolitan imperative'. It did not propose to decentralize or to alter drastically the role and physical character of the central business district, and in fact it heartily endorsed the principle of continued peripheral expansion and hoped to provide for institutions and physical facilities which would underline unity and social integration as the desired expansion proceeded (Mayer and Wade 1969).

More militant *national* reforms were introduced during the Progressive Era, especially between 1906 and the end of the First World War. It was a time for what John Dewey called 'constructive social engineering', which saw the abandonment of *laissez-faire* and a strong mandate for renewal which encouraged all parties to call in their 'expert planning advisors'. Urban housing, as in Britain, was the focus of most public concern at this time, and led directly towards an increasing pressure upon local governments to take steps towards controlling the physical pattern of the city, to provide new services and to restrain the socially harmful activities of individuals. Between 1900 and 1917 over 100 towns undertook some form of comprehensive planning, and this number included half of the nation's fifty largest cities; the principle of land-use 'zoning' was not at first popular with the middle-class reform groups, but it was widely publicized and eventually successfully introduced, in New York City in 1916 and later in Chicago. In this same period the American City Planning Institution was founded, urban planning courses in various guises were offered at the universities, and in 1909 the first National Conference on City Planning and Problems of Congestion—later entitled more simply the N.C.C.P., dropping the second half of the original name—was convened at Washington. Supported by the Russell Sage Foundation, the publications of the N.C.C.P. offered the chief forum and promotional agent for planning ideas. Also in that notable year of 1909, when Patrick Abercrombie performed the same function at Liverpool's School of Civic Design, J. S. Pray introduced his 'Principles of City Planning' course to a class at Harvard. In addition, Benjamin Marsh's textbook *Introduction to City Planning* first appeared and Harrison's and Kellogg's impressive *Pittsburgh Survey* was completed, with its extensive repertoire of statistical and cartographical techniques representing a wealth of data on population, health, housing, building use and condition, traffic, property values, school areas and other impedimenta which were to become so familiar to the growing army of professional planners (Walker 1949; Scott 1969).

*

The development of professional town planning in the Western World during the twentieth century cannot be understood without reference to its major antecedents—without considering, in some detail, two types of motivation which were frequently interrelated but had significantly different philosophical origins and modes of expression. The first was based upon a deep concern for urban form and a search for the ideal city from an architectural viewpoint; the other was the search for the ideal community. Differences in approach between the young planning organizations in the United States and Britain at the end of our period should not be exaggerated: clearly, there were these similar antecedents and the situation in each country was of course still very fluid. Yet planning in Australia was undoubtedly influenced by all the developments we have described, and the preliminaries to this final section would therefore be incomplete if it was not pointed out that a relatively wider concept of planning, with a peculiarly modern flavour, was then being proclaimed in America at the highest levels of the new profession.

There was more than an echo of Patrick Geddes' social philosophy in the 1910 address of N.C.C.P. president Frederick Law Olmsted jr, who spoke of the planners' recognition of the city as 'one great social organism whose welfare is in part determined by the action of the people who compose the organism today, and therefore by the collective intelligence and good will that control those actions'. Olmsted and his senior colleagues were agreed that their profession should not be totally concerned with the physical structure of the city, and that it need not always be involved in patching up or in mere beautification. Urban planning had indeed to become properly engaged with its client, the public, in the identification, expansion and communication of available options; it had to become an agent for enhancing city life in a rapidly changing, increasingly urban world. Their acceptance of an essentially reformist attitude towards the urban environment as a vital and complex resource was obviously based upon a growing recognition of the city as a dynamic human system which could be directed and improved to some degree by deliberate public action, which they understood to include the ideal of comprehensive planning. The rhetoric continued to improve, but town planning remained for the most part a middle-class movement, within and outside the profession itself. In addition, in the United States as in Britain, there was usually insufficient appreciation of the close relationship between some of the declared social objectives of the town planners and the need for radical *economic* planning. And in both countries the original vision became more clouded, was even betrayed, in later years; yet the promise remains.

12 Urban Management and Town Planning in Australia

> Eutopia, then, lies in the city around us; and it must be planned and realized, here or nowhere, by us as its citizens—each a citizen of both the actual and the ideal city seen increasingly as one (Geddes 1915: vii).

Three successively larger building booms between 1860 and 1890 absorbed about one-third of Australia's total investment, transformed the urban scene, created enormous problems for the cities' managers and led directly to the depression of the 'nineties. Most importantly, suburban expansion and the rapid development of the commercial cores quickly outstripped the ability of the local authorities to provide basic services and the resulting deterioration of living conditions eventually provoked a good deal of public concern, which led to a sustained and forceful restatement of each facet of the old question: what were the human consequences of urbanization for all classes of society, and how would these effects be accurately measured; how were Australians to cope with growing inequities in the urban environment and with the increasing centralization of population and power; how might they attempt the alternative or associated strategy of some form of decentralization? Even in the booming 'eighties some doubts were expressed about the trend of events, and by the early twentieth century the infant town planning movement was gaining ground in each State in its campaign for the introduction of 'rational' urban development programmes.

God Against Mammon, Postponed

The port-capitals were tight bottlenecks of British and European capital and it was often claimed that the investors' representatives in Australia had little or no interest or experience beyond the main cities. This was exaggerated, but it is not difficult to imagine the availability of overseas funds assisting directly or indirectly in stirring the frenetic land boom of the 'eighties. From the viewpoint of the history of urban management, however, it is more useful to concentrate upon the local actors.

The contradictions in the contemporary image of urban land as a resource were more apparent than real, and the image itself was clearly the inheritance of earlier experience in town and country. Nourished in the high optimism of the 'eighties, one distinctive feature of the great suburban dream was certainly the distortion of the old ideal of a rural Arcady. The widespread yearning for security—and for comfort, status, even a degree of independence —after so many years of uncertainty, and of locational and occupational mobility, was at least as well satisfied by a decent house on its own piece of the city's periphery as on a back-breaking country selection. There was indeed an abundance of testimony by this time, including the best of practical testimony from actual participants, to support a rejection of the traditional 'yeoman' ideal. In addition, the urban situation presented quite as many opportunities as the rural sector for outright speculation or sober investment.

Speculation was a particularly well-established trait in the Australian Colonies, and land continued to provide the obvious outlet. When rationalization was required, the conservative view was always available. It asserted the inalienable right of the individual to own private land, and extremists of this persuasion proceeded logically enough to reject all forms of State interference in the investment of capital in private property—so that, with the exception of the useful tariff umbrella in Victoria, any attempt to direct the choice of land utilization was also indignantly brushed aside. Furthermore, it had been argued from the earliest days of Wakefieldian theorizing, and was still stoutly proclaimed, that the attainment of property ownership was an integral part of the immigrant's assimilation and therefore a most worthy goal, almost a measure of acceptance, or identity, for every patriotic citizen. In contrast, the land reformers naturally took their arguments from J. S. Mill, Henry George and others, often via the *Age's* David Syme and other local savants who passionately insisted on the sanctity of land, which they placed above all other types of property (*Age*, 1 January 1881). Significantly, however, their proposals for well-regulated land-use controls, community ownership, leasing and so on won far more approval from urban residents and their elected representatives when they were pointed towards the management of the *rural* environment.

The extraordinary success of the building societies, first established in the 'forties, contributed massively to the process of suburban expansion. They survived and prospered by identifying the simple utilitarian dream and by vigorously promoting it, while at the same time demonstrating an unmatched capacity to deliver the desired product. The *Age* (14 April 1881) claimed that the societies had absorbed a far greater proportion of the savings of the ordinary working families than in any other part of the world, and it was plain enough that the strategy they employed was usually pointed at the working classes: 'the first, the paramount duty of a working man is to acquire a home' (*Australian Financial Gazette* 1890). In 1891 there were thirty-two Land Banks, Building and Investment companies in Sydney, with assets of almost £8 millions; in the same year Victoria had eighty-one registered Building Societies which were owed £8.5 millions in the city and suburbs. Many of the latter were said to be *de facto* banks, and efficient covers for a wide range of speculative activity (Campbell 1970). Yet in general, the services provided by these institutions facilitated a more rapid and possibly more profligate expansion than might otherwise have been possible. They normally lent up to 80 per cent on a £40-£50 deposit and although their clients were predominantly drawn from the less wealthy classes—who for a time fared better thereby than they had ever hoped—inadequate supervision from the societies and from Government permitted that unfortunate Australian tradition of cheap and repetitive, speculative building to become more deeply entrenched. Our present suburban townscapes still display this ambiguous record.

It is difficult to over-estimate the social value of the work that has been done by building societies. In the suburbs of large towns you see whole townships built entirely by these societies; every inhabitant of these townships in the course of a few years becomes a proprietor, and the society further aids him by making loans to him on mortgage of his property. It is the defect of these townships that the houses are all as alike as one another as peas in a pod—four-roomed squares or six-roomed oblongs built of red brick, and with every detail exactly the same; but their plainness and similarity does not detract from their manifest virtues (Twopeny 1883: 37).

The urban land rush accelerated existing trends and effected an environmental transformation which was certainly more subtle but possibly no less drastic or durable than that produced by the gold-miners of an earlier generation. The miner himself was then a little less busy in the provinces, but most of the cast in this new and elaborate metropolitan production were also experienced contributors to the colonial scene—the politician, speculator, administrator, builder, developer, immigrant group, merchant, building society, architect, industrialist, real estate agent, transport company and, of course, the Australian public as crowd, general chorus and financial backer. The functional geography and social ecology of the city was moulded by their interaction and a powerful framework was thereby erected to dominate all subsequent developments in the urban environment.

Speculators and merchant princes built their stately homes at the end of the railway and tramway lines, and the developers and real estate agents combined to ensure the emergence of socially distinct suburban areas and a maximum profit for themselves. Two successful International Exhibitions, less magnificent than Chicago's incomparable Columbian Exposition but similar in their influence upon local ideas, were held in Sydney in 1879 and in Melbourne during the following year. Melbourne's Exhibition Building was constructed at a cost of over £250,000 and with its annexes it covered almost twenty-two acres, all of them packed with modern promotions and the whole resounding with the announcement that Victoria was swiftly becoming one of Britain's leading colonies in industrial as well as agricultural affairs. 'The hybrid Florentine French' style of the major building encouraged an orgy of display and decoration in the new business houses and suburban mansions of the boom era. The mass production of intricate and showy ornamental cast iron, zinc ornamental roofing finishes, metal ceilings, highly modelled and decorative plasterwork and the like, enabled Australians of every class to indulge their lavish and often eccentric tastes in some way. The first passenger lift to be exhibited in Australia was shown at the Sydney Exhibition. It was then possible to erect taller buildings for a more intensive and profitable use of the central business districts for giant hotels, insurance houses and department stores. At first, this met the increasing pressure of higher land prices following the improvements in rapid transit and the parallel development of mass commuting, but inevitably, in the absence of intervening controls, the same process set up a chain reaction which continues today.

In urban as in rural Australia individuals and groups discovered that the inadequacies of the broader management setting forced them to set about achieving their own solutions, according to their own perception of the changing situation. But the major result for cities was that most physical change was brought about by 'private interests under public auspices for speculative purposes', and the weakest members of society were pushed to the wall.

17   The Elaborate New South Wales Court at the Melbourne Exhibition, 1880

There was always vigorous competition between New South Wales and Victoria, which were considered to be the two most successfully 'developed' of the young Australian Colonies. Each used the Exhibition to announce its achievements and advertise its wares—to display its faith in the honoured symbols of material progress. Rural and urban environments throughout Australia had other tales to tell, but the quest for profit and material security entirely consumed the attention of all but a small number of prominent groups and individuals.

Urban Australia did not suffer the extremes of wealth and poverty which had produced such fine humanitarian responses and community experiments in Britain and the United States; nor was there the ethnic heterogeneity which posed so many problems in the great North American centres. The mix of social problems in the Australian cities was not essentially different, however, except in its types of emphasis and the generally smaller scale. And, since it was another nominally Christian nation, one expects the Christian churches to have had some impact upon the general response.

Yet throughout Australia the churches were wracked with internal theological disputes and inter-denominational rivalry, and their reactions to the challenge of science frequently resulted in prolonged and agonizing public debates. Nevertheless the leading Christian denominations still exercised an important influence in the management of social problems in each Australian city, even though their definitions of what constituted a social issue were often as narrow and disappointing as their solutions. In the United States the strong negative response to new immigrants in the inner urban areas was based upon an image of the anti-Christ, anti-American ghetto of strange languages or accents, overcrowding and poverty, and an equally 'foreign' townscape punctuated by saloons, Roman Catholic churches and synagogues. In Melbourne several Protestant churches in the inner city were virtually empty in the 'eighties; their diminishing congregations had moved off to the prosperous suburbs, sometimes to dwindle still further. The replacement population in the central districts was largely Irish and Catholic, together with working-class Protestants and other groups who knew little about what the churches were offering. By 1890 the high-status Wesley Church in the heart of the city was an isolated and besieged island surrounded by 'low-class Roman Catholics, in great numbers, and the fallen and criminal classes, with a large admixture of Jews, Chinese and Indians', and the bitter and frustrated ministers of the Church of England archipelago complained that 'more and more of the respectable classes are pushing out into the suburbs, and leaving behind them a great mass of semi-heathenism for us to cope with' (Howe 1972). In the 'eighties few senior churchmen or prominent lay-men of any denomination chose to question the consuming materialism of the day; with some notable exceptions there were no major demands for a thorough investigation of the inequities in the expanding city, no urgent and sustained campaigns for an alternative means of channelling the desired development to benefit all classes. This was particularly unfortunate, for institutionalized religion continued to wield considerable influence, despite its problems. Political parties and organized pressure groups were not yet strongly defined and the churches consequently had great political po-tential. But their most energetic work was based upon a superficial diagnosis which did very little at first to counteract the most pernicious effects of rapid urbanization. They became engrossed in the treatment of a small selection of symptoms which were principally affronts to their own brand of moral conscience, seldom recognizing a number of other distressing features of city life which faced the majority of the poorer residents. Evangelical Pro-testantism, for example, was particularly strong in Melbourne, where several inter-denominational groups were formed to purge that city of its immorality. In 1880 the Melbourne United Evangelistic Association published a short pamphlet entitled *Melbourne and its Sin*, an interesting document which proved to be remarkably popular. In 1882 the Society for the Promotion of Morality was revived with great success and launched a very lively campaign for temperance reform, Sunday observance and new legislation against pro-stitution. Melbourne's reputation as the headquarters of Australian 'wow-serism' was assured; yet some of the leading wowsers could have been justly accused of having or condoning double standards, since they included within their ranks a number of the city's busiest speculators (Cannon 1966; Dunstan 1968). The unusually liberal Presbyterian Dr Charles Strong; the Baptist Minister S. Chapman; Dr John Singleton and a few other prominent Chris-tians, chose instead to address themselves to the slum problem. Then the Salvation Army set up its first corps, at North Melbourne in December 1882, and it achieved far better results in its practical social work than any of the established churches; by the end of the 'eighties its British leader General William Booth proudly recorded the favourable public and official recog-nition the Army had won in Victoria for its work with convicted and habitual criminals and among the destitute and unemployed (Booth 1890: 275-6;

Serle 1971: 153-75; for a general statement on this period see Howe 1972). With the deepening of the depression in the 'nineties there was an intensification of much of this work to redeem the inner city, and in the harbour districts of Sydney, for example, Archdeacon F.B. Boyce predicted dire catastrophes for the slum dwellers if they were not rehoused and their vile hovels demolished. Some of the best energy of 'Christian Socialism' at this time, however, was also directed towards a wholesale condemnation of the city as an environment for decent family life, and this antagonism was a prime motivation in the formation of scores of those 'Village Settlements' already mentioned, in which thrift, temperance and Sunday observance were almost as frequently prescribed as the ideal of co-operation itself.

Australia's cities in the late nineteenth century had obviously failed to develop efficient management systems to deal with their problems and make the most of their opportunities, and the work of the voluntary organizations did not compensate for fundamental weaknesses in the administrative machinery. Yet, as in Britain and North America, there was a growing realization in some quarters of the benefits to be gained by increasing the scale of spatial organization and administrative co-ordination. So in Melbourne in 1874 a municipal conference proposed the formation of a Board of Works to examine and supervise a wide range of problems and facilities for the area within a radius of ten miles of the city centre, including water supplies, sewerage, river control, noxious trades, parks, tramway systems and hackney carriages. The issue was then shelved, but the general acceptance of the well-publicized, real and supposed relationship between water supply, sewerage and public health virtually guaranteed some major administrative reform (cf. Powell 1973a). Shortly after the report of the Royal Commission on the Sanitary Condition of Melbourne, the Melbourne and Metropolitan Board of Works was created in 1890 and modelled on the lately deceased and unlamented London and Metropolitan Board of Works. The M.M.B.W. was granted considerable autonomy in its designated function as the supreme authority for water supply and sewerage, and was indeed subject only to Parliament rather than to any individual minister, but the same degree of autonomy was retained over the years as the Board accumulated more and more responsibilities, until it became the example *par excellence* of *ad hoc* institutional growth—and possibly Australia's most frequently cited obstacle to adaptive comprehensive planning. It is therefore useful to recall that its first commission was particularly large, obvious and very basic, as yet another invited overseas consultant reminded his Victorian audience.

Accustomed as I have been in most towns for the last 30 years to the use of a decent water-closet, I found some of the appliances in vogue in Melbourne sickening and digusting.

In a few of our north country towns the pail system still exists with as little excuse as in Melbourne, but it is gradually dying out. The consensus of opinion among sanitarian experts is in favour of the immediate removal of all human refuse from the proximity of human habitations without the assistance of manual labour.

I hold this opinion very strongly. The material does not improve by keeping. The true policy is to get it off the premises as rapidly as possible (Mansergh 1890: 18).

The visit of Beatrice and Sidney Webb contributed less than it promised to the debate: despite their proven administrative skills and varied practical experience, their diary shows an unfortunate blend of insularity and puritanism which surely reduced their value as observers and advisers (Austin 1965). Interest in the 'metropolitan' solution was then running high in each of the Australian capitals, but it proved too difficult to disentangle the competing strategies of 'unification' and 'federation'. The creation of the M.M.B.W. was one of many compromises. Rather than remodel the existing inefficient structure, politicians, public servants and technicians chose the easier way of forming a mixture of *ad hoc* bodies or government departments to provide the expensive services required by the urban community, and one of the results was that the various municipalities found themselves competing with each other and with the new agencies and departments when they were seeking financial aid (Laverty 1972). The chaotic and capricious development resulting from this excessive fragmentation produced a situation which would have been both alarming and challenging for the most gifted practitioner of integrated planning. There were few enough of those in the late nineteenth-century world, and none in Australia.

Yet in this respect Australia once again had the good fortune to attract some immigrants of extraordinary ability and determination who lifted the standards of service provided by their own profession. The accomplished architect John Sulman, for example, arrived in Sydney in 1885 at the age of thirty-six. He had then established a fine reputation in Britain and had already been elected president of the Architectural Association, which carried with it an entitlement to a seat on the council of the R.I.B.A., when he decided instead to emigrate to the warmer climate of Australia in an effort to seek a cure for his wife's tuberculosis. Perhaps only the aggressive Canadian immigrant John Horbury Hunt did more than Sulman to raise the professional standards of the architects of New South Wales during this period (Freeland 1971), but Sulman had a wider influence throughout Australia and was closer than most of his colleagues to the ideas of the nascent town planning movement in Britain. The private anguish behind his decision to emigrate to Australia can only have reinforced his professional commitment to the promotion of a new ethic of public service which placed community welfare above the claims of the individual client. On a number of occasions within a few years of his arrival, but especially in an address to the Melbourne meeting of the A.A.A.S. in 1890, he questioned the freedoms allowed to private owners and developers and insisted on the right and duty of the State to impose stricter controls over preparatory planning. Public health and amenity were his principal concerns, and although his ideas did not gain the publicity they deserved, he soon built a small nucleus of support which included several leading architects, engineers and surveyors.

Sulman was made Secretary to the Research Committee appointed to consider his important paper, and the succinct report presented to the Association at its next meeting in Christchurch, New Zealand, heartily endorsed his arguments. The Committee recommended that urgent steps be taken to persuade the colonial governments to pay due consideration to such factors as the choice of healthy sites and the necessity for fixing a minimum size for building allotments. It also noted the desirability of establishing and maintaining the combined acreage of streets and reserves at about one-third of the total area leased or sold, and favoured the restriction of 'towns and suburbs'—which they defined as sub-divisional schemes containing allotments of less than one acre—to areas of no more than two square miles, divided one from the other wherever possible by belts of reserved land at least one-eighth of a mile wide. One member suggested in a separate statement that the land devoted to recreational purposes alone should be at least one-third of the total and arranged so that no part of the built-up area was more than half a mile from a reserve; he also emphasized the potentially complementary roles of road engineers and landscape architects. The final recommendation was a call for more official recognition of the 'professional' principles of thorough preparation and expert supervision.

> 7. That, to give effect to the above, plans of every town or suburban sub-division be submitted to a specially-appointed official or board for approval, and that without such approval no sale or lease be valid. That the official or board veto the plan if any of the foregoing stipulations be not complied with, and further require that a satisfactory scheme of surface-drainage, sewerage, and water-supply be submitted for future realisation, such scheme to show contour-levels and all natural features (Report on Towns 1892: 541).

In his Presidential Address at the same Christchurch meeting, Sulman hammered home this point when he expressed the hope that a general planning council would soon be established to control all town planning affairs in New South Wales; and the great day did arrive, *seventy-two years later* (Sulman 1892).

But there was little discussion in the closing years of that century about the related processes of city growth and the development of 'city-regions', and therefore nothing significant was said, apparently, about the opportunities a new country could offer for the creation of integrated systems of new towns. The best of ideas during this period were derivative and selective; even dated, to some extent. The principle of participatory planning underlying the reasonably democratic administrative system proposed by Ebenezer Howard, for example (Figure 16), received very little attention in the young Australian democracy before the First World War. Sulman himself, despite his relatively progressive thinking, seems to have honestly believed that the function of the technical expert included telling people what they required and what they should expect to get; like many future planners he found it difficult to concede that democratic controls ought to be built into every phase of the planning process, that the work of planners should never be insulated from the political process. This is not to diminish a man who was then so far ahead of his contemporaries in several respects; if this type of criticism is to be made at all about his work, it is more relevantly put in the context of our next section, which deals with the later years. In fact, far more interest was aroused before the turn of the century in the continuing controversy over the expansion of metropolitan forms of government—two interesting but inconclusive 'Greater Sydney' conferences were held in 1900 for example—and there were undoubtedly many who, like the designers of Chicago's famous plan, were fully prepared to accommodate to what they saw as the inevitability of increasing urbanization. So Hayter,

Victoria's excellent Government Statistician, predicted an acceleration of the recent trends and yet looked confidently to suburbanization and the provision of urban open space to offset the disadvantages of the continuing metropolitan concentration of Australia's population. His statistical guides already incorporated a 'Greater Melbourne' division to take in the area within ten miles radius of the city centre (Hayter 1893).

People and Planning, 1900-14

The dire prophecies of Archdeacon Boyce were horribly realized in March 1900 when bubonic plague wrought havoc in the Rocks area of Sydney, a deprived and criminally neglected district near the wharves around Darling Harbour. The Rocks Resumption Board was hastily assembled in May 1901 and the 'Redevelopment' of blighted areas henceforth became as important to the architects as the debates on suburban design. The 'structuralist' or environmentalist approach was again displayed in the recommendations made by a Royal Commission which reported unsuccessfully at the end of the decade on the pressing need, felt mainly by engineers and architects, for further demolition and redevelopment, the extension of surface and underground transportation facilities, and so on. To be fair, it should also be recorded that the Commissioners recommended the provision of additional housing within the financial reach of poorer citizens, and they called for new legislation after the pattern of the British 1909 Act to empower local councils to undertake their own planning schemes (Winston 1957). Another important sequel in New South Wales was the appointment of a powerful statutory authority, the Sydney Harbour Trust. This decision was heavily criticized by local Labor politicians because the Trust was not an elected body; the basic idea was of course welcomed by those who shared John Sulman's view that politics was a harmful 'intrusion' into a situation demanding only technical expertise and thoroughly professional co-operation (Sulman 1907). The opposing argument for municipal and social reform above all other considerations was best presented by Labor's knowledgeable spokesman J. D. Fitzgerald (1906). Following the election of a Labor Government, however, and the advice and encouragement of R. F. Irvine, the Professor of Economics at Sydney University, Sulman and Fitzgerald actually joined forces to plan Daceyville Garden Suburb in 1912-13.

To some extent these immediate pre-war years did mark the culmination of an extremely significant burst of activity in every State and, notably, 1913 also saw the formal inauguration of Canberra, 'the city beautiful of our dreams' (Sydney Morning Herald, 27 December 1913). But it would be incorrect to say that a definite turning point had been reached, for the two major streams of thought which fed the planning movement still favoured different courses: deliberate and sincere efforts were made to combine them from time to time, but the union was neither complete nor reliable. Nevertheless, in Sydney Town Hall on 17 October 1913, Australia's first Town Planning Association was formed, its membership sporting the expected colour range from the purest of blues to a most violent crimson, and including a rich mixture of architects, municipal administrators, social reformers, engineers, surveyors and, need it be said, some of Australia's most astute real estate men. Although the choice of dominant hues varied from State to State, each of the other town planning groups naturally exhibited the same generous colour range.

In Melbourne the debate on metropolitan unification or federation consumed most of the energies of those engaged in the planning movement, but in the prevailing social and political climate this frustrating episode merely wasted valuable time. The municipal franchise still favoured property owners, the ultra-conservative Legislative Council retained its power to check the efforts of the Lower House, and the wealthier municipalities jealously protected their privileged positions from any attempt which they perceived as a 'revolutionary' design to swamp them with the voting strength of the lower orders. In the circumstances, it was easier to create a series of new and independent metropolitan authorities, or to graft still more limbs on to the lumbering octopus of the M.M.B.W.—the beast of all burdens with an astonishing capacity to convert energy into muscle, which soon enabled it to provide for its own prodigious growth.

The urban-based Labor movement was gaining strength in Victoria, however, and the housing issue became a central plank in its reform platform. In 1913 a Joint Select Committee was appointed to consider metropolitan housing and the witnesses called at seven useful meetings included Arthur Pearson, president of the Minimum Allotment, Anti-Slum and Housing Crusade Committee and John Baxter Huggan, its Secretary; W. H. Renwick, the organizer of the Free Trade and Land Values League; James William Barrett, a well-known physician; also town clerks, surveyors, police constables with experience in Port Melbourne, South Melbourne, Fitzroy and Carlton, the Commonwealth Statistician George Handley Knibbs and Dr John Smyth, the principal of Melbourne's Teachers' Training College. Poverty, crime, health, education, administration, land reform: what was to be done for a youthful patient suffering from so many complaints? The British Act of 1909 was repeatedly quoted. Pearson emphasized the need for similar legislation, not only to provide for housing reform and urban renewal, but also to guarantee certain minimum standards for active and passive recreation space—that 10 per cent of any newly developed area should be set aside for parks, recreational reserves and children's playgrounds, and garden space around each new dwelling should be at least twice as great as the area occupied by the house. Like Irvine in Sydney, Barrett's particular concern was the absence of decent and inexpensive housing: 'It is futile to abolish slums without providing some place where the slum population can live. It is equally futile to erect houses, the rents of which are quite out beyond the reach of the slum dweller'. In areas such as Collingwood, it would be preferable to improve existing properties and to engage in the renovation and restructuring of the general environment; children's playgrounds were especially needed in these areas. Barrett was also an ardent supporter of Garden Cities and Garden Suburbs. Fisherman's Bend on the Yarra, he suggested, offered a good opportunity for a small experiment along these lines and, if necessary, British experts should be invited over to act as design consultants. Smyth's disturbing testimony revealed that, since the British minimum standard for school playground space was then fifty square feet per child, and although the London County Council had had to settle for a mere thirty square feet, the situation in several of the schools in Melbourne's inner suburbs was surely the worst of advertisements for a new country—Faraday Street School in Carlton, with 650 children, had eighteen square feet of playing space per child; the school at Princes Hill had twenty-two square feet for each of its 1,100 pupils; the 700 school-children at Rathdown Street were comparatively fortunate, with an average of about thirty-nine square feet, but this was still less than 80 per cent of the standard British allowance. As statistical data of all kinds was amassed in every part of the world, bold comparisons like this were made to serve a variety of purposes. Yet Smyth's timely observations appeared to be particularly well calculated to challenge New World pride, to produce the type of unsettling effect which often leads to a healthy revision of attitudes, improved adaptation, even innovation. Huggan's efforts to demonstrate that many municipalities had less than 5 per cent, frequently less than 2 per cent, of their areas devoted to parks, gardens and recreation areas, should be seen in the same light.

The Commonwealth Statistician might have contributed similar ammunition, but he restricted his evidence to the presentation of data relating to population and housing densities per municipality in 1901 and 1911 in Melbourne and Sydney. Allowing for the much greater topographical variety in the Sydney region, the picture was basically similar in each city, with heavy concentration in the centre and a decline towards the periphery. The density of population and occupied dwellings per acre had increased in every Melbourne municipality and in most areas of Sydney between the two census years, although there was a significant decline in Sydney's commercial heart. The most densely populated municipalities in Melbourne were Fitzroy and Collingwood, with thirty-seven and thirty people respectively per acre in 1911, and the density declined rapidly with distance from the inner districts to less than 0.5 per acre on the outer periphery; the ratio of occupied dwellings per acre declined comparably from 7.3 and 6.2 in Fitzroy and Collingwood to less than 0.5 in the outer suburbs, but the pattern was not maintained in the average number of occupants per house, which ranged from about four to six over the entire region. Several of Sydney's inner areas were more crowded than Melbourne's—Darlington, Newtown, Paddington, Redfern, Erskineville and Glebe were all more densely populated than Fitzroy, and each of the first four of these municipalities accommodated over fifty people to the acre in 1911 (Report on Housing 1913).

Whatever the deficiencies of these statistics they did suggest the practical importance of adding a spatial dimension to the interpretation of the changing urban fabric. As social scientists in North America, Britain and Europe were then discovering, the urban process had its own momentum, its own pathology; and simple statistical indices were found to have great potential as management guides, for they located distinct areas of need and could be made to yield a battery of alternative social and physical geographies of the city, illustrating new textures for more efficient forms of spatial organization. Similar investigations were clearly being pursued in Australia in the immediate pre-war years, but with few tangible results. One promising achievement which emerged from the Melbourne meeting was the *Workers' Dwellings Act*, which received formal assent on 3 February 1914. This Act authorized municipal councils to obtain, by voluntary or compulsory purchase, any land in their municipality which they believed to be suitable for the erection of workers' homes—that is, for the construction and leasing of modest houses to individuals with annual incomes of less than £2,000, provided they did not already own a home. If necessary, councils could borrow up to £50,000 to assist in such purchases. When the final report of the succeeding Royal Commission on the subject was presented in 1918 not a single municipality had taken advantage of the new provisions and it was suggested that their reluctance was mainly due to the leasing restriction: had they been able to sell freehold rights, the councils would have tackled the situation with energy, without losing the confidence of their ratepayers (Report on Housing 1918).

The Victorian Town Planning Association had been formed in 1914 and, like its sister organizations in the other States, its early work was dominated by British influences. A senior architect in the Public Works Department, J. C. Morrell, visited Britain and prepared a detailed official report on recent developments in practice and theory, emphasizing the environmentalist arguments and demonstrating the social and economic necessity for integrated or comprehensive forward planning, as opposed to repeated patching-up operations (Morrell 1915). The impression gained from these years is that there was a definite intensification of the old feeling of isolation and insecurity among many of Australia's professionals. They were now very concerned that they might be falling seriously behind their colleagues in other countries, and in the planning movement at least these fears were highly contagious. Hence the despatching of Morrell to Britain, which was a match for Irvine's commission to investigate the European and American situation for the New South Wales Government. The Western Australian reaction was similar, as Webb (1968) has shown. In 1910 Perth's Town Clerk, W. E. Bold, convinced his council of the value of British, continental European, American and Scandinavian developments in city management, and in 1913 it was decided to finance him on an international tour, which included visits to Garden Cities and Suburbs, new housing estates and the like, and a stopover at the Imperial Health and Town Planning Conference, where he encountered Ebenezer Howard and other celebrities. Bold's subsequent activities in Western Australia included a major role in the campaign for the comprehensive planning of a 'Greater Perth' region, preparing the way for the formation of the local planning association in 1916.

The Webb's description of Adelaide, the most English of Australia's cities, was one of the few useful and generous observations made by the patronizing pair during their tour. Its parklands offered some warm familiarity, a reminder perhaps of the agreeable juxtapositions in the park and office environment of central London. So Sidney Webb, who had contributed so much to the modernization of London's own administration, was moved to declare the South Australian capital 'a charmingly attractive city—wisely planned and full of amenity, unostentatious and refined, courteous and homely'. It was worthy indeed to be compared with the German 'Residenzstadt', the capital of a small principality, and with 'more chance than any other Australian city of becoming the Weimar or, more precisely, the Stuttgart of the Southern Hemisphere' (Austin 1965: 93-4). Certainly, Colonel Light's great design had given the South Australians a type of Garden City about seventy years before Ebenezer Howard's plans began to take shape in Britain, and Adelaide's managers were justifiably proud of the local masterpiece. But they had also become dangerously complacent, too content with the original importation, reluctant to consider more recent developments overseas.

Whereas New South Wales, Victoria and Western Australia had chosen humbly to send out their own reporters to improve their contact with the wider world, the good news was brought to South Australia by Charles C. Reade, a New Zealand journalist who had achieved prominence as a leading member of the Garden Cities and Town Planning Association of Great Britain. Reade arrived in Adelaide on 18 April 1914 bearing 1,000 lantern slides illustrating the ancient and recent history of town planning, and the headlines in the *Adelaide Advertiser* (20 April 1914) conveyed precisely the type of image he hoped to promote during his lecture tour: 'GARDEN CITIES / A Growing Movement / Beauty, Health, and Utility' — a grand announcement, no doubt supplied by Reade himself. He made his first enemies within a few days of his arrival. At a small mayoral reception, Reade was asked by the Acting Mayor, Alderman Lewis Cohen: 'what possible improvements could be made to Adelaide, with its present magnificent parks and gardens', to which the New Zealander calmly replied that there was definitely too much being spent on roads by the various councils and that, so far as he was aware, there was little or no provision for further areas of open space in the expanding suburbs (*Advertiser*, 23 April 1914). The smug Adelaide establishment was further scandalized by Reade's lecture entitled 'Garden Cities versus Adelaide slums and suburbs' and, together with his supporters in the newly-formed South Australian Town Planning and Housing Association, he continued to expose the evils inherent in the *laissez-faire* attitude to urban management.

Reade's skill and persistence eventually won sufficient political and professional support to make a major impact in South Australia, where he was to perform admirably as Government Town Planning Adviser after 1916. The analysis of his later contribution lies beyond the scope of this book; it is admirably discussed in Leonie Sandercock's recent socialist critique of the historical and political development of Australian town planning in the twentieth century, a most persuasive and sustained argument which should very soon gain the wider circulation it requires and deserves (Sandercock 1974). For our present purposes it is important and relevant to mention the Australasian lecture tour jointly undertaken by Reade and another visitor, W. Richard Davidge, which waved the town planning banner very profitably indeed, and the publication of a valuable pamphlet summarizing their main recommendations (Reade and Davidge 1915). Pointing again to the economic and social benefits of prior *planning* as opposed to haphazard *sub-divisioning*, they also stressed the protection of the community's financial investment where planning controls resulted in an increase in land values, the extension and strengthening of regulatory powers and zoning legislation, the provision of cheap, rapid and government-controlled transport systems in every new scheme, and the preservation of green belts, reserves and areas of specific scientific, scenic or historical interest. And they still found time to extol the virtues of the prototype Garden Cities and Garden Suburbs.

*

With increasing knowledge of the relationship between urbanization and regional development, a wider setting was given to the analysis of the city's own problems of 'apoplexy at the centre and anaemia at the extremities'. In Melbourne a report on traffic congestion favoured an extension of the tramway system and produced a useful array of statistical data on urban travel behaviour (Report on Traffic 1919), and in the same city a special commission on the drift of population from the country districts to the metropolis emphasized that the prime task was to discover 'the deficiencies and disabilities surrounding country life, and the exploration of the undeveloped resources of country districts'. Indeed in Victoria, as in every other State, the young Country Party seemed convinced that the welfare of the rural sector was the major concern of 'decentralization'. The Melbourne report discussed the importance of formulating an integrated 'Country Life Policy' in which 'the keynote...must be organization, and a director or specialist will be required to lay out, direct, and supervise the organized methods which the policy involves, and all that is deemed necessary for the development of the resources of each part of the State'. It envisaged the production of detailed regional inventories of soils, climate, natural resources and marketing and transportation facilities, the promotion of farmers' and other community associations, a reformed system of technical education and surveys of regional 'adaptability' (Report on Population 1918).

Two Australasian Town Planning Conferences towards the end of the war, in Adelaide in 1917 and in Brisbane during the following year, advertised the arrival of planning as a recognized profession and at the same time the material presented illustrated the continuing dominance of architects and administrators. Problems of poverty, speculation, traffic engineering, and the financial viability and commercial utility of planning were also discussed, however, and it was clear that one or two of the leading figures had expanded their vision of the tasks before them. Sulman, for example, moving closer to American and British thinking, was now arguing for fully balanced and virtually self-contained suburbs separated one from the other by rural land, none to contain more than 30,000 inhabitants; and Fitzgerald, that same Fitzgerald, was demonstrating that planning was a good business proposition for any city. But there was still deep disagreement over the fundamental basis of *power:* should the crucial decisions be taken by an 'independent' body of technical experts in each State, or should the final control be the local council? The Adelaide conference recommended in favour of local authorities with the right of broader control reserved to the State Government; this recommendation was later diluted when the Brisbane conference opted for a useless midway position and the issue is still unresolved. The planners, like the administrators, showed proper professional decorum. The inspirational reformist zeal was on the wane; increasingly, when they spoke of people, they meant themselves.

V Australian Approaches to Environmental Management: a Conclusion

THE historical-cultural perspective attempted in this book is no more than a tentative exploration of a number of themes of recognized significance today, acknowledging that it would be premature to attempt a more comprehensive treatment of any of the selected areas at this stage. Australia's changing society urgently requires further descriptive and critical analyses of the evolution of present management systems for the natural and built environments, and the type of preliminary survey offered here is simply intended as a small contribution towards the clarification of a relevant and challenging field for teaching and research, which recent developments suggest will soon command its due attention in this country.

More specialized interpretations are required for each of the major resource areas mapped out in this book; indeed, with other researchers, I may revise some of the opinions stated here as we increase our meagre knowledge of the early management of Australia's land, water, forests and cities. Detailed interpretations of environmental attitudes and behaviour in these crucial areas seem to be fundamental to a more general understanding of the ways in which Australian society has used and abused its natural and man-made environments. Yet even within the present framework, rather more attention could and possibly should have been paid to the role of scientific and technical innovations, and the development of techniques for the diffusion of those innovations: soil, seed, harvesting and livestock-breeding improvements, climatological and zoological research, changing methods of exploration, extraction and conservation in the mining industry, and so on, could all be included within the broad interpretation of 'resource management' outlined in the introductory statement. Were it possible to treble the size of the present volume these would represent the major additions I would prefer to make, while also intensifying the present social, economic and political perspective on each of the selected themes.

The materials for a more expanded discussion may soon be available. Investigations of transportation innovations, for example, both technical and managerial, are highly relevant, especially where they are concerned with the perception and management of distance and location, dynamically interrelated resources of central importance in examining the Australian experience. Entrepreneurial activity and improved methods of marketing and investment behaviour, on the foreign and domestic scenes, could be added to the list; so too could the study of changing emphases in education, especially the development of new forms of technical education. And there is clearly a need for further examination of the part played by 'regional identity' in the management of resource allocation and settlement evolution— the significance, that is, of the identification and elucidation of specific natural regions, as well as the social and political implications of some forms of territoriality: of the attachment to place, the deep sense of regionalism occasionally manifested in certain areas of Australia. In these latter respects the mystique of the 'desert heart', the enigmatic tropical north, and the implications of 'new States' movements for the spatial organization of resource management, demand intensive effort of the kind which some commentators persist in calling 'interdisciplinary'. Too much of the present analysis has had to be concentrated on the favoured sectors of the continent where the vast majority of its people have sought a living, but these were always parts of a much greater unit and however convenient their dissection, the investigation cannot be accepted as complete without further careful consideration of the interrelationships within the broader setting.

When compared with some of the more rigorous methodology employed increasingly in the social sciences, the breadth of choice presented by any demanding type of historical-cultural approach must to some greater degree expose the predilections and scholarly deficiencies, and the doubts, convictions and commitments—social and therefore also political—of the individual worker. But the judgement or opinion it yields need not be less valuable for discarding the comfortable cloak of anonymity. Suggestions have been made directly or implicitly throughout the book for specialist research into certain issues and the activities of particular groups and little-known personalities, but a few more general observations are now required to complete this brief summation.

Australia was seldom without a number of highly talented individuals in each of the fields of environmental management with which we have been concerned; they usually kept fully abreast of the latest developments and some of them built lasting international reputations. Notably, many were immigrants, and it is high time they were accorded due recognition as *pioneers* in and for their new country: they shared a distinctive commitment to community service as they defined it and were often dedicated to the building of respected professional institutions with high technical and ethical standards. But for many years these gifted individuals were less frequently harnessed and rewarded in Australia than their counterparts in, for example, the United States. Baron von Mueller, for instance, who always lived most frugally on his Government salary, is said to have spent £20,000 during his remarkable career to finance his own research, and generally to advance the cause of science in Australia and elsewhere. When he died he left a little over £1,000 and his will invited the Victorian Government to remember his sacrifices and make better provision for his heirs. This small point is still worth recording. The conventional wisdom has been ungenerous in its definition of the 'pioneer' image. It has deprived the pioneer of some of his most vital equipment: to the horses, telescopes, picks, shears, axes, fire-brands, weatherboard cottages and all the rest, we must at least be prepared to add the microscope, pen, theodolite, drawing-board, debating-chamber and lecture-hall.

After his traverse of Victoria in the 1830s Sir Thomas Mitchell expressed the hope that the development of the new territory 'might be trained according to one general system, with a view to various combinations of soil and climate, and not left to chance, as in old countries—or, which would perhaps be worse, to the partial or narrow views of the first-settlers'. It presented, he said: 'a fair blank sheet, for any geographical arrangement, whether of county divisions—lines of communications—or sites of towns, etc.', a perfect opportunity to improve upon the confused and rudimentary forms of regional planning which had been attempted in the older districts. Increasingly, the colonial governments attempted to observe, analyse and direct the evolution of settlement, yet the tradition of relatively independent mobility and empirical testing, already firmly entrenched in every sphere of settlement activity by mid-century, remained the dominant control over the pattern of resource appraisal and management, and Mitchell's hopes were never realized in any part of Australia. During the latter half of the century, Australia's technicians and natural scientists did respond to the perceptive statement by George Perkins Marsh which suggested that the challenge of environmental management in their country might be a most important measure of man's future capacity to live less dangerously as a dominant ecological agent (above, p. 59). There followed a hard but losing fight against the exploitative, expansionist attitudes which characterized the 'seventies and 'eighties, during which time the numbers and professional respectability of the scientists and technologists also increased and, possibly assisted by the duplication of public services in the system of separate Colonies, they were gradually moved into bureaucratic labyrinths. Their ideas on conservation and rational planning often remained remarkably advanced for their day, but there was always an unfortunate lack of synchronization; in addition, they only succeeded in communicating their hopes and fears to the public as a whole where it could be shown, as in certain types of agricultural practices and above all in water management, that 'Australia's development' depended upon the employment of their expertise. By the end of the century much of the reformist zeal from this small sector had evaporated. On the other hand, with the exception of the comparatively neglected foresters, the 'experts' were then in a position to contribute more directly towards the honoured goal of efficiency and rational development, which usually included the promotion of various utilitarian philosophies of conservation, if not always the ecological and aesthetic versions. Though it picked up its full momentum only in later years and was more dependent on overseas influences, the Australian experience of urban management was essentially similar: a rich development of technical skills, bureaucratization and an increasing divorce from the public.

It is insufficient to say that, in spite of the commendable commitment and advanced scientific and technical knowledge displayed by the leading figures, there were always too few Australians who knew enough or cared enough about their environment to press for any rapid or lasting changes in its management—though certainly, particularly before the 'nineties, the marked isolation of the small group of middle-class intellectuals we have encountered here could scarcely have helped their cause, and it is true that most of them showed a certain disdain, or at least a feeling of discomfort and an unfortunate naiveté towards the political process. That they achieved anything at all during that rush for material progress is only in part a testimony to their skill and persistence. They were too easily fobbed off with interminable committees and Royal Commissions and although their evidence was occasionally sieved through by a few politicians who were beginning to show some interest in the more comprehensive involvement of the State in resource allocation and development, especially in the advancement of agricultural settlement, too often it was shelved and added as much to the frustrations of the reformers in each Colony as it did to the slowly increasing store of knowledge concerning the extent and causes of environmental damage and the possibilities for improvement. It is more difficult to account for the apolitical attitudes of those who expressed concern for the management of the urban environment after the turn of the century, when the various groupings in the colonial parliaments began to take on more clearly defined party identities and the issues with which the reformers were concerned were of vital and immediate concern to every sector of the urban population. Perhaps by that time the determination to achieve the goals of respected 'professionalism' was an especially strong motivation, and there were certainly signs of a deep reluctance to politicize their activities being woven into the very fabric of the group as it attempted to make its mark on the national urban scene.

As Encel (1970) and others have pointed out, the elevation of the practical 'expert' to a position of reasonably high social status was one way of solving the problem of reconciling the Australians' anti-intellectualism with their growing awareness of the needs of a modern industrialized nation for trained intellects. But the notable preference for recruiting armies of technicians, administrators and scientists into ever-expanding government departments, a preference for bureaucratization which was apparently largely shared by the experts themselves, is a widely recognized peculiarity of the Australian experience. Underlying these developments was the idea of channelling and enforcing the demands of an egalitarian social philosophy by means of authoritarian, legal-rational controls, a practice which was well established by the early years of this century. Visiting commentators were frequently impressed with the show of egalitarian democracy in Australia, but as one pessimistic critic in New South Wales reminded them, if some twentieth-century de Tocqueville came to Australia he would be similarly impressed at first by the apparently esteemed luxury of an extensive range of elected bodies, yet on second view would be bound to change his mind.

> ... out of the multitude of these political counsellors a quaint form of wisdom has been evolved. We have not yet had sixty years' experience of untrammelled self-government in Australia, and some of the States have had a good deal less. But our experience has been sufficient to have enabled us to make the discovery that Parliaments and Cabinets cannot be expected to do their own work themselves ... [In New South Wales] we have had more time for experiment. The result is that we are gradually but surely taking administrative power out of political hands, and entrusting it to the care of commissions. The tendency is to put everything into commission (*Sydney Morning Herald,* 20 May 1905).

The similarly egalitarian, anti-intellectual Americans also established major Government agencies imbued with modern concepts of utilitarian conservationism, but in large measure they achieved this result through the efforts of local and nationally-based social and political movements which often retained much of their impetus after the establishment of those powerful agencies, and their continued vigilance ultimately gained further tangible successes in the promotion of aesthetic and ecological modes of conservational thought. In contrast, the Australians casually eschewed public campaigning, direct action, open debate, intensive lobbying and the like. Australian society maintained its heavy dependence upon recommendation by Royal Commission well beyond the period reviewed here—between the late 1850s and the beginning of the Second World War, for example, the record shows an average of six or seven Royal Commissions in session for each year—and there is still a depressingly uniform propensity to delegate the power of decision making to technical and professional specialists in administrative or quasi-judicial rule-making bodies. The continuing innocent reliance upon the expertise, anonymity and impartiality of government bureaucracies has not exhibited or encouraged the type of democratic involvement in environmental management wherein our hope for a better type of survival surely lies.

References Cited

ADELAIDE ADVERTISER, 1914.

AGE, 1865, 1871, 1881, 1883, 1902, 1907.

ALEXANDER, J.A., 1928: *The Life of George Chaffey*, Melbourne.

ALTSHULER, A. A., 1969: *The City Planning Process: a Political Analysis*, Ithaca and London; first published 1965.

ARGUS, 1865, 1871, 1881, 1883, 1884, 1890, 1901, 1902, 1904, 1907.

ARMYTAGE, W. H. G., 1958: 'The Chartist Land Colonies, 1846-48', *Agricultural History*, 22, 87-96.

ASHWORTH, W., 1954: *The Genesis of Modern British Town Planning*, London.

AUSTIN, A. G. (ed.), 1965: *The Webbs' Australian Diary, 1898*, Melbourne.

AUSTRALASIAN, 1873.

AUSTRALASIAN BUILDER AND LAND ADVERTISER, 1856.

AUSTRALIAN FINANCIAL GAZETTE, 1890.

BAKER, D. W. A., 1958: 'The Origins of Robertson's Land Acts', *Historical Studies, Australia and New Zealand*, 8, 166-82.

BAKER, I. G., 1951: 'Elwood Mead in Australia; an Historical Survey', *Aqua*, 2, 3-11.

BARDWELL, S., 1974: The National Park Movement in Victoria, Ph.D. thesis, Monash University.

BARRETT, A. H. B., 1971: *The Inner Suburb; the Evolution of an Industrial Area*, Melbourne.

BELL, C.N., 1893: Presidential Address, Engineering and Architecture Section, *Australasian Association for the Advancement of Science*, Hobart, 1892, 4, 185-99.

BENNETT, G., 1862: *Acclimatisation: its Eminent Adaptation to Australia*, Melbourne.

BERGER, C., 1966: 'The True North Strong and Free', in P. Russell (ed.), *Nationalism in Canada*, Toronto, 3-26.

BERNDT, R. M. and BERNDT, C. H. (eds), 1965: *Aboriginal Man in Australia*, Sydney.

BIDIE, G., 1869: 'Effects of Forest Destruction in Coorg', *Proceedings, Royal Geographical Society*, 13, 1868-69, 74-83.

BLACKBURN, T., 1894: 'Importance of Ascertaining the Distribution of Australian Fauna', *Australasian Association for the Advancement of Science*, Adelaide Meeting, 1893, 5, 446-51.

BLAINEY, G., 1966: *The Tyranny of Distance*, Melbourne.

BLEASDALE, J. J., 1871: *New Industries*, Melbourne.

BLIGH, B., 1973: *Cherish the Earth. The Story of Gardening in Australia*, Sydney.

BOGUE, A. G., 1963: *From Prairie to Corn Belt*, Chicago.

BOOTH, W., 1890: *In Darkest England and the Way Out*, London; facsimile edition 1970.

BRIDE, T. F. (ed.), 1969: *Letters from Victorian Pioneers*, facsimile edition, Melbourne; first published Melbourne 1895.

BRIGGS, A., 1969: *The Age of Improvement, 1783-1867*, London; first published 1959.

————1971: *Victorian Cities*, Harmondsworth and Ringwood; first published London, 1963.

BROWN, J. E., 1881: *A Practical Treatise on Tree Culture*, 2nd edition, Adelaide.

BROWN, R. H., 1948: *Historical Geography of the United States*, New York.

BUCKINGHAM, J. S., 1849: *National Evils and Practical Remedies*, London.

BURCH, W. R. jr, 1971: *Daydreams and Nightmares: a Sociological Essay on the American Environment*, New York.

BURROUGHS, P., 1967: *Britain and Australia, 1831-1855. A Study in Imperial Relations and Crown Lands Administration,* Oxford.

BUTLIN, N. G., 1964: *Investment in Australian Economic Development 1861-1900,* Cambridge.

CAMERON, J. M. R., 1974: 'Information Distortion in Colonial Promotion: the case of Swan River Colony', *Australian Geographical Studies,* 12, 57-76.

CAMPBELL, J., 1970: The Settlement of Melbourne, 1851-1893: selected aspects of urban growth, unpublished M.A. thesis, Melbourne University.

CANNON, M., 1966: *The Land Boomers,* Melbourne.

————1972: *Land Boom and Bust,* Melbourne.

CARSTENSEN, V., 1958: *Farms or Forests: Evolution of a State Land Policy for Northern Wisconsin, 1850-1932,* Madison.

CHADWICK, G. F., 1966: *The Park and the Town,* London.

CHERRY, G. E., 1970: *Town Planning in its Social Context,* London.

CLARK, C. M. H., 1963: *A Short History of Australia,* New York.

CLARKE, M., 1876: 'Preface' in A. L. Gordon, *Sea Spray and Smoke Drift,* Melbourne.

CLARKE, W. B., 1876: 'Effects of Forest Vegetation on Climate', *Journal and Proceedings, Royal Society New South Wales,* 10, 179-232.

COGHLAN, T. A., 1887: *The Wealth and Progress of New South Wales, 1886-87,* Sydney.

COLEMAN, B. I., 1973: *The Idea of the City in Nineteenth-Century Britain,* London.

CORBETT, A. H., 1957: 'The History of Engineering and Engineering Education in Australia', *Australian and New Zealand Association for the Advancement of Science,* Dunedin Meeting, 101-16.

————1969: 'Australian Engineering, 1788-1969', *Journal Institution of Engineers, Australia,* 41, 141-7.

————1973: *The Institution of Engineers Australia: a History of the first Fifty Years, 1919-1969,* Sydney.

CREESE, W. L., 1966: *The Search for Environment,* New Haven and London.

DALEY, C. S., 1924: 'Baron Sir Ferdinand von Mueller, K.C.M.G., M.D., F.R.S.; Botanist, Explorer and Geographer', *Victorian Historical Magazine,* 10, 23-32, 34-75.

DALLAS, K. M., 1969: *Trading Posts or Penal Colonies: the Commercial Significance of Cook's New Holland Route to the Pacific,* Hobart.

DAVISON, G., 1969: The Rise and Fall of 'Marvellous Melbourne', 1880-1895, unpublished Ph.D. thesis, Australian National University, Canberra.

DAVITT, M., 1898: *Life and Progress in Australasia,* London.

DAWSON, R., 1831: *The Present State of Australia,* London.

DUNSTAN, K., 1968: *Wowsers,* Melbourne.

DUTTON, G. (ed.), 1964: *The Literature of Australia,* Melbourne.

DYOS, H. J. and WOLFF, M. (eds), 1973: *The Victorian City, Images and Realities,* 2 vols, London and Boston.

DYSTER, B. D., 1965: The Role of Sydney and the Roles of its Citizens in New South Wales, 1841-1851, unpublished M.A. thesis, Sydney University.

EAST, L. R., 1954: 'Irrigation in Victoria—the First Hundred Years', *Aqua,* 5, 7-18.

EAST, L. R., GREEN, K. D. and HORSFALL, R. A., 1958: 'The Development and Use of Water Resources in Victoria', *Journal Institution of Engineers, Australia,* 30, 35-64.

EATON, J. H. O., 1945: *A Short History of the River Murray Works,* Adelaide.

ELLIOTT, B., 1967: *The Landscape of Australian Poetry,* Melbourne.

ENCEL, S., 1970: *Equality and Authority: a study of class, status and power in*

Australia, Melbourne; reprinted 1972.

FIELD, B., 1819: *First Fruits of Australian Poetry*, Sydney; 2nd edition 1823.

————1825: *Geographical Memoirs on New South Wales*, London.

FINER, S. E., 1952: *The Life and Times of Sir Edwin Chadwick*, London.

FITZGERALD, J. D., 1906: *Greater Sydney and Greater Newcastle*, Sydney.

FITZPATRICK, B., 1941: *The British Empire in Australia: an Economic History, 1834-1939*, Melbourne; reprinted 1969.

FOREST CONSERVANCY PAPERS, 1874: Papers Relating to Forest Conservancy, *Victorian Parliamentary Papers*, 1874, 3, No. 86.

FRANCIS, J., 1972: 'Sir Joseph Banks, architect of science and empire', *Proceedings, Royal Society of Queenland* (1971), 83, 1-19.

FREELAND, J. M., 1971: *The Making of a Profession. A History of the Growth and Work of the Architectural Institutes in Australia*, Sydney.

GAFFNEY, M. S. and HIBBS, G., 1968: *Social Sciences and the Environment*, Madison.

GEDDES, P., 1904: *City Development. A Study of Parks, Gardens and Culture-Institutes*, Edinburgh.

————1915: *Cities in Evolution. An Introduction to the Town Planning Movement and to the Study of Civics*, London.

GILBERT, L. A., 1966: 'The Bush and the Search for a Staple in New South Wales, 1788-1810', *Records, Australian Academy of Science*, 1, 6-17.

————1970: 'Plants, Politics and Personalities in Nineteenth-Century New South Wales', *Journal Royal Australian Historical Society*, 56, 15-35.

————1971: Botanical Investigation of New South Wales, 1811-80, unpublished Ph.D. thesis, University of New England, Armidale.

GILL, W., 1894: 'Deforestation in South Australia: its Causes and Probable Results', *Australasian Association for the Advancement of Science*, Adelaide Meeting, 1893, 5, 527-36.

GOLLAN, R., 1960: *Radical and Working Class Politics: a Study of Eastern Australia, 1851-1910*, Melbourne.

GOODWIN, C. D., 1964: 'Evolution in Australian Social Thought', *Journal of the History of Ideas*, 25, 393-416.

GREEN, H. M., 1961: *A History of Australian Literature, Pure and Applied*, 2 vols, Sydney.

GREEN, J. R., 1909: *A History of Botany, 1860-1900*, London.

GREER, S., 1964: *The Emerging City: Myth and Reality*, New York.

HANCOCK, J. L., 1967: 'Planners in the Changing American City, 1900-1940', *Journal of the American Institute of Planners*, 33, 290-304.

HANCOCK, W. K., 1972: *Discovering Monaro: a study of Man's Impact on his Environment*, Cambridge.

HARRISON, G. L., 1954: *R. M. C. The Work of the River Murray Commission*, Canberra.

HAYS, S. P., 1957: *The Response to Industrialism, 1885-1914*, Chicago; reprinted 1966.

————1972: *Conservation and the Gospel of Efficiency*, New York; first published Cambridge, Mass., 1959.

HAYTER, H. H., 1893: 'The Concentration of Population in Australian Capital Cities', *Australasian Association for the Advancement of Science*, Hobart Meeting, 1892, 4, 541-6.

HEATHCOTE, R. L., 1965: *Back of Bourke, A Study of Land Appraisal and Settlement in Semi-Arid Australia*, Melbourne.

————1972: 'The Visions of Australia, 1770-1970', in A. Rapoport (ed.), *Australia as Human Setting*, Sydney, 77-98.

HEDLEY, C., 1894: 'The Faunal Regions of Australia', *Australasian Association for the Advancement of Science,* Adelaide Meeting, 1893, 5, 444-6.

HIBBARD, B. H., 1965: *A History of Public Land Policies,* New York; first published 1924.

HIGHSMITH, R. M., JENSEN, J. G. and RUDD, R. D., 1962: *Conservation in the United States,* Chicago.

HISTORICAL RECORDS OF AUSTRALIA, 1788-1848, Series 1, Governors' Despatches, 26 vols, Sydney.

HISTORICAL RECORDS OF NEW SOUTH WALES, 1893-1898, Sydney.

HOARE, M. E., 1967: 'Learned Societies in Australia: the Foundation Years in Victoria, 1850-1860', *Records, Australian Academy of Science,* 1, 7-29.

————1968: 'Doctor John Henderson and the Van Diemen's Land Scientific Society', *Records, Australian Academy of Science,* 1, 7-24.

HOLTZE, M., 1894: 'A Plea for a Rational Popular Nomenclature for Australian Plants', *Australasian Association for the Advancement of Science,* Adelaide Meeting, 1893, 5, 443-4.

HORNE, R. H., 1859: *Australian Facts and Prospects,* London.

HOWARD, E., 1898: *Tomorrow: a Peaceful Path to Real Reform,* London.

HOWE, R., 1972: The Response of Protestant Churches to Urbanization in Melbourne and Chicago, 1875-1914, unpublished Ph.D. thesis, Melbourne University.

HOWITT, W., 1972: *Land, Labour and Gold; or, Two Years in Victoria, with visits to Sydney and Van Diemen's Land,* facsimile edition, Sydney; first published London, 1855.

HUTCHINS, D. E., 1916: *A Discussion of Australian Forestry,* Perth.

HUTH, H., 1957: *Nature and the American. Three Centuries of Changing Attitudes,* Berkeley; reprinted Lincoln, Neb., 1972.

INSKO, C. A., 1967: *Theories of Attitude Change,* New York.

ISE, J., 1961: *Our National Park Policy: A Critical History,* Baltimore.

JACOBS, M. R., 1957: 'History of the Use and Abuse of Wooded Lands in Australia', *Australian and New Zealand Association for the Advancement of Science* (*Australian Journal of Science,* 19), Dunedin Meeting, 132-9.

JEANS, D. N., 1966a: 'Crown Land Sales and the Accommodation of the Small Settler in New South Wales, 1825-1842', *Historical Studies Australia and New Zealand,* 12, 205-12.

————1966b: 'The Breakdown of Australia's First Rectangular Grid Survey', *Australian Geographical Studies,* 4, 119-28.

————1972: *An Historical Geography of New South Wales to 1901,* Sydney.

JEVONS, W. S., 1858: *Social Survey of Australian Cities, 1858* (ms.). 'Remarks upon the Social Map of Sydney', Mitchell Library, Sydney.

————1886: *Letters and Journals of W. Stanley Jevons, edited by his wife* (Harriet A. Jevons), London.

JONES, R., 1969: 'Fire-Stick Farming', *Australian Natural History,* 16, 224-8.

KIDDLE, M., 1961: *Men of Yesterday; a Social History of the Western District of Victoria, 1834-1890,* Melbourne.

KLUCKHOHN, C., 'Myths and Rituals: a General Theory', in J. B. Vickery, *Myth and Literature,* Lincoln, Neb., 33-44.

KOLLMORGEN, W. and KOLLMORGEN, J., 1973: 'Landscape Meteorology in the Great Plains Area', *Annals, Association American Geographers,* 63, 424-41.

LA NAUZE, J. A., 1949: *Political Economy in Australia,* Melbourne.

————1965: *Alfred Deakin: a Biography,* Melbourne.

LANSBURY, C., 1970: *Arcady in Australia. The Evocation of Australia in Nineteenth-Century English Literature,* Melbourne.

LAVERTY, J. R., 1971: 'Town Planning in Brisbane, 1842-1925', *Royal Australian Planning Institute Journal,* 9, 19-26.

————1972: 'Greater Brisbane: A Response to Problems of Metropolitan Government', *Australian Journal of Politics and History*, 18, 34-51.

LEADER, 1885.

LEIGHLY, J., 1958: 'John Muir's Image of the West', *Annals, Association of American Geographers*, 48, 309-18.

LEWIS, R. A., 1952: *Edwin Chadwick and the Public Health Movement, 1832-1854*, London.

LOWENTHAL, D., 1958: *George Perkins Marsh; Versatile Vermonter*, New York.

————1964: 'Introduction', in Marsh, 1964: ix-xxix.

MACASKILL, J., 1962: 'The Chartist Land Plan', in A. Briggs (ed.), *Chartist Studies*, London, 304-41.

MACKAY, H., 1903: 'Forestry in Victoria', *Victorian Year-Book*, 1903, Melbourne, 411-16, 473-8.

————1914: 'Forestry in Victoria', A.M. Laughton and T. S. Hall (eds), *Handbook to Victoria*, British Association for the Advancement of Science, Melbourne, 310-33.

McCASKILL, M., 1966: 'Man and Landscape in North Westland, New Zealand', in S. R. Eyre and G. R. J. Jones (eds), *Geography as Human Ecology: methodology by example*, London, 264-90.

McCOLL, H., 1883: Memorial, Surface Irrigation Canals, *Victorian Parliamentary Papers*, 2nd session 1883, 1, C 10, C 11.

McCOLL, J. H., 1917: 'Hugh McColl and the Water Question in Northern Victoria', *Victorian Historical Magazine*, 5, 145-63.

MANSERGH, J., 1890: *Report on the Sewerage and Sewage Disposal of the Proposed Melbourne Metropolitan District*, Melbourne.

MARKHAM, C. R., 1866: 'Destruction of Forests, and the Indian Water Supply', *Proceedings, Royal Geographical Society*, 10, 1865-66, 266-9.

MARSH, G. P., 1964: *Man and Nature, or, Physical Geography as Modified by Human Action* (edited by D. Lowenthal), Cambridge, Mass.; first published New York, 1864.

MARTIN, C. S., 1955: *Irrigation and Closer Settlement in the Shepparton District*, Melbourne.

MARTIN, J., 1838: *The Australian Sketch Book*, Sydney.

MARTIN, JEAN, 1970: 'Suburbia: Community and Network', in A. F. Davies and S. Encel (eds) *Australian Society: a Sociological Introduction*, Melbourne, 2nd edition, reprinted 1972; first published 1965, 301-39.

MAYER, H. M., and WADE, R. C., 1969: *Chicago: the Growth of a Metropolis*, Chicago.

MEAD, E., 1903: *Irrigation Institutions: a Discussion of the Economic and Legal Questions Created by the Growth of Irrigation Agriculture in the West*, New York.

————1914: 'Irrigation in Victoria', in A.M. Laughton and T. S. Hall (eds), *Handbook to Victoria*, B.A.A.S. Meeting, Melbourne, 255-68.

————1920: *Helping Men to Own Farms: a Practical Discussion of Government Aid in Land Settlement*, New York.

MEINIG, D. W., 1954: 'The Evolution of Understanding and Environment: Climate and Wheat Culture in the Columbia Plateau', *Yearbook of the Association of Pacific Coast Geographers*, 16, 25-34.

————1970: *On the Margins of the Good Earth: the South Australian Wheat Frontier, 1869-1884*, Adelaide; first published Chicago, 1962.

MEREDITH, L. A., 1844: *Notes and Sketches of New South Wales*, London; facsimile edition Harmondsworth and Ringwood, 1973.

MILLS, R. C., 1968: *The Colonisation of Australia, 1829-1842: the Wakefield Experiment in Empire Building*, London; first published 1915.

MITCHELL, T. L., 1839: *Three Expeditions into the Interior of Eastern Australia*

. . . ., London.

————1848: *Journal of an Expedition into the Interior of Tropical Australia, in Search of a Route from Sydney to the Gulf of Carpentaria*, London.

MOON, K., 1969: 'Perception and Appraisal of the South Australian Landscape 1836-1850', *Proceedings, Royal Geographical Society of Australasia (S. A.)*, 70, 41-64.

————1970: 'Aesthetic Qualities of the South Australian Landscape: the Views of the Early Settlers', *Flinders Journal of History and Politics*, 2, 18-27.

MORRELL, J. C., 1915: *Town Planning*, Melbourne.

MOZLEY, A., 1967: 'Evolution and the Climate of Opinion in Australia, 1840-76', *Victorian Studies*, 10, 411-30.

MUELLER, F. VON, 1876: *Forest Culture in its Relation to Industrial Pursuits*, Melbourne.

————1890: Inaugural Address, *Australasian Association for the Advancement of Science*, Melbourne Meeting, 1890, 2, 1-26.

MULVANEY, D. J. (ed.), 1971: *Aboriginal Man and Environment in Australia*, Canberra.

MUMFORD, L., 1946: 'The Garden City Idea and Modern Planning', in F. J. Osborn (ed.), *Garden Cities*, 29-40.

NASH, R., 1967: *Wilderness and the American Mind*, New Haven; reprinted 1971.

————1972: 'American Environmental History: a New Teaching Frontier', *Pacific Historical Review*, 41, 363-72.

NORMINGTON-RAWLING, J., 1962: *Charles Harpur, an Australian*, Sydney.

O'RIORDAN, T., 1971: *Perspectives on Resource Management*, London.

OSBORN, F. J. (ed.), 1946: *Garden Cities of Tomorrow* (E. Howard), London.

OXLEY, J., 1820: *Journals of Two Expeditions to the Interior of New South Wales . . . 1817-18*, London.

PALMER, V., 1971: 'The Legend', in C. Wallace-Crabbe (ed.), *The Australian Nationalists*, Melbourne.

PATTISON, W. D., 1964: *Beginnings of the American Rectangular Land Survey System, 1784-1800*, Chicago; first published 1959.

PEARSON, A. N., 1900: *The Scientific Directing of a Country's Agriculture*, Melbourne.

PIERSON, S., 1973: 'The Way Out', in Dyos and Wolff, *Victorian City*, 2, 873-89.

PERRY, T. M., 1966: 'Climate and Settlement in Australia 1700-1930: some theoretical considerations', in J. Andrews (ed.), *Frontiers and Men*, Melbourne, 138-54.

PHILIPP, J., 1971: *A Great View of Things: Edward Gibbon Wakefield*, Melbourne.

PINCHOT, G., 1947: *Breaking New Ground*, New York.

POTTS, E. D. and POTTS, A., 1970: *A Yankee Merchant in Goldrush Australia: the Letters of George Francis Train, 1853-55*, Melbourne.

POWELL, J. M., 1968a: 'A Pioneer Sheep Station: the Clyde Company in Western Victoria, 1836-40', *Australian Geographical Studies*, 6, 59-66.

————1968b: Settlement and Land Appraisal in Victoria, 1834-1891. Rhetoric, Reality and the Public Domain, with special reference to the western plains, Ph.D. thesis, Monash University, 2 vols; published in part in Powell, 1970a.

————1969: 'The Squatting Occupation of Victoria, 1834-1860', *Australian Geographical Studies*, 7, 9-27.

————1970a: *The Public Lands of Australia Felix. Settlement and Land Appraisal in Victoria 1834-91 with special reference to the western plains*, Melbourne.

————1970b: 'The Victorian Survey System, 1837-1860', *New Zealand Geographer*, 26, 50-69.

————1972: 'Images of Australia, 1788-1914', *Monash Publications in Geography*, 3, 21pp.

————1973a: 'Medical Promotion and the Consumptive Immigrant to Australia', *Geographical Review*, 63, 449-76.

————(ed.), 1973b: *Yeomen and Bureaucrats: the Victorian Crown Lands Commission 1878-79*, Melbourne.

————1973c: 'Arcadia and Back. "Village Settlement" in Victoria, 1894-1913', *Australian Geographical Studies*, 9, 134-49.

————1973d: 'An Australian Utopia', *Australian Geographer*, 12, 328-33.

POWELL, J. M. and WILLIAMS, M. (eds), 1975: *Australian Space Australian Time*, Melbourne.

POWELL, J. W., 1879: *Lands of the Arid Regions of the United States,* Washington.

PROGRESS REPORTS 1885, 1887: Progress Reports of the Royal Commission on Water Supply, *Victorian Parliamentary Papers*, 1885, 2, 19; 3, 51; fourth progress report, 1887, *Irrigation in Egypt and Italy*, Melbourne.

PROSHANSKY, H.M., ITTELSON, W.H. and RIVLIN, L.G. (eds), 1970: *Environmental Psychology: Man and his Physical Setting*, New York.

RAKESTRAW, L., 1972: 'Conservation Historiography: an Assessment', *Pacific Historical Review*, 41, 271-88.

READE, C. C. and DAVIDGE, W. R., 1915: *Australian Town Planning Tour: Recommendations in Regard to Planning*, Adelaide.

REISSMAN, L., 1964: *The Urban Process*, New York.

REPORT, 1856-7: Report ... Mining Resources of the Colony of Victoria, *Victorian Parliamentary Papers*, 3; Nos 21 and 24.

REPORT, 1871: Progress Report of the Royal Commission on Foreign Industries and Forests, *Victorian Parliamentary Papers*, 1871, 3, No. 60.

REPORT, 1879: Annual Progress Report of the Forest Reserves, and Forest Conservancy Generally, *South Australian Parliamentary Papers*, 1879, 3, No. 83.

REPORT, 1880: Supply of Water to the Northern Plains, *Victorian Parliamentary Papers*, 1881, 2, No. 18.

REPORT, 1882: Supply of Water to the Northern Plains (Irrigation), *Victorian Parliamentary Papers*, 1882-83, 3, No. 74.

REPORT, 1885: *First Progress Report, Royal Commission on Water Supply. Irrigation in Western America, in so far as it has relation to the circumstances of Victoria*, Melbourne.

REPORT, 1890: Report of the Conservation of Forests for the Year Ending 30 June 1890, *Victorian Parliamentary Papers*, 1890, 4, No. 202.

REPORT ON FORESTS, 1865: 'Report on the Advisableness of Establishing State Forests', *Victorian Parliamentary Papers*, 1864-65, 4, No. 77.

————1873: Report on Forest Reserves, *South Australian Parliamentary Papers*, 1873, 3, No. 135.

REPORT ON HOUSING, 1913: Progress Report from the Joint Select Committee upon the Housing of the People in the Metropolis, *Victorian Parliamentary Papers*, 1913-14, 1, D4.

————1918: Final Report from the Royal Commission on the Housing Conditions of the People in the Metropolis and in the Populous Centres of the State, *Victorian Parliamentary Papers*, 1918, 2, No. 19.

REPORT ON POPULATION, 1918: Report of the Select Committee upon the Causes of the Drift of Population from the Country Districts to the City, *Victorian Parliamentary Papers*, 1918, 1, D1.

REPORT ON TOWNS, 1892: 'Report of the Committee ... appointed to Consider and Report upon the Location and Laying-out of Towns', *Australasian Association for the Advancement of Science*, Christchurch Meeting, 1891, 3, 540-1.

REPORT ON TRAFFIC, 1919: Report of the Board Appointed to Investigate the Problem of Relieving Congestion of Traffic in Melbourne, *Victorian Par-*

liamentary Papers, 1919, 2, No. 8.
REPORT ON WATER, 1871: Report by Lieutenant-Colonel Sankey, R.E., on Water Supply, *South Australian Proceedings of Parliament,* 1871, 2, No. 97.
RIBBENTROP, B., 1900: *Forestry in British India,* Calcutta.
RICHARDSON, E. R., 1962: *The Politics of Conservation: Crusades and Controversies,* Berkeley.
RIMMER, P. J., 1975: 'Politicians, Public Servants and Petitioners: Aspects of Transport in Australia 1815-1901', in Powell and Williams, 182-225.
ROBBINS, R. M., 1964: *Our Landed Heritage. The Public Domain, 1776-1936,* Lincoln, Neb.; first published 1942.
ROBERTS, S. H., 1968: *A History of Australian Land Settlement, 1788-1920,* Melbourne; first published 1924.
ROBINSON, K. W., 1975: 'The Geographical Context of Political Individualism 1860-1914', in Powell and Williams, 226-49.
ROKEACH, M., 1970: *Beliefs, Attitudes and Values,* San Francisco; first published 1968.
RULE, A., 1967: *Forests of Australia,* Sydney.
RUTHERFORD, J., 1974: 'Interplay of American and Australian Ideas for Development of Water Projects in Northern Victoria', in J. M. Powell (ed.), *The Making of Rural Australia,* Melbourne, 116-34; first published 1964.
SANDERCOCK, L., 1974: The Politics of City Planning in South Eastern Australia, 1900-1973, unpublished Ph.D. thesis, Australian National University, Canberra.
SCHMITT, P. J., 1969: *Back to Nature,* New York.
SCHOENWALD, R. L., 1973: 'Training Urban Man. A Hypothesis about the Sanitary Movement', in Dyos and Wolff, *Victorian City,* 2, 669-92.
SCOTT, M. G., 1969: *American City Planning since 1900,* Berkeley.
SERLE, A. G., 1963: *The Golden Age, a History of the Colony of Victoria, 1851-1861,* Melbourne.
————1971: *The Rush to be Rich,* Melbourne.
————1973: *From Deserts the Prophets Come. The Creative Spirit in Australia, 1788-1972,* Melbourne.
SHAW, A. G. L., 1969: *The Economic Development of Australia,* London; first published 1944.
SHEPHERD, T., 1836: *Lectures on Landscape Gardening in Australia,* Sydney.
SIDNEY, S., 1852: *The Three Colonies of Australia: New South Wales, Victoria, South Australia,* London.
SLADEN, D., 1888a: *A Century of Australian Song, 1788-1888,* London.
————1888b: *Australian Ballads and Rhymes: Poems Inspired by Life and Scenery in Australia and New Zealand,* London.
————1888c: *Australian Poets, 1788-1888,* London.
SMITH, B., 1960: *European Vision and the South Pacific. A Study in the History of Art and Ideas,* Oxford; reprinted 1969.
————1962: *Australian Painting, 1788-1960,* Melbourne; reprinted 1972.
SMITH, H. N., 1950: *Virgin Land. The American West as Symbol and Myth,* Cambridge, Mass.
SMYTH, R. B., 1855: 'On the Influence of the Physical Character of a Country on the Climate', *Transactions Philosophical Society of Victoria,* 1, 203-21.
————1869: *Goldfields and Mineral Districts of Victoria,* Melbourne.
SPATE, O.H.K., 1951: 'The Growth of London, A.D. 1600-1800', in H. C. Darby (ed.), *An Historical Geography of England before 1800,* Cambridge, 529-48.
————1971: *Australia,* London; first published 1968.
SPOONER, P., 1974: 'Man and Landscape in Australia: History of Gardening', unpublished paper, *Australian U.N.E.S.C.O. Committee for Man and the Bio-*

sphere, Canberra Conference, 9pp.

STREHLOW, T. G. H., 1965: 'Culture, Social Structure, and Environment in Aboriginal Central Australia', in Berndt and Berndt, 121-45.

———1970: 'Geography and the Totemic Landscape in Central Australia: a Functional Study', in R. M. Berndt (ed.), *Australian Aboriginal Anthropology*, Nedlands, W. A., 92-140.

SULMAN, J., 1892: 'The Architecture of Towns', *Australasian Association for the Advancement of Science*, Christchurch Meeting, 1891, 424-33.

———1907: *Improvement of the City of Sydney*, Sydney.

SUTCLIFFE, J. T., 1921: *A History of Trade Unionism in Australia*, Melbourne.

SYDNEY MORNING HERALD, 1844, 1905, 1913.

TENCH, W., 1961: *Sydney's First Four Years*, Sydney; first published 1789 and 1793.

THOMPSON, K., 1970: 'The Australian Fever Tree in California: Eucalypts and Malarial Prophylaxis', *Annals, Association American Geographers*, 60, 230-44.

THORNTHWAITE, C. W., 1936: 'The Great Plains', in C. Goodrich, B. W. Allin, C. W. Thornthwaite *et al.*, *Migration and Economic Opportunity*, Philadelphia, 202-50.

TOMPSON, C., 1826: *Wild Notes from the Lyre of a Native Minstrel*, Sydney.

TUAN, YI-FU, 1974: *Topophilia. A Study of Environmental Perception, Attitudes and Values*, Englewood Cliffs, N. J.

TUNNARD, C. and REED, H. H. jr, 1955: *American Skyline: the Growth and Form of Our Cities and Towns*, Boston.

TURILL, W. B., 1959: *The Royal Botanic Gardens, Kew*, London.

TURNER, F., 1890: 'Fodder Plants and Grasses of Australia', *Australasian Association for the Advancement of Science*, Melbourne Meeting, 1890, 2, 586-96.

TURNER, I., 1964: *The Australian Dream*, Melbourne.

TWOPENY, R. E. N., 1883: *Town Life in Australia*, London; facsimile edition Ringwood, 1973.

URLICH CLOHER, D., 1975: 'A Perspective on Australian Urbanization', in Powell and Williams, 104-49.

VINCENT, J. E. M., 1887: *The Colonisation of Greater Britain—Viticulture, Fruitgrowing in Australia*, Melbourne.

WACE, N. and LOVETT, B., 1973: *Yankee Maritime Activities and the Early History of Australia*, Canberra.

WALKER, R. A., 1949: *Urban Planning*, Chicago.

WARD, D., 1971: *Cities and Immigrants: a Geography of Change in Nineteenth-Century America*, New York.

WARD, R. B., 1958: *The Australian Legend*, Melbourne.

WATERSON, D. B., 1968: *Squatter, Selector and Storekeeper. A History of the Darling Downs, 1859-93*, Sydney.

WEBB, M. J., 1968: 'Planning and Development in Metropolitan Perth to 1953', *Australian Planning Institute*, Perth Congress, 5pp.

WEBER, A. F., 1963: *The Growth of Cities in the Nineteenth Century: a Study in Statistics*, New York; first published 1899.

WHITE, M. and WHITE, L., 1962: *The Intellectual Versus the City*, Cambridge, Mass.

WILLIAMS, M., 1966a: 'Delimiting the Spread of Settlement: an Examination of Evidence in South Australia', *Economic Geography*, 42, 336-55.

———1966b: 'The Parkland Towns of Australia and New Zealand', *Geographical Review*, 56, 67-89.

———1974: *The Making of the South Australian Landscape*, London.

———1975: 'More and Smaller is Better: Australian Rural Settlement, 1788-1914', in Powell and Williams, 61-103.

WILLIS, M., 1949: *By Their Fruits: a Life of Ferdinand von Mueller, Botanist and Explorer,* Sydney.

WILSON, J. F., 1865: 'Dessication of Orange River Basin', *Proceedings, Royal Geographical Society,* 9, 1864-65, 106-9.

WINSTON, D., 1957: *Sydney's Great Experiment: the Progress of the Cumberland Plan,* Sydney.

WOOLLS, W., 1879: *Lectures on the Vegetable Kingdom,* Sydney.

WRIGHT, J., 1963: *Charles Harpur,* Melbourne.

———1965: *Preoccupations in Australian Poetry,* Melbourne; reprinted 1966.

YEAR BOOK, 1905: *Year Book of Agriculture for 1905,* (Dept Agriculture), Melbourne.

GENERAL CONVERSION FACTORS

1 acre	=	0.4047 hectare
10 acres	=	4.05 hectares
640 acres	=	259.0 hectares
1 mile	=	1.609 kilometres
10 miles	=	16.1 kilometres

Index